Praise for *Crafty Screenwriting*

"Finally, a book about the craft of screenwriting that sweeps away two decades of mystification and cant. From the most elevated artistic concerns to the mundane details of how many brads to bind your script with, Alex Epstein shines the light of common sense and experience on this tricky, delicate, and profitable art. Every page sparkles with wisdom, plain-speaking, and wit. It is my new answer to the dozens of questions I'm asked by new writers eager to get it right: 'Read Alex Epstein.' "

—Don Roos, writer-director, *The Opposite of Sex* and *Bounce*

"Alex Epstein brings a screenwriting professional's honesty, skill, and expertise to a field otherwise crowded with how-to-write quacks."

—John Badham, director, *Saturday Night Fever, War Games,* and *Stakeout*

"This is that rare kind of book about screenwriting which is truly helpful. I recommend it to anyone seriously wanting to write screenplays that get produced. It's full of detailed and no-nonsense guidelines about what writers should do to make their scripts better, and about what they must do if they want their scripts to be considered for production. It's a how-to book on how to write not merely a script that shows you off—but a script that convinces producers to make it into a movie. It's a book that genuinely wants to help—and does."

—Eleanor Bergstein, screenwriter, *Dirty Dancing*

"I wish more writers knew what makes a script worth producing—not just how to structure a plot and write good dialogue, but how to come up with a story that people want to see on the screen. *Crafty*

Crafty Screenwriting explains all of that in a clear and often hilarious way. I hope a lot of writers read this book; then I'll get more screenplays I want to make into movies."

—Paul Colichman, producer, *Gods and Monsters, Tom & Viv,* and *One False Move*

"*Crafty Screenwriting* is an INVALUABLE TOOL for anyone attempting to penetrate the dangerous thickets of Hollywood, with an idea in their hand and not much else. It is totally impressive how this book somehow gives you under one cover an actual, workable ROAD MAP that if followed with a strict loyalty to your OWN creativity, will guide you through the often terrifying journey of confusion and rejection toward the bright realization of your singular talent!"

—Henry Jaglom, writer-director, *Déja Vu, Always,* and *Eating*

"*Crafty Screenwriting* explains what no one else seems to be explaining: how to write a screenplay that's not only a good read, but a good movie project that a producer can make into a good movie. Shrewdly realistic and funny."

—Pieter Kroonenburg, producer, *The Hotel New Hampshire* and *To Walk With Lions*

"This refreshingly undogmatic book crystallizes the knowledge that really skilled screenwriters all have, and lays it out plainly for anyone to absorb. I don't think there are many writers (or producers and executives, for that matter) who won't learn a great deal from this book."

—Roger Spottiswoode, director, *Tomorrow Never Dies, The Sixth Day,* and *And the Band Played On*

"Finally a book on screenwriting that gets it all right. Over and over again, Epstein names the key points to writing a script that sells. I'm going to pass this thing out like Lifesavers."

—Ed Elbert, producer, *Anna and the King* and *The Mighty Quinn*

CRAFTY TV WRITING

Also by Alex Epstein

Crafty Screenwriting

CRAFTY TV WRITING

THINKING INSIDE THE BOX

ALEX EPSTEIN

A HOLT PAPERBACK
HENRY HOLT AND COMPANY ■ NEW YORK

Holt Paperbacks
Henry Holt and Company, LLC
Publishers since 1866
175 Fifth Avenue
New York, New York 10010
www.henryholt.com

A Holt Paperback® and HP® are registered trademarks of Henry Holt and Company, LLC.

Distributed in Canada by H. B. Fenn and Company Ltd.

Library of Congress Cataloging-in-Publication Data

Epstein, Alex.
Crafty TV writing : thinking inside the box / Alex Epstein—
1st Holt paperback ed.
p. cm.
Includes index.
ISBN-13: 978-0-8050-8028-5
ISBN-10: 0-8050-8028-7
1. Television authorship. I. Title: Crafty television writing. II. Title.

PN1992.7.E67 2006
808.2'25—dc22 2005055534

Henry Holt books are available for special promotions and premiums. For details contact: Director, Special Markets.

First Edition 2006

Designed by Victoria Hartman

Printed in the United States of America

3 5 7 9 10 8 6 4

For Robin Spry

who believed . . .

Contents

Acknowledgments xv

Introduction: Why You Want to Write TV xvii

Part One: THINKING INSIDE THE BOX

1 ▪ The Hidden Structure of a TV Series 3

What Makes Great TV? 4

A Hook 8

An "Attractive Fantasy" 11

Characters We Never Get Tired Of 14

A Place Where Stories Walk in the Door 28

Episodic vs. Serial Stories 33

Demographics and Networks 36

The Show Bible 38

2 ▪ Great Episode Ideas 41

The Springboard 42

What Makes a Great Springboard? 46

How to Come Up with Great Springboards 51

What Makes a Bad *Story Idea* 56
Mixing and Matching 62
Themed Shows 63

3 ▪ Writing the Script 65
Teasers and Tags 66
Act Outs 67
Breaking Story 74
Time Compression 76
Weaving Stories Together—The Beat Sheet 77
No Hand Waving, Please 80
The Most Powerful Screenwriting Tool in the World 82
Mix It Up 83
The Rule of One 84
Tracking Expectations 86
Treatments 92
Going to Pages—the Script 93
Dialogue 101
Action 104

Part Two: THE WRITER'S TOOLKIT

4 ▪ Bad Writing and How to Fix It (Or at Least Get Away with It) 111
When Is Your Draft Done? 112
Contracts and Drafts 115
Taking Criticism 116
The Flavors of Bad Writing 119
Pulling vs. Pushing 120
Geography 123

Suspension of Disbelief 125
Offscreen Story 130
Go-Tos 133
Point of View 136
Communicating Without Dialogue 138

5 ▪ Bringing the Funny 142
What's So Funny? 143
Great Comic Premises 144
Plausible Surprise 145
Funny Word Last 146
Commitment 147
Juxtaposition 147
Squiggy 149
Comedy Is in the Characters 151
Comedy Is in the Pauses, Too 153
Don't Break the Frame 155
Joke on a Joke 156
Bric-a-brac 156
Up and Back 157
Trivia 158
Underwriting 159
Overwriting 160
Learning to Be Funny 162
Stand-up Comedy 162

Part Three: WORKING IN TV LAND

6 ▪ Preparing to Be a TV Writer 167
Writing Partners 170
Film Schools and Classes 173

The Free Alternative Film School 176
Seminars and Workshops 179
Awards and Competitions 180
The Spec Script 182
Spec Pilots as Samples 190
Screenwriting Software 191

7 ▪ Breaking In 195
Getting an Agent 195
Staffing Season 199
L.A., the Big Nipple 200
The Back Door 203
Other Back Doors 207

8 ▪ Getting Hired 208
Killer Story Pitches 209
Be Fun 211
Just Do It 213
Be Flexible but Passionate 214
Writing Your Freelance Script 217
Multiple Jobs 221

9 ▪ Moving up the Food Chain: Writing on Staff 223
Who Are All These People? 224
Story Editors 225
Your Master's Voice 228
Credit Where Credit Isn't Due 231
Production Notes 232
Playing Nice with the Other Kids 234
How to Run a Writing Room 236
Surviving Getting Fired 243

10 ▪ The Holy Grail: Creating Your Own Show 248
Spec Pilots for Real 251
Pitching Festivals: Any Use? 254
The Pilot Episode 255
Coming Up with a TV Show 257
Enjoying the Process 266
A Parting Word 268

Appendix 1 ▪ Resources 269

Appendix 2 ▪ Writing Contests and Fellowships 273

Appendix 3 ▪ Final Draft vs. Screenwriter 275

Appendix 4 ▪ Scale Payments 279

Appendix 5 ▪ Samples 281

Appendix 6 ▪ Script Pages 289

Glossary 303

Notes 311

Index 315

Acknowledgments

This book owes a deep debt to:

The many working writers who have taught me
what they know . . .

The readers of my blog and website, who let me know
what they wanted to know . . .

The producers and network executives who have
generously paid me to learn how to write TV . . .

And my family, who make all my achievements
into celebrations.

Introduction

WHY YOU WANT TO WRITE TV

When I was first coming up in the biz, movie writers looked down at TV writers. "If this doesn't work out," they'd say, "there's always TV." TV writers had an inferiority complex: "I'd love to work in movies. But I can't afford it." (Even then, TV writers made more money.) A movie could be made for a niche audience, but not TV. The three networks only aired shows that the entire country could watch. It was the '80s, and *Miami Vice* was the most innovative thing on television.

Then cable blossomed. Now everyone from HBO to the Playboy Channel to PAX to FX to Showtime is producing their own flavor of programming. Groundbreaking pay cable shows like *The Sopranos* and *Six Feet Under* have forced the networks—now five of them—to push the envelope on language, nudity, moral darkness, and narrative invention. Today, the sheer appetite that all these channels have for programming means that an offbeat story has more of a chance of finding a home on TV than it does in a movie theater.

That's all good. But it's not why you want to write TV.

A movie is a one-night stand. Every movie invents its own world, its own characters, its own tone, its own dialogue style, its own way of coming at a story. Even sequels change the rules—just look at the difference between *Alien* and *Aliens*. You spend a night with a movie, and you move on. That's exciting, but it's limiting. How deep can your audience's relationship with a movie be? How much can you, as a writer, show the audience about characters they'll never spend more than two hours with? For the writer, a movie has the frustrations of a one-night stand: all that emotion, and in the morning it's over.

A TV series is a relationship. Its world lasts, whether it's lost dinosaurs, cops 'n' DAs, or yuppies competing for a job working for Donald Trump. Each episode shares that world and fleshes it out. We get to know the same core characters better, coming to love or hate them. A series tells stories with a consistent tone, reusing the same narrative structure, allowing it to concentrate on the richness of those stories.

As a writer, you're the person who'll spend the most time with your characters and their stories. If you're a movie writer, you'll be the one creating the world and then losing it—especially if, as usual, you're not the one asked to write the sequel, or even the shooting draft. If you're a TV writer, you can get to play in the world you and your fellow writers have created for as long as your show runs.

That's fun. It also means that TV is about twice as hard to write as movies. How do you find a format that can sustain 100 episodes? How do you create characters who will be consistently compelling over that many stories? How do you find a tone you want to sustain from fall through to spring? How do you lure the same viewers back week after week?

The answer is in the *template*. Every TV show, whether drama or comedy, fiction or "reality," has hidden rules that define what it does—the format of the storytelling, the goods that every episode must deliver. Delivering those goods according to the template's hidden rules, while still keeping your stories surprising and compelling, makes TV writing hard. Delivering those goods regularly and *on time,* facing notes from everybody from the assistant director to the head of the network to the actor calling from the set, makes TV writing harder. If writing a movie is a one-night stand, writing TV is like a marriage. There are a lot more rules, and you have to work at it harder. But you get an experience that's richer and deeper, that can fulfill you for years or even decades.

To write TV, you have to know about twice as much as you need to know to write a movie. You need to know everything a feature film writer needs to know, plus a whole 'nother basket of knowledge about "act outs," "core cast," character revelation, and how to play nice in the writing room.

The hours are longer, and more people scream at you in TV.

That's *definitely* not why you want to write for television—though, if you're tempted by a challenge, you're in luck.

But.

But.

Because it's harder, television writers are in an entirely different ball game than movie writers. You heard the old joke about the dumb actress in Hollywood—she slept with the *writer*? Movie writers are often banned from the set. They are rewritten willy-nilly by the director, the producer, and the star. Sometimes the writers aren't even invited to the premiere.

TV writers run the asylum. In American television, the person running the show is almost by definition an experienced writer who is in charge of the show's creative vision. Usually the showrunner came up with the idea for the series in the first place. TV writers get respect. We have clout. Oh, we're not the only ones with clout. After all, we're playing with the network's money; and ultimately we all work for the audience. But if we don't get final say, we get *first* say.

We have to take notes, but we get to decide how to take them, at least until we're fired.

It's our show to win or lose.

That's why you want to write TV.

How do you write TV? What do you need to know about a show's "template"? How do you find out what it is?

How do you integrate notes from the producer, network, director, star, and production staff, all while episodes are hurtling toward an airdate that cannot be put off? How do you work in a medium where writer's block is *verboten*?

How do you get a job? How do you move up the food chain? How do you get to the point where you can create your own show?

Crafty TV Writing will show you how working TV writers do it—how they look at and create television series.

Then you can run the asylum, too.

CRAFTY TV WRITING

▪ PART ONE ▪

THINKING INSIDE THE BOX

1

THE HIDDEN STRUCTURE OF A TV SERIES

You're reading this book for one of a handful of reasons:

- You're a student of television, and you want to understand how it works from a writer's perspective.
- You want to break into television. You're writing, or planning to write, two killer "spec scripts" that will get you an agent, who'll get you a job writing on a show. (A spec script is a script you write purely as a sample. More on that later.)
- You broke into television, you're writing a freelance script, and you want some more insight into how to make it great, so you'll get hired as a story editor.
- You're a staff writer or story editor or, Lord knows, maybe even a showrunner. You know how to write television, but you'd like to crystallize your own thinking. Or, you are procrastinating, and you can't justify reading the latest Stephen

King, because it's been optioned already. Anyway, you're always looking for a few new tools for your toolkit.

No matter which one it is, the first thing to understand is what makes a TV show great.

What Makes Great TV?

The essence of a successful TV show is consistency. Audiences tune in every week to see compelling stories told in a consistent way. They tune in each week to see the *same thing*. On the surface, it's obvious what this thing is:

- On *CSI,* the forensics team will solve a couple of murder cases.
- On *Law & Order,* the cops will crack a case in the first half, and then the prosecutors will prosecute the alleged perp in the second.
- On *The Apprentice,* some yuppies will compete against each other, stooping at nothing, and then one of them will get fired.
- On *I Love Lucy,* Lucy will come up with a harebrained scheme. It will backfire, and she'll have to try to hide the aftermath from Ricky.

It's no use showing the audience something different, no matter how good. If you're making a glamorous soap opera, when viewers tune in to your show they want to see glamour and soapy plot lines. If you start writing the show as if it's a gritty drama, you'll lose your viewers. Meanwhile, the viewers who actually like gritty dramas will be over at another channel watching the latest incarnation of *The Shield/The Wire/Hill Street Blues/NYPD Blue/Homicide*. So you won't get them, either. No matter how quirky a movie is, it can build its unique audience through word of mouth and reviews; a TV episode comes and goes in an evening.

CSI might get away with one episode played for dry comedy, but two in a row and its audience gets confused and clicks the remote. If *Lucy* had tried a serious episode in which it turned out Lucy was a closet alcoholic—well, it never would have got that far, because Desi would have canned all the writers.

From the moment a show establishes what it is, it needs to stick to whatever that is. If it does that thing well, its audience will build. If no one really wants to see that thing, its audience will drift off and the show will get canceled. But if it can't figure out what that thing is, it's going to get dropped even faster.

It's pretty easy to see what the goods are that most shows are trying to deliver. Some more examples:

- On *The X-Files,* two FBI agents will investigate a mysterious paranormal phenomenon that has a scientific explanation.
- On *Battlebots,* we'll meet some robots and their designers, and then the robots will bash the heck out of each other.
- On *America's Next Top Model,* the wannabe models will learn about part of the modeling biz, and then someone will get sent home.
- On *Queer Eye for the Straight Guy,* five fabulous gay designers will descend upon some clueless straight guy, identify his style problems, fix them, and then party.
- On *NYPD Blue,* Detective Andy Sipowicz and his partner will investigate a horrible crime, find a suspect, and beat a confession out of him.

You get the idea.

But shows have to be consistent below the surface, too. A series has to maintain its tone. Viewers tune in to a show with a certain frame of mind, and if they're looking for dark, the show better deliver dark. A series has a core cast. Viewers tune in to see characters they've come to love, and if the episode doesn't show those characters in compelling stories, those viewers are going to feel dissatisfied. A show may have a preferred sort of ending. If viewers expect the cops to get their man, and they don't, they'll feel cheated.

Even the level of consistency stays consistent: an offbeat comic drama like *Moonlighting* can get away with an outrageous spoof like its classic "Atomic Shakespeare" episode, in which the characters reenact *The Taming of the Shrew; CSI* and *Law & Order* never stray from their procedural format.

Every show has territory it's willing to explore and territory where it won't go. There's no infighting on a *Star Trek* crew, no jockeying for the captain's favor, and no one betrays anyone else unless under some malign external influence. *24* doesn't do flashbacks; every event in an episode takes place during the same hour of the same day. On the other hand, anyone on *24* can turn out to be a traitor, and *Star Trek* not only does flashbacks, its crews even travel back in time. Every TV series has a deep structure, a *template,* which is simply the sum of all the things that must remain consistent from episode to episode.

When a show strays from its template, it begins to fail. When John Wells took over the helm of *The West Wing* from Aaron Sorkin, he changed the show in fundamental ways. Under Sorkin, the show was like the various *Trek* shows: a small band of colleagues who would lay down their lives for one another, each doing their part to promote the common purpose. They might argue about the best way to do things, but they never fight one another.

Under Wells, the show became a different animal. It became a workplace soap, like other John Wells shows: *Third Watch, ER, China Beach*. From a show about politics, it became more of a show about political workers: their infighting, their personal dramas. Wells's show did an episode in which CJ visited her sick father; it could easily have been a plotline from any other workplace soap. Sorkin's *West Wing* would never have spent more than three minutes on a personal matter unless it had political ramifications.

The show immediately took a hit. A lot of people stopped watching. Fans even created a website to petition the network to cancel the show, to put it out of its misery. Later on in Season 5, it struck out in a new direction, getting back to politics, but changing the shape of the show. The show may survive if it remains consistent in its new direction, and if the storytelling is good enough to attract a new audience. But a show with a less devoted audience—or a less sophisticated one—might simply have disappeared.

Many fascinating shows never manage to nail down exactly what goods they're delivering; or if the writers know, the audience can't figure it out fast enough. That's why shows sometimes find a home on DVD. In that medium they can build an audience over time, the way movies do, by word of mouth and reviews. Joss Whedon's science-fiction/western drama *Firefly,* killed after eleven aired episodes, found its second wind on DVD, selling over 200,000 units, justifying a movie (*Serenity*).

Some of the elements of a show's template are:

- A hook
- An attractive fantasy
- Characters we never get tired of
- Its venue
- Its genre
- Its tone
- Its program length
- Its network and time slot

A Hook

In the movies, a *hook* is a basic premise that makes you want to read the script if you're a producer or agent, and makes you want to see the movie if you're an audience member. In television, a show has a hook when its basic situation makes people want to watch the show before they've heard anything else about it.

- A family of goofy aliens lives in the suburbs (*Third Rock from the Sun*).
- A thriller that takes place "in real time" over the course of a single day, each hour-long episode shows one hour of the day (*24*).
- A wrongly convicted doctor hunts for the one-armed man who murdered his wife, while fleeing from the law (*The Fugitive*).
- A student by day is a sexy CIA superspy by night (*Alias*).

What about reality shows? They're all about the hook, each one more original than the next:

- A motley bunch of people live in a house together, watched by cameras; each week they vote someone out of the house (*Big Brother*).
- A motley bunch of people live on an island together, watched by cameras; each week they vote someone off the island (*Survivor*).
- A motley bunch of singers perform for the audience; each week, the judges and then the audience vote someone off the show (*American Idol*).
- A motley bunch of actresses perform for some judges; each week, the judges vote someone off the show (*The Starlet*).

Obviously some hooks are for some people and not for others:

- A Hong Kong detective transfers to L.A., where he uses his martial arts to fight crime (*Martial Law*).
- A Shaolin monk, a master of kung fu, flees bounty hunters through the Old West *(Kung Fu*).
- A teenage suburban girl battles vampires with the help of her friends (*Buffy the Vampire Slayer*).
- A vampire with a soul battles supernatural evil (*Angel*).

People who don't like martial arts won't be watching *Martial Law* or *Kung Fu*. People who don't care about vampires or martial arts won't be watching *Buffy* or *Angel*. I won't be watching any reality shows, thank you. That's okay. So long as you're hooking *enough* people, the show stays on the air. That's what modern television is all about.

Not all TV shows have conceptual hooks. Many sitcoms are vehicles for a star or for a hot comic talent the network hopes will become a star. The conceptual one-liner for *Roseanne* wouldn't be that appealing:

- A grouchy white-trash mom waddles through life, bitching about stuff.

Add Roseanne Barr, and you have:

- Roseanne Barr plays a grouchy white-trash mom who waddles through life bitching about stuff.

Now it's funny—if you know Roseanne Barr. The show was based on her stand-up comedy act, which was pretty much her grouching and bitching about stuff. Her success in stand-up led network execs to develop a show for her, hoping it would attract an audience.

The premise for *Home Improvement* wouldn't attract a crowd:

- An absentminded dad hosts a home improvement show on TV; at home he's even more confused.

But you add Tim Allen, and the show is a hit. Tim Allen's stand-up comedy act was about, among other things, the differences between men and women, sometimes as epitomized by their attitudes toward power tools.

- Ray Romano plays a put-upon dad whose parents live next door and won't stay there (*Everybody Loves Raymond*).
- Jerry Seinfeld plays a comic whose friends get obsessive about petty things (*Seinfeld*).
- Pamela Anderson plays a book clerk (*Stacked*).

It's not just sitcoms. Some dramas are first and foremost star vehicles, too:

- Dick Van Dyke plays a doctor who investigates murders (*Diagnosis Murder*).
- Rob Lowe plays a Washington lawyer (*The Lyon's Den*).
- Rob Lowe plays a casino doctor (*Dr. Vegas*).

A show can be a star vehicle for nonhumans as well:

- Learn stuff from furry monsters and an eight-foot-tall canary (*Sesame Street*).

Some vehicles work. Some don't. Sometimes the star can't carry a show. The jury is still out on whether audiences want to see Rob Lowe in his own show, though he was great in *The West Wing*.

Sometimes it's the wrong vehicle for what people like about the star. Sometimes, the scripts just suck.

A show doesn't have to have any conceptual hook at all:

- Six friends live in two New York apartments and hang out at a coffee shop a lot (*Friends*).

Before *Friends,* none of the cast was a major star. When *Friends* came out, Jennifer Aniston had played Ferris Bueller's sister in the abortive TV series based on *Ferris Bueller's Day Off,* and David Schwimmer had played Cop #2 in *Wolf.* The show's creators, David Crane and Marta Kauffman, had created a series before, but weren't star showrunners by any standard. But the writing and acting were magic.

- A bunch of losers hang out at a bar. Some of them work there (*Cheers*).
- The lives and cases of some tough New York detectives (*NYPD Blue*).
- The lives and cases of some tough Baltimore homicide detectives (*Homicide*).

Shows like *Friends* and *Cheers, NYPD Blue,* and *Homicide* are simply platforms for great characters to get involved in great stories; or to put it another way, they're platforms for great television writers to tell great stories.

An "Attractive Fantasy"

If a hook gets us watching, what keeps us watching?

We watch some shows because the characters are in a situation that we'd like to be in. In *The O.C.,* the characters have personal problems we can all relate to (romance, family, money), but they're young, slim, and beautiful, and live in spectacular houses under the Southern California sun. Most of us have the problems without the spectacular houses and the sun. We feel we could be them; by watching the show, we get to enter their lives. As Lee Rich, creator of *Dallas,* says, "People are looking at it saying, 'See, they have problems too, regardless of how much money they have.' "[1]

On *Sex and the City,* four thirty-something women get to live in the most glamorous parts of the most glamorous city in the world. They wear fabulous clothes and they have fabulous apartments. (On TV, everyone in New York has a fabulous apartment, even if they work at a coffee shop.) They not only have time to go out and breakfast, dine, and party with one another *several times a week,* they all like one another enough to do it. Does anyone over twenty really have friends like that? We wish we did . . . and by watching, we get to step into their world, and they become our friends, too.

On *Happy Days,* the characters live in the simpler, happier 1950s of memory.

The attraction may be that the characters' lives feel more important than ours. In *ER,* the characters save lives; in *Homicide,* the characters catch killers. Like us, they worry about making the rent, and falling in love. But their jobs are immediately, viscerally urgent. We get to step out of our lives and into theirs.

These are the fantasies that attract us to the worlds of these shows. Whatever keeps us coming back to spend time in the world of the show is what I call the show's *attractive fantasy*. A show can also have a *negative fantasy*. The characters are dealing with problems like the ones we face but worse.

We watch *The Sopranos* because our family is just like that, but at least no one's getting whacked.

We watch *Oz* because at least we don't live in a maximum-security ward, where we can be stabbed to death with a spoon. We can step outside *anytime we like*.

We watch *Lost* because it's exciting to think about being stranded on a mysterious and dangerous desert island, so long as you know you can change the channel at any moment, and the beast is not actually going to chase *you*.

Comedy is often based on a negative fantasy. We watch *Seinfeld* because Jerry and his buddies are just like us, only even more shallow and selfish. On *All in the Family,* Archie Bunker is a worse redneck bigot than most people's parents, and Edith is much more of a ditz. *Everybody Hates Chris* is about how bad it was to grow up being Chris Rock. If we can see the comedy in other people's lives, we can laugh at our own.

Shows often offer both attractive and negative fantasies. In *Buffy the Vampire Slayer,* the characters are usually in immediate mortal peril, but they also have skills and powers we don't have. The attractive fantasy is that Buffy gets to save the world; the negative fantasy is that she has to. In *Miami Vice* the negative fantasy is that the cops are up against arrogant, violent criminals flush with drug money; the attractive fantasy is they get to wear really slick clothes and live in Miami.

What both fantasies have in common is that *everything on TV is exciting*. TV is *compressed time*—life without the dull bits. Trying to get a promotion in your own job may involve years of work and politicking, much of it irritating or boring. There's no scutwork on TV. On *The Apprentice,* within a dozen hours, someone is going to win the job and the rest are going to get fired. Immediate gratification—for the viewers, anyway.

You can't really choose whether to have an attractive fantasy or a negative one. It's inherent in the premise. But understanding what the attractive fantasy of a show *is* enables you to deliver the goods for that show. If you're writing an episode of a show like *The O.C., Beverly Hills 90210, Miami Vice,* or *The Fresh Prince of Bel Air,* remember that people are watching at least partly because it's set in a community that most of America would like to live in, with characters who never have to worry about the rent. If you're not selling that fantasy, you're not delivering the goods.

Characters We Never Get Tired Of

A TV show doesn't *need* a hook. You can get people to tune in by running promotions day and night. It doesn't *need* an attractive fantasy. The characters of *Murphy Brown* or *The Mary Tyler Moore Show* or *Sanford and Son* live in the ordinary workaday world. Hell, the characters of *WKRP in Cincinnati* live in Cincinnati.

The one thing no television show can live without is a great cast of characters.

With rare exceptions, a movie *is* its plot. The characters exist to flesh out a story. If you know what the movie's story is, you can create the characters you need to tell that story. (See the section on retro-engineering the cast of *The Mummy* in my last book, *Crafty Screenwriting,* if you like.) When you describe a movie to someone, you talk about its plot.

When a network greenlights a TV series, traditionally they are buying a format they hope will be able to support at least 100 episodes. That's *100 stories*—more if there are multiple stories in each episode—almost none of which the writers have come up with yet.

In sitcoms, stories almost always come from challenging your characters' flaws, longings, and fears. Even in procedural dramas (*CSI, Law & Order*), where plots are often external, the strongest stories are still those that hit the characters where they live. Your characters are a *source* of most of your stories.

But much more important, characters are why the audience keeps tuning in to a show.

People tune in to shows because they care about the characters and want to see what's going to happen next in their lives. We get to know characters like Lucy Ricardo, Cliff Huxtable, Captain James T. Kirk, and Tony Soprano. They become members of our extended family.

We want to know what's happening with them. Will Ross get back together with Rachel? Will Dave and Maddy ever sleep together? How's Andy Sipowicz doing with his sobriety? What is Archie Bunker or Fred Sanford carrying on about this week? Will Carrie Bradshaw find true love, or will she push it away yet again?

The exception to this rule is the anthology show: *The Twilight Zone, Outer Limits, Red Shoe Diaries, The Hunger*. In these cases the show has to tap in to a very specific yearning in its niche audience, and deliver very tightly defined goods to fulfill it: here, creepy science fiction or sex. Anthology shows are rare because it's hard for them to sustain an audience, precisely because they have no characters for us to return to. That's why they often have a host—The Crypt Keeper, etc.—to give the show a familiar face.

TV characters populate our lives in some of the ways real friends do. We worry about them. We think about what we would do in their shoes. We talk about them behind their backs. We can't wait to see them again, and if we discover they're off on a vacation somewhere, incommunicado, we feel disappointed and a little lonely. And if we find ourselves alone in a hotel somewhere in the dark of night with no one to call and we can spend a little time with them, we're relieved, and not so lonely anymore. John Rogers (*Cosby, Global Frequency*):

> Movies, you go and you watch that story and those people are cool for that one time. TV is much more about those characters and that world. You'd want them at your barbecue. It's like you develop an addiction for them. So writing TV requires a much more thorough knowledge of the human psyche.

Note that we may not necessarily *like* all the characters on a TV show. We just have to *care* about them. Wanting desperately to see Caleb or Julie Cooper on *The O.C.* get their comeuppance is just as good as wanting Ryan or Seth to find love and happiness. J. R. Ewing practically personifies *Dallas* but you wouldn't really want him to be your uncle—or business partner. On the other hand, there is a general belief among network executives that characters, particularly central characters, should be likable. Chris Abbott (*Magnum, P.I.*) disagrees:

> I don't think there is a need to make characters likable. You need to make them interesting. Executives feel they need to be part of a process, and there are two things they can say: "This doesn't make sense" and "this character isn't likable enough." I wrote a pilot once. The central character was an unlikable guy but brilliant and he drove the show and was the engine for the whole family. But they couldn't get past that he was unlikable. There are too many people involved in creative decisions that shouldn't be. The cable shows were doing so much better, not because of sex or violence, which I can do without, but they could widen out the literary field and bring us people who weren't necessarily likable. Tony Soprano can be unlikable. *The L Word* the same way. Look at *Roseanne* when she came on—not a likable family. I think the real "L word" is "likable," and let's get rid of that.

And Barbara Hall (*Joan of Arcadia*):

> When I was pitching *Joan of Arcadia,* a studio executive asked me if Joan would be "heroic" in nature. I said, "No, she's a teenager, so she's narcissistic, sulky, self-obsessed." The executive said, "Well, I'm having trouble finding the good guy in all this," to which I replied, "Well, God is going to be pretty good."[2]

The same applies to reality shows. Characters have to be compelling and watchable, but not necessarily likable. The motley members of a *Survivor* cast are carefully chosen in much the same way a cast of characters is created. They're all distinct individuals, interesting in different ways, with personalities that will surely come into conflict with one another. We want to love most of them for different reasons, but we love to hate Rob and Amber. On every *America's Top Model,* there are some obviously wicked pretty models, some normal-looking girls we'll root for but who will never make the final cut, and some brats we'll get to enjoy watching take a fall.

A TV show *is* its characters. When you describe a TV show, you're describing the characters and the situation they're in.

The TV audience can get very attached to a show's characters. Once they feel they know them, woe betide the show if the writers change them too much. To the viewers, this will feel as though they've betrayed the character. I abandoned *Felicity* at the beginning of Season 2 after she chose Ben over Noel. It seemed out of character—at least, the character as I'd grown attached to her. Some of *Felicity*'s audience abandoned the show after Keri Russell got a short haircut (supposedly without warning the producers!).

The audience can grow so attached to characters that they have trouble imagining the actors playing a different role. Leonard Nimoy never really escaped Spock, in spite of his methinks-the-lad-doth-protest-too-much autobiography *I Am Not Spock*. When Susan Lucci, star of *All My Children,* goes out in public, do people shout out her name? No, they call her Erica. No movie actor has ever been so closely identified with a role.

When CBS thought the audience would need an explanation of why Mary Richards was still unmarried at thirty (the early 1970s, people!), the creators of *The Mary Tyler Moore Show* suggested she be divorced. But the network was concerned that viewers would somehow feel she'd divorced Dick Van Dyke—she'd played his wife for years on *The Dick Van Dyke Show*—

and they'd never forgive her for it. So the new story was she'd been engaged and then dumped.

So watch out. If you get a character wrong when you're writing a freelance script, you'll just get rewritten. If you get a character wrong when you're writing a spec script, you won't get the job. If you get a character wrong on a beloved show when you're doing the last pass on the script, and the actor doesn't catch it, there will be people out there who feel you've violated a member of their family. They will hunt you down and kill you like a dog in the street.

Characters are the whole deal. We'll tolerate huge plot problems if we're loving the characters and the way they deal with their extraordinary lives. Javier Grillo-Marxuach (*Charmed, Lost*):

> [You can] put characters in the most ridiculous situations, and if they're good characters, people will laugh at the situations and buy the jeopardy. I wrote an episode [of *The Chronicle*] where they were fighting Elvis impersonator vampires. You should not, by any reasonable standard, be able to take that seriously, and yet the three main characters of that show were fun and really developed—we *could* have them fighting a man-eating oven or a monster that is attracted to cell phone radiation. . . . If you look at *Buffy* and *Angel,* they didn't always have the budget to do everything that they needed to do convincingly, but the audience will forgive a lot of those things if you have characters that they care about—you can have all the fun in the world if your characters are consistent and their jeopardy is believable.[3]

Who are these characters we tune in to watch?

Lead Character

Your lead is, obviously, the role your star plays, the character who has most of the screen time in any episode, the character in the thick of the main story in any episode.

Unlike mainstream movies, TV has room for lead characters who aren't traditional heroes, from Tony Soprano, who can be homicidal, to Bart Simpson, who is merely horrible, to Drew Carey, who's fat, sarcastic, and irritating, to Archie Bunker, who's bigoted and overbearing. A movie hero can be cruel, but never petty. TV leads are petty all the time, from Larry David on *Curb Your Enthusiasm* to Jerry Seinfeld on *Seinfeld* to Roseanne to Jackie Gleason to, well, most comedy leads.

Though almost every movie has a main character, not every TV show does. It's hard to imagine *The Cosby Show* without Cliff Huxtable, or *Chico and the Man* without Chico. But is it possible to imagine *The O.C.* without Ryan? If Ben McKenzie dropped dead, would you have to recast someone else as Ryan or cancel the show? Or could you keep the show going without him?

How about *Beverly Hills 90210* if Shannon Doherty stomped off in a salary dispute and you had to do without Brenda Walsh?

How about *NYPD Blue* if David Caruso wanted too big a salary increase to play Detective John Kelly?

Whoops, sorry, David Caruso. It turns out The Show Must Go On.

Unlike movies, true ensemble shows are not rare on television. The *Friends* cast made a point of negotiating their salaries as a group because they knew perfectly well that any one of them could be written out. *Cheers* survived the departure of co-star Shelley Long, and when Valerie Harper insisted on a major salary bump on *Valerie,* her very own star vehicle, she had to watch the show become *Valerie's Family,* and then *The Hogan Family,* staying on the air for another four years without her.

That said, almost all TV shows do have a star, and if that star leaves the show, he has to be replaced by another star (usually Jimmy Smits).

Writing for stars—or actors who are convinced they are stars—is tricky. The more an actor plays a part, the more he feels he owns the role. (He may be right.) If you give an actor scenes or dialogue or stories that he feels are wrong for the character, he will balk. If this happens when the story is still just a springboard, all you've lost is a springboard (a story idea in a nutshell); if it happens on the set, you're in trouble.

It is true for any character, but particularly for a lead, that he is defined as much by what he would *never* do as what he will *usually* do. Captain Kirk will break the Prime Directive at the drop of a hat, but he would never leave a crew member behind. Jack Bauer might leave a crew member behind, but he would never betray his country. Homer Simpson would betray his country, but he would never think too deeply about it.

One way to look at the core cast you need, says Tom Chehak (*Diagnosis Murder*), is "what's the tenth episode of the third season all about? Then you start backtracking from there and see what you need to get there. Do I need a love interest—do I need pathos, love, hate etc." James Nadler (*PSI Factor*) likes to have at least one romantic triangle in his core cast, as an endless source of friction.

Point-of-View Character

Your lead character may also be a *point-of-view (POV) character,* through whom we see all the stories unfold. On *Sex and the City,* Carrie Bradshaw narrates all the stories and puts them in perspective for you. On *My So-Called Life,* Angela Chase tells you what the stories she's living through mean to her. But having a POV character doesn't require having her narrate, only that the stories are told through her emotional point of view.

Note that this is not the same as the character's *physical* point of view. Emotional point of view includes everything that happens to her, plus anything that she's going to find out about sooner or later, plus things she doesn't find out about but that are going to affect her during the story. (I go into this in more detail in *Crafty Screenwriting*.) If you have a point-of-view character, nothing can happen in the show that she never finds out about, or that doesn't affect her strongly in some way. If there are secondary stories (B stories and C stories), they usually start as part of the point-of-view character's life and then spin off to continue without her.

The point-of-view character doesn't have to be a lead. She doesn't even have to be alive. *Desperate Housewives* is narrated from beyond the grave, *Sunset Boulevard*–style, by Mary Alice, an apparent suicide victim. That makes establishing her point of view a little trickier. But everything that happens still has to be, in some sense, "her story."

Having a POV character makes the storytelling more intimate. We're seeing the show through someone's soul. If TV characters are members of our extended family, it's like having a member of your family tell you something that happened to them. However, a show's format may not lend itself to having a point-of-view character. A show like *West Wing* is really *about* conflicting viewpoints, so having a point of view would actually *reduce* the richness of the stories. Procedural shows like *CSI* and *Law & Order* are really *about* solving crimes; any interpersonal drama is just gravy. Telling the stories from one point of view might not add anything.

Core Cast

The core cast are the characters you see in every episode of a show. They're the people you see on the poster, and the people featured in the main title sequence. If a TV show "is" its characters, they're the characters that "are" the show.

The core cast are the characters for whom the audience is watching the show. They're the ones the audience has let into their extended family. For each core cast member, you can assume that at least some of the audience is watching the show solely to see what that character is up to this week.

If a core cast member isn't in an episode, their fans are going to be disappointed. Disappointed fans drift off to watch other shows. Your ratings fall. You are canceled. You are fired. You take to drink. Your marriage disintegrates. You have to move back to Oklahoma and take that job at Uncle Jake's feedlot, and watch other people's television shows at the strip mall bar.

So, when you're writing a show, *you have to serve your core cast.* Every episode must have at least one story involving each member of the core cast. On *Friends,* for example, each of the six friends is featured in every episode in at least one story line. On *Will & Grace,* it's Will, Grace, Karen, and Jack. On *I Love Lucy* it's Lucy and Desi, Fred and Ethel.

Not everyone uses the term "core cast." A related term is "series regulars." The series regulars are those cast members who appear in the opening title sequence of every episode; their contract is by the season. But they may actually only be contracted to appear in a limited number of episodes. A series regular need not necessarily be core cast.

Not everyone in the core cast has their own stories, either. On *I Love Lucy,* only Lucy has stories. On *Alias,* all the stories are about Sydney Bristow. The characters who have their own A stories are the *stars* of the show, whether or not the actors who play them are actually TV stars. On classic *Star Trek,* for example, Kirk, Spock, and McCoy are the stars. Scotty, Uhura, Sulu, and Chekhov appear in every show, but they're not carrying the show. On *Desperate Housewives,* the four women are the stars; their husbands and boyfriends are series regulars, at least until death does them part.

Core cast members would almost never go missing from an episode without a strong offscreen reason—for example, if core cast members were sick, or somehow managed to convince the showrunner to let them take off a couple of weeks to do a movie. When they do, moreover, the episode needs a good onscreen reason why they're not there; e.g., in dialogue you hear that the character is sick, or has gone on vacation.

Core cast members are almost never absent from stories; stories are almost never without core cast members. Even a C story will usually revolve around a core cast member.

From a budget point of view, the core cast are "free": they have already been guaranteed a certain amount of money per episode whether you use them a little or a lot. This can run from the big—say $50,000 per week—to the monstrous—a million bucks an episode. But that's already factored into the budget. The more you can keep the episode restricted to core cast, the happier your line producer is.

This contractual guarantee is why, when a show drops a core cast member, it's almost always done between seasons. You can always add a core cast member by simply writing an actor into every episode. Dropping a core cast member means you're going to be paying for them for the rest of the season, but not having them onscreen. The money people hate that.

Relationships

Another way of looking at the cast of a TV show is not as a bunch of characters but as a web of relationships. TV characters don't define themselves in a vacuum. They define themselves by how they relate to the other characters on the show. Lucy on her own is a bit of a whiner and a screwup; Desi on his own is a straight man. Put them together and you get an adorable relationship to watch. The ongoing success of *The Amazing Race* is precisely that rather than pitting individuals against one another, it pits couples who already have relationships against each other. How those relationships are tested by the competition is the essence of that show. Whether a show is scripted or semi-scripted ("reality"), it's the relationships between the characters that define the show.

TV Characters Don't Change

Characters rarely develop on TV. Generally, *TV characters don't change*. Their relationships with other characters change, and we learn new things about them. They may change jobs. But they don't change who they are. This is changing as television gets more sophisticated and storytelling gets more linear. But it is still fundamentally true.

In movies, characters are supposed to develop. But on TV, they don't. They may learn a lesson during an episode but they always seem to forget the lesson by the beginning of the next episode. That's because on TV, you never know how long you're going to be telling your stories. Your show may be canceled after six episodes, or fourteen, or after its first season. It may go on for ten years, as *Friends* did. You never know. As Johnny Depp remarked on another subject, "Bugs Bunny never changed, and it never stopped working."[4]

If your characters change, the dynamic between them changes. The conflicts between your core characters should be an endless source of stories; if those conflicts get resolved, or no longer become important to a character because he's moved on in his life, you've removed a source of dramatic conflict. That means you've just lost a source of stories.

An alcoholic never stops being an alcoholic; if he's lucky, he becomes a *recovering* alcoholic. In the same way, a character on television never fills the hole in his soul that you put there; he'd stop being interesting if he did. Instead he will continue to attempt to fill it in different ways; and there's your stories. The moment a character is contented, after all, his story's over.

This is more like real life, anyway. Real people rarely change. They may get a little wiser. They may occasionally recognize their patterns and know when they're heading into disaster. But they change their behavior slowly if at all; and they almost never change their attitudes. Happy, positive people tend to stay happy and positive even in adversity. Bitter, resentful people tend to stay bitter and resentful even when they're riding high. Workaholics don't stop working when they get rich. A maternal woman doesn't stop mothering when her kids go off to college, she just finds someone or something else to mother.

What replaces character development is character *revelation*. As a series goes along, you'll see the characters flesh out. You'll learn more about them. You'll understand better who they are and how they got that way. They'll never change who they are, but they'll become deeper and richer characters.

This is one reason why many TV writers *don't* try to create a lot of *backstory* for their characters. (A character's backstory is whatever happened to her before the stories that the writers are telling about her began.)

Movies often show character by flashing back to the past or having a character relate some pivotal, life-changing event. In contrast, we often know almost nothing about a TV character's past at first. What was Lucy's life like before she married Ricky Ricardo? Who cares? We get to know them the way we get to know real people, by watching what they do and how they *are*.

As with real people, occasionally bits of information slip out. We rarely get a character aria about what someone's parents' marriage was like, but we might get a revealing comment or two:

```
                    CHANDLER
The Bings have horrible marriages. They
yell. They fight. And they use the pool
boy as a pawn in their sexual games.
```

```
                  ROSS
Chandler, have you ever put on a black
cocktail dress and asked me up to your
hotel room?

                CHANDLER
No.

                  ROSS
Then you are neither of your parents.[5]
```

The reason TV writers usually skip the big backstory upload is that it may block future stories. Aaron Sorkin, talking about *The West Wing:*

> Why don't you [wait till you] get to an episode where, if you have a really good story for Bartlet and his father then, well, now his father's alive, that's the way it is from now on. But if you want to tell stories about sort of the ghost father, and living with the idea that Bartlet's father never liked him, well, now he's died. It wasn't until I wrote "Two Cathedrals"—the second season finale—that we knew that Bartlet's father was physically abusive."[6]

And here's Lee Goldberg (*Diagnosis Murder*):

> The only people who don't seem in-the-loop on this are development executives, who often want to know before the pilot is written every detail of the hero's life . . . who all his relatives are and what they do . . . and who his best friend was in preschool. But the fact is . . . none of that matters. And even if the writers tell you, it's bullshit."[7]

As a general rule, the less backstory, the better—unless it's crucial to the episode's story. If you have a revelation to make, don't throw it away as exposition. Make an episode out of it. When we finally saw pre–nose job Rachel and fat Monica on *Friends,* it was an event.

As with all rules, you can break this one if it's fruitful. Some series are all about the past. Every episode, *Lost* flashes back to the pre-crash life of one of the characters. *Angel,* about a vampire with a soul who fights evil, is as often an exploration of Angel's evil past as it is a contemporary story. (But then, as a 250-year-old vampire, he has a little more past than the rest of us.)

Network execs, by the way, often want to know everything about the character's backstory. And so does the audience. That doesn't mean you should tell them. It's not bad to leave them wanting to know more. That pulls them into the story. John Rogers:

> Miranda is captured. And she tells them they have to let her go because "she knows what happened in Tecumseh, IL." And they let her go. Now the whole audience is wondering—what the hell happened in Tecumseh? We've convinced them that this world is real, not self-contained. People forget they're watching a story—they're hanging out in a world.
>
> It drives execs crazy. Because they feel that you're cheating. But three years later when [the audience sees] an episode called "Tecumseh" coming up on their TiVo, they're gonna cream their pants.

Recurring Characters

Recurring characters are characters who keep coming back, but who don't have to be in every episode. They may grow into core cast if their story lines work out—or if the actors are compelling onscreen. One joy of writing TV is discovering a great actor and then writing her part bigger and bigger. But usually, recurring cast belong to aspects of the main characters' lives that aren't always part of the story you're telling: parents, spouses, and kids. In an externally driven show, the villain is generally recurring or even episodic, since at some point the hero may actually defeat him.

Unlike core cast, recurring characters *can* change. They can even resolve their issues with the core cast, because, after all, you can toss them away when you're done telling their stories.

A Place Where Stories Walk in the Door

Some concepts lend themselves to TV, and some don't. Often, it's a question of venue. By and large, TV shows are shot on much smaller budgets than movies. The most expensive movies these days may cost $200 million for their two hours. Of that, above-the-line talent (cast and directors) rarely top $50 million. (Say $20 million for the star, $15 million for the remaining cast, and $10 million for a top director. Don't talk to me about what the writers are getting. It don't much figure.) So you can shoot a movie for up to $75 million *per hour,* not including cast.

TV shows don't get to play with that kind of money. Sure, TV stars can rake in huge amounts of money. In the last seasons of *Seinfeld,* each of the four core cast was making a million bucks an episode—over twenty million a year for each of them. But the production budget—the amount of money spent on the crew—is much smaller. If you don't count the actors, the average sitcom episode costs a million dollars to produce.[8]

A "half hour" of television is about 20 minutes of new footage; the rest of the airtime goes to commercials, promos, and the title sequence. So a sitcom's production costs are about $3 million per hour—or 4 percent of the per-hour costs of making a high-budget movie.

Time is an even more important factor. A new James Bond film might have six months to shoot two hours' worth of story. That's

120 days of production for the main unit, plus untold days of second-unit production and computer graphics; or one day of production per minute of airtime.

A TV series needs a new show every week. By airing the occasional rerun, a show can shoot up to 8 days per episode with the main production unit. (The main unit is directed by the episode director and shoots the actors acting. The second unit is directed by a second-unit director and shoots things like car drive-bys, helicopter shots, and inserts. If the second unit shoots an actor, he's doing something that doesn't involve dramatic acting—walking into a building, say.) A typical single-camera half-hour show shoots four and a half days (there's some overlap) per episode; a three-camera sitcom tries to get the whole show shot in a day.

So a television show shoots about one day of production per *five* minutes of airtime, or about 20 percent of the production period of a movie.

So TV isn't allowed to cost as much to shoot as movies can. And it isn't allowed to take as long to shoot as movies can. How does TV do it?

A TV show will usually have *standing sets:* a fictional setting created in a totally controllable soundproof studio where as much of the weekly action as possible takes place. In the case of a sitcom, this may be almost all of the show. Think of the early days of *Friends*. The episodes take place in two apartments and a coffee shop, and were actually filmed on a stage with an audience watching. Later when the show became a huge hit, they opened the show up and allowed more and more location shooting. But most of the episodes still took place in those two apartments and that coffee shop. Think of *Cheers,* which initially took place entirely on one bar set.

Even a show like *24,* whose main character, Jack Bauer, is driving all over Los Angeles, has a major standing set to which the show keeps returning: the Counter Terrorism Unit's headquarters.

Every time you're on standing sets, your production manager is happy. Your director may be miserable—standing sets never look as good as real locations, though they make camera moves and lighting easier. But if TV directors wanted to shoot in the real world, they should have become movie directors.

When a TV show does have to go on location, it tries to restrict its locations to those places where the characters will spend a fair amount of time. Every time the production company has to wrap up the equipment and move somewhere else, it takes an hour, not counting travel time. That's an hour of everyone's time—we're talking fifty to a hundred people, all on the clock—when nothing is getting shot. So if you go to a warehouse, at least five minutes of the show, say, should take place in or near that warehouse. If you, God forbid, go to a boat, at least five minutes should take place on or near that boat.

From a production point of view, it's tough to have a TV show that has no narrative home. TV lends itself to shows that have one or two basic venues and don't go gallivanting all around the globe. That's why so many TV shows are set in a home, a workplace, or a home and a workplace. *Melrose Place* is based on an apartment complex. *De Grassi Jr. High* is based on a school. *Corner Gas* is based on a gas station and a diner. *The Honeymooners* is based on two apartments. *Will & Grace,* an apartment. *St. Elsewhere,* a hospital. *L.A. Law,* a law office. *Babylon 5,* a space station. And so on.

If a show's concept allows stories that take place in, say, one home and one workplace, that's going to put much less strain on the budget and the schedule.

Often you have to get creative. If your show is about a fugitive who's never in the same place twice, then you can at least build some standing sets showing the headquarters of the cops trying to track him down. Also, you can make sure that at least each episode takes place at only one basic setting. Dr. Richard Kimble comes to a farmhouse . . . next episode, Dr. Richard Kimble gets a job at a hospital . . . next episode, Dr. Richard Kimble gets a job at a garage . . .

Likewise, your classic *Star Trek* episode takes place on the *Enterprise,* with the away team sent to a single "planet surface" location—itself either a set built just for that episode or a single natural environment (usually Vasquez Rocks in Agua Dulce).

You don't have to have a single standing set. The first season of *Buffy,* for example, typically had Buffy's House (Living Room, Dining Room, Foyer, Buffy's Room, etc.); Sunnydale High School; the graveyard set; and the Bronze (a student bar). There would be one or two "swing sets" that could be used if an episode needed a visit to, say, the zoo. Almost everything was shot on a set in the first few seasons. (Later seasons had bigger budgets, hence more locations.)

If you're trying to come up with good TV pitches, remember that the ideal TV series venue is one where fresh stories naturally walk in the door every week. That way you don't have to send your core cast out into the wide world. On *ER,* almost all of the show takes place inside the hospital, that is, on a hospital set that lives on a soundstage somewhere in Southern California. No need to go out looking for stories; every week, new sick people fly in the door. On *The West Wing,* most of the show takes place inside the West Wing of the White House. No need to go out looking for stories; every week, new problems walk in the door or come in via the media.

Any situation involving complicated production—for example, anything involving animals that are expected to react in certain ways (think *Turner and Hooch*), or anything involving *Roger Rabbit*–style CGI/live interaction—may not be feasible on TV. If you do it anyway, it may look lame.

That said, TV shows are constantly trying to break the home-and-workplace mold. There are two ways to achieve this:

1. Spend more money. (Hah!)
2. Block shooting.

Block shooting is a rarely used technique in which the entire series, or at least a "block" of episodes, is shot all at once. That means if you go to a shoeshine kiosk once in each of eight episodes, you shoot all the shoeshine scenes for all eight episodes on the same day. It saves a ton of time for the production unit and allows the writers to use a location that wouldn't be justified otherwise. If a location comes up only once an episode, but comes up in several episodes that are being shot in the same block, then it's just as efficient for production as a location that's used several times in one episode.

Block shooting is rare because it's a nightmare for directors and actors to keep track of where their characters are emotionally over the course of multiple episodes. It drives wardrobe crazy, too, and it has ramifications you might not think of—essentially it means an actor can't get a shorter haircut mid-season, because you can't go back to the old haircut when you're shooting scenes from the earlier episodes. If you're shooting in the fall, you may have trouble matching the color of the leaves!

As a writer, you have no control over whether your show is block shot. It is or it is not. If it's block shot, you'll have a little more latitude in using a location for only one or two pages in an episode. But if it's not (and you can assume it's not), you'll want to avoid specialized locations unless a reasonable chunk of the story (two or three scenes, say five pages plus) takes place in them.

Nondescript (ND) locations are almost always safe, though. If you set something on `EXT. STREET--DAY`, they can always shoot around the corner from wherever else they're shooting that day. They can always find an `EXT. PHONE BOOTH--DAY` around the corner, too, and if they can't, they can rent a phone booth and plant it on the `EXT. STREET--DAY`.

Episodic vs. Serial Stories

To what degree do story lines carry over from one episode to another?

Daytime soap operas are serial. Story lines develop over many episodes or over the entire season. Characters hook up or break apart. To really appreciate what's going on in a soap opera episode, you need to have seen the preceding episodes. Prime-time soaps like *Everwood* and *Rescue Me* and *Dawson's Creek* and *Dallas* also play out their relationship arcs over many episodes. Who's dating whom? Who's breaking up with whom? Who shot J.R.?

It's not just soap operas. The prime-time thriller *24* is all but impossible to follow if you have not been keeping up with the unfolding narrative, and if you watch a later episode, it will kill your enjoyment of any earlier episodes you might have missed. You'll know what the secrets are, who the traitors are, what the villains' secret plans are, and so on.

Other shows are largely episodic. You can watch the episodes from one season in any order and they'll make as much sense. You don't need to have seen the previous *Simpsons* episode to appreciate this one; you don't even need to have seen any previous episodes, though knowing the characters makes the jokes funnier. Many crime and medical shows are episodic. You can watch any *Law & Order* and immediately understand what's going on; at most, you might miss the flavor of the core characters' personal lives. That's because the show isn't really *about* the private lives of the core characters, it's really about their cases. It's a "franchise show."

Most shows are somewhere in between. Each episode is a self-contained story, but the characters are involved in longer "story arcs" that give the season as a whole a story to tell. The comic situations in any episode of *Friends* are funny whether you've seen the show before or not; but the show develops the characters' personal relationships over the course of each season, and viewers have an ongoing soap opera–style story to follow. Will Ross break up with Rachel? Will Ross get back together with Rachel? Whose baby was it? And what about Naomi?

Networks prefer episodic shows because they don't have to worry whether viewers miss one. Dedicated viewers might watch 80 percent of a show's episodes when it first airs, but you want to be able to pull in any viewer that decides to give the show a shot mid-season. Later, when the episodes reappear in syndication, viewers drift in and out. The more serial a show is, the harder it is for it to pull in new viewers in mid-season. The more serial your show is, the more trouble your audience will have following the story when, inevitably, the network preempts your show two weeks in a row to run the World Series, or your audience abandons your show en masse for the finale of a long-running and beloved sitcom. And what happens if your show gets moved from Tuesday at 8 P.M. to Thursday at 10? You'll lose some old viewers and get some new ones. The easier the show is to get into, the more of those new viewers you'll get to keep.

Networks don't, amazingly, always air episodes in order. The *Firefly* pilot didn't air; the show started with episode #2. We had the same surprise on the first show I (co-)created, *Naked Josh:* after we'd worked hard to establish all the characters and their relationships in our pilot, the US network aired the second episode first.

Episodic shows are easier to write, too, because the writer only has to worry about what's happening this episode, not the ramifications of a whole season arc. But writers like to write serial shows because it makes the overall story richer and deeper. If it were up to the writers, many shows would be immediately released on DVD, so the shows could be seen in complete order, without those pesky commercials. Show creators have to choose between riskier but more satisfying serial storytelling and simpler but shallower episodic storytelling.

Naturally, the more episodic a show is, the easier it is to spec. (We'll get into spec scripts in a bit. For now, a spec is a sample episode of a current show, which you write in order to demonstrate your writing ability.) All you need to write a *Law & Order* spec is an intriguing case and some compelling perpetrators. Moreover, whoever's reading your spec of an episodic show needs to know very little about where it fits in the current season, or even what season it belongs to, assuming the core cast has not changed. But it would be quite a challenge to slip your own episode into the *24* time line, since every hour of Jack Bauer's day is accounted for, and your reader will need to know what happened right before and what will happen right after your story.

On the other hand, rising to a challenge is one way to impress readers. If you *can* figure out how to slip an episode into a time line without leaving your intended readers behind, then you'll show your chops. It's the sort of problem that occurs on real shows, when suddenly you need a spare episode to play between two episodes that are already plotted. On *Charlie Jade* my staff and I had to come up with an episode all of whose stories would take place during the night between the end of one already written episode and the beginning of another already written episode.

Demographics and Networks

Demographics are the makeup of the audience for the show. *The O.C.*, for example, is a "co-viewing" show: it's aimed at both teenagers and adults. The conventional wisdom is that adults want to watch stories about adults and kids mostly want to watch stories about kids. Therefore every episode of *The O.C.* features stories about some adults—Sandy and Kirsten Cohen—and some kids—their son, Seth Cohen, their adopted son, Ryan Atwood, and the boys' respective flames, Summer Roberts and Marissa Cooper. On the other hand, *Mighty Morphin Power Rangers* is a kids' show, so the heroes are all kids. The only adults are the scary-hair-villains-of-the-week.

Different time slots have different demographics. At midday, the audience is primarily homemakers and the unemployed. Afternoon and Saturday morning are kids. Prime time is the whole family. In late prime time and late night, the only people watching are adults and naughty kids. In the *Medium* writing room, showrunner Glenn Caron is said to be fond of saying, "It's a ten o'clock show. Somebody's gotta get f***ed, somebody's gotta get killed."

Each network has its own intended demographic. The networks have always tried to grab the entire family, but of the networks, CBS has traditionally been aimed at older adult audiences, while the WB goes for younger adult audiences. UPN has generally been more interested in African-American audiences than the other networks. Nickelodeon is aimed at kids; Lifetime is "television for women"; Disney is family-safe; PAX is family-safe for Mormons; and Playboy is for lonely single guys who don't get enough porn spam. An April 2005 *New York Times Magazine* article, "Our Ratings, Ourselves," reported:

> The average American household now sees 8 hours 1 minute of TV every day and has access to more than a hundred channels and several different sets—often tuned to different channels in different rooms. Industry types call this phenomenon audience fragmentation. The days of a family gathering together on the couch are dying out for good. We're in pieces. Or as Steve Morris, the Arbitron CEO, put it more gently, "People are dividing." Every age group, every cultural group and every demographic group, Morris added, is in the process of getting media packaged expressly for its members.[9]

The demographics of a show ought to be fairly simple, though sometimes a show will attract a secondary audience no one counted on, such as the gay audience watching *SpongeBob SquarePants,* the lesbians watching *Xena: Warrior Princess,* and the hip twenty-somethings watching *Pee Wee Herman.* Then you are writing for two audiences at once, which can be tricky, but also a good deal more fun.

If you are not sure of the demographics of a time slot and channel, don't just watch the shows that air then, watch the commercials. If they're selling brightly colored plastic toys, it's a kids' show. If they're selling BMWs, the show has a large number of rich adults in its audience.

You can do this for individual shows, too. If you want to know if the Miss America Pageant is aimed at horny young guys or at girls who want to be beauty queens, watch the commercials. If they're selling Miller Beer, Jeep Wrangler, and Gillette Mach Three razors, the audience is mostly young guys. If they're selling Stay-Free Maxi Pads and hair color, the audience is mostly girls. If they're selling Viagra, it's dirty old men who ought to be ashamed of themselves.

You can approach demographics from the chicken or the egg. If you're writing a show *about* kids, it's almost certainly a show *for* kids. That means you're aiming for an afternoon time slot on a network, or any time on a kids' channel. Or, if you want to create a prime-time show, then you know the audience is the whole family, which means you better be pitching a show that attracts at least teens-on-up and is suitable for the whole family to watch.

You should know a show's demographics before you write it. Before you tell a story, you should know whom you're telling it *to*. You don't need to see the market research. But you do need to be able to picture the audience in your mind's eye. *You are telling stories to an audience*. Demographics are who that audience is. You need to know if the people around your campfire are Cub Scouts or Girl Scouts or your old buddies from college.

The Show Bible

A show's template is theoretically laid out in a document called the show's *bible*. In practice, there may be no bible, only the scripts and the episodes. Some of the elements of the template may live only in the showrunner's head. Some elements may even creep into the show without anyone quite realizing it, not even the showrunner, until someone writes an episode that breaks the show's unwritten rules, and everyone has to figure out what went wrong.

If you're writing for an established show, either as a freelancer or as a staff writer, they'll give you the bible, if there is one. However, even if there is one, the bible rarely contains all the information you need, and it often contains lots of information you don't.

Information you don't need often includes yards of backstory for the characters and their world. Unless the episode you're writing is about that backstory, most of it is likely to be irrelevant to your story. Do you really need to know about Mary Sue's parents' divorce in order to write Mary Sue? Does anyone really need to know that the planet was settled after the Vogon War? You may be tempted to try to get some of that backstory out to the audience. Resist the temptation. Worse than irrelevant is backstory in the bible that's been contradicted or superseded in the episodes. In that case, what happened in the episodes is much more important, because the audience has seen them, while it will never see the bible.

Information you need that isn't in the bible is either in the episodes or in the heads of the writing staff. Before you bother the writers, you want to watch as many of the episodes of the show and read as many of the scripts as you can. Then, if you still have questions, ask the writing staff to clarify. The template may be described in the bible, but it really lives in the episodes and in the writing staff.

If you can't get the episodes on DVD or from the show, you can watch them at the Museum of Television and Radio, with branches in New York and Beverly Hills. Their library is quite current.

If you are writing a spec script, your agent, if you have one already, may be able to get you a copy of the show bible. Generally, though, you're going to have to retro-engineer the bible from the episodes you've seen and the scripts you've been able to get your hands on. You can tell from the episodes and their scripts who the core cast are, what the standing sets are, how much of the show is shot exterior, and so on.

Remember, though, that nothing in the bible actually goes on TV. What goes on TV are episodes. Anything in the bible is up for grabs. As Lee Goldberg (*Diagnosis Murder, Martial Law*) says, "They're gonna toss the bible as soon as they get the series order."[10] What's in the episodes is the *show*.

Getting your hands on sample scripts is easier. Many scripts are available for free on the Net, at sites such as Drew's Script-O-Rama (www.script-o-rama.com), Simply Scripts (www.simplyscripts.

com), and Twiz TV (www.twiztv.com). Many shows have thoughtfully given copies of scripts to the Writers Guild of America Library in Los Angeles. The Margaret Herrick Library at 333 South La Cienega Boulevard in Beverly Hills also carries scripts.

You can also read published compilations of scripts, but these are long out of date by the time they hit bookshops. Compared to television, publishing works at a glacial pace. Heh.

You can buy scripts on eBay (ebay.com), as well as Planet MegaMall (www.planetmegamall.com), Script Shack (www.scriptshack.com), and DV Shop (www.dvshop.ca/dvcafe/writing/tvscripts. html). They're not cheap, though.

Script City (www.scriptcity.com) and other sites (see Appendix 1) sell TV scripts for around ten bucks a pop. That's steep if you're buying more than a couple. I'm not clear on how they can legally sell scripts, which are copyrighted material. Maybe they've got a royalty deal going. Who knows? They do, however, have an impressive collection; for example, around twenty *Third Rock from the Sun* scripts, and they will e-mail scripts to you upon payment.*

---

* Note that in buying a script that was actually used on set, you're buying someone's legitimate physical property that he or she has a right to sell. In buying an electronic copy of a script, or a script that was photocopied in order to be sold, you may be pirating software. Someone owns that script and if he or she is not getting paid for it, you're buying stolen property. On the other hand, if that someone is a studio or network, you may not feel too bad about it. If they'd published the script, you'd have bought it, right?

2

GREAT EPISODE IDEAS

What makes a good episode?

A good episode *delivers the goods on the show's template.* It provides all the elements in the show's template (hook, attractive fantasy, core characters, etc.) that people are tuning in for. If it's an episode of a series where there is always a moral issue at stake, there's a moral issue at stake. If it's for a show where there's supposed to be a karate fight, there's a karate fight.

A good episode has an *emotional heart.* We have to care about what's going to happen, and the story has to move us.

Unless the show is entirely episodic, a good episode also moves the characters' individual stories forward and develops the season story lines. (A great spec script, obviously, won't do this, because it exists outside the season time line, but then, a great spec is not entirely the same as a great episode.)

A great episode gives us fresh insight into the characters and, maybe, ourselves. A great episode also leaves the viewer wanting to watch the next episode *as soon as possible.*

The Springboard

In the beginning is the *springboard:* simply a promising story in a nutshell.

- Aunt Bee gets a chance to do a nightly cooking show, but she's guilty that there's no one to cook for Andy and Opie. So they concoct an imaginary housekeeper and cook for themselves. Too bad they can't cook! (*The Andy Griffith Show,* "The Mayberry Chef")
- When Krusty the Clown is busted for robbing the Kwik-E-Mart, Bart has to prove that Krusty was framed by Sideshow Bob. (*The Simpsons,* "Krusty Gets Busted")
- Scooby Doo and his friends investigate a dude ranch haunted by a 150-year-old ghost. They discover the ghost is really the dude ranch's assistant, who's trying to scare away guests so he can buy the ranch cheap. (*Scooby-Doo, Where Are You?,* "Mine Your Own Business")
- Bobby steals his mother's stash and gets caught with it, but Jack takes the heat. (*Jack and Bobby,* "Better Days")
- When the new city commissioner tries to run a freeway through the Addams Family's house, Gomez has to find a way to stop it. (*The Addams Family,* "Progress and the Addams Family")
- Mulder and Scully investigate a series of "locked room" killings. They discover the killer is a mutant who can squeeze through impossibly tight spots. (*The X-Files,* "Squeeze")
- When Dawson and Joey finally spend a night together, everything's perfect . . . until Dawson gets a call from an old girlfriend. (*Dawson's Creek,* "The Song Remains the Same")
- When Cordelia wishes that Buffy had never come to Sunnydale, a vengeance demon makes her wish come true, with

nightmarish consequences (*Buffy the Vampire Slayer,* "The Wish")

A springboard, by the way, is not exactly the same thing as the episode's "logline," the one-liner that appears in the channel listings in the paper or in *TV Guide,* though they can look similar. A logline is all sizzle: "When Caleb makes a shocking announcement, the revelation rocks the Cohen family, right in the middle of their Chrismukkah celebration." The springboard gives away the mystery: "When Ryan invites Lindsay over to Chrismukkah, Sandy convinces Caleb to reveal that Lindsay's his daughter—how will the Cohen family take the news?" Likewise, the springboards give away the mutant in *The X-Files,* the fake ghost, and Sideshow Bob's guilt.

A good *story,* in TV or any other medium, has these basic elements:

1. A compelling central *character*
2. with a *goal,* a *problem,* or an *opportunity*
3. who faces *obstacles* and/or an *antagonist.*
4. If he succeeds, he and/or the world wins something he didn't have before (*stakes*), and/or
5. if he fails, he and/or the world is worse off than if he hadn't tried (*jeopardy*).

A springboard should contain these elements, either implicitly or explicitly.

- Your central character will be one of the show's core cast. All of them should be compelling.
- The goal, problem, or opportunity may be implicit. On *NYPD Blue,* Andy Sipowicz's lifelong goal is to be a good cop and protect the innocent from evil by putting scum

behind bars. Each crime he investigates gives him an opportunity to do that. On *Dawson's Creek,* Dawson's goal is to find romantic happiness; spending the night with Joey has given him an opportunity to do it. Or, it may be explicit. On *Buffy,* Cordelia's wish turns Sunnydale into a realm of nightmare, creating a problem for everyone.

- In an externally driven show, there's usually an antagonist—the serial killer in "Squeeze," the dude ranch's assistant in "Mine Your Own Business." In an internally driven show, the core cast themselves are often each other's antagonists. When Dawson gets a call from an old girlfriend, Joey becomes his antagonist (sometimes called an "intimate opponent," if you want to get fancy about it) because she doesn't trust him; or, from Joey's point of view, Dawson's old girlfriend becomes an obstacle to her relationship with Dawson. Aunt Bee's guilt over abandoning the family kitchen is an obstacle to keeping her cooking show. In *The Amazing Race,* the other competitors are antagonists; time, distance, and difficulty are obstacles.
- Your protagonist, or his world, should have something to gain (the stakes). Aunt Bee's having a cooking show is at stake in "The Mayberry Chef." Dawson's romantic relationship with Joey is at stake in "The Song Remains the Same." On *NYPD Blue,* the stakes are subtler: Andy's reputation as a good cop, and his satisfaction at putting scum behind bars.
- Your protagonist, or his world, should be in jeopardy. The Addams Family's house is in jeopardy in "Progress and the Addams Family." The mutant's future victims are in jeopardy in "Squeeze." Dawson's *friendship* with Joey is in jeopardy in "The Song Remains the Same" (that's the danger in dating your best friend). All of Sunnydale is in jeopardy in "The Wish."

All of these elements add up to a story whose outcome we care about.

In television, jeopardy is probably more common than stakes. That's because the world doesn't change much on a TV show—if it did, you'd break the consistency of the show. While a poor guy in a movie can win a million dollars and end up rich, if that happens on TV, your show about a poor guy is now about a rich guy, which changes the entire dynamic. When Diane Chambers finally gets a break as a writer on *Cheers,* she's no longer a wannabe writer, she's a real one—and she's off the show.

When a character actually wins something big, the show has to deal with the consequences. Roseanne did win the lottery on *Roseanne,* and the show lost its grounding in trailer-trash reality. When Dave finally slept with Maddy on *Moonlighting,* the show lost its romantic tension.

(When the air goes out of a show, it's said to have "jumped the shark." The phrase was invented by a website—naturally, www.jumptheshark.com—for the *Happy Days* episode in which Fonzie jumps over a shark on water skis, after which, some feel, the show never recovered its credibility.)

It's easier to put something at risk that the characters already have. Then they can win—succeed in keeping it—without changing the setup of the show.

Jeopardy is endless. Cop shows, for example, regularly deal with people who break the rules and hurt people. Their victims are in jeopardy. The cops reestablish the normal world by arresting and convicting them. Medical shows are about people who are sick or wounded; the doctors are just trying to make them healthy again.

The jeopardy or stakes may be implicit, but they must be clear. We have to have something to root for or root against. That's what draws us into the story.

What Makes a Great Springboard?

A great story springboard perfectly fulfills the show's template. *It uses the show's central conflict to tell a new story or deepen an old one.*

In a properly constructed show, the main character wants something he's never going to get—not while the show's still running. On *Friends,* Ross wants Rachel to think he's cool; Rachel wants Ross to respect her. On *I Love Lucy,* Lucy wants Ricky to be impressed with her. On post–Shelley Long *Cheers,* Sammy wants to sleep with Rebecca. On *The Sopranos,* Tony Soprano wants peace within his family. On *Bewitched,* Samantha wants to avoid using witchcraft because her powers unnerve Darrin.

Every episode of *The Apprentice* is about who'll win the job. How the competitors struggle to stay in the game—by cooperating or sabotaging one another—is the essence of each episode.

How the characters struggle to get what they want is the essence of any show. In a great episode, the central conflict takes the characters into new story territory. It gives them new wounds, creating new reasons to separate them from what they want. Or it takes them deeper into old territory, making their old wounds deeper, intensifying the old reason they can't have what they want.

A great story idea challenges your characters. Characters are defined by their strengths and weaknesses. A great episode challenges a character's weakness or strength—it forces a character to overcome or at least face one of his flaws, or turns one of his virtues into a risk factor.

WEAKNESSES:

- Sam Malone is definitely not an intellectual. So when Diane teases Sam about the dumb women he dates, Sam tries to prove her wrong by dating someone smart. (*Cheers,* "Sam's Women")

- Grissom's going deaf. So when Grissom investigates the murder of a man who's been pushed off a building, his increasing deafness pushes him off the case. (*CSI,* "High and Low")
- Buffy never wanted to be the Slayer. So when she wakes up in an asylum and the doctors tell her that her being the Slayer and everything that's happened on the series are part of a massive hallucination she has to fight, she desperately wants to believe them. (*Buffy the Vampire Slayer,* "Normal Again")
- Clark Kent is vulnerable to kryptonite. So when he gets a class ring set with red kryptonite, he loses his morals. (*Smallville,* "Red")
- Josh is shy with women. So what's he going to do when he's dating two of them? (*Naked Josh,* "The More the Merrier")

Edith Piaf used to say, "Use your faults; use your defects. They will make you a star." It's our flaws that make us distinct. But our strengths, too, make us distinct.

STRENGTHS:

- Jed Bartlet is intensely moral. But when a Qumari minister turns out to have been plotting terrorism in the United States, he has to order him killed in a secret assassination. (*The West Wing,* "We Killed Yamamoto")
- Sandy Cohen is a devoted family man—and a liberal lawyer. So when an old lover shows up, on the run from the law, he feels he has to protect his family by keeping her reappearance a secret. What happens when Kirsten finds out? (*The O.C.,* "The Accomplice" and "The Second Chance")

- When Clark Kent's friend Pete loses a race, he asks Clark to use his superpowers to help him win—but the only real winners will be the thugs that run the race. (*Smallville,* "Velocity")
- Mal is more decent than he'd like to admit. So what will he do when a shipment he's been hired to steal turns out to be badly needed medicine for a community suffering from disease? (*Firefly,* "The Train Job")
- Andy Brown moved to Everwood to protect his kids from the big city. But when his son gets a girl pregnant, Andy is concerned that the knowledge will wreck his son's life. Will he tell the truth? Or try to protect his son from the consequences of his actions? (*Everwood,* "The Day Is Done")
- When nebbishy returnee Carl Morrissey discovers he has super-strength and super-speed, he decides to clean up his favorite park and chase out the muggers who hang out there. But is he invulnerable, too? (*The 4400,* "The New and Improved Carl Morrissey")

Or as the proverb says, "No good deed goes unpunished."

In all of these cases, it's the character's strength or weakness that *causes* the situation to be a problem. A less moral president than Jed Bartlet wouldn't blink an eye about assassinating a terrorist. A smarter, more intellectual man than Sam Malone (say, Frasier Crane!) wouldn't have any trouble finding smart women to date. It's the flaw or the strength that makes it a story. (If Hamlet were in Othello's shoes, and vice versa, neither play would happen. Clever Hamlet would spot Iago's treachery in a moment, and decisive Othello would kill the usurper the moment he got back from Wittenberg.)

Everyone has the virtue of their vices and the vices of their virtues. An episode in which an articulate character talks himself *into* trouble, or a brave character puts his friends in danger, is always worth a shot.

Another way of looking at the same thing is that a character is defined by what he *tends* to do, and by what he would *never* do willingly. Challenging those aspects of his personality is always promising story territory. If there's something your character would *never* do, then putting him in a situation where doing exactly *that* is apparently his only way out, is a good way of creating a convincing story.

A great story springboard uses the show's template to do something another show can't do. You want your audience to watch your show and not some other show, don't you? A great episode tells a story no other show can tell:

- In *Star Trek: The Next Generation*'s "A Perfect Mate," Captain Picard falls for an "empathic metamorph," a woman who changes her personality to suit whatever man she's with. But she's a diplomatic gift from one planet's ruler to another, intended to help stop a war—so Picard can't have her. The science-fiction premise allows the show to illuminate how ordinary women are expected to change their personalities to suit their men, without getting preachy about it.
- On the *Punk'd* pilot, Ashton Kutcher's gang show up at *NSYNC star Justin Timberlake's house and pretend they're repossessors looking for the $900,000 in back taxes he supposedly owes. Where else do you get to see stars made fools of on TV? Intentionally, I mean.
- On *Charlie Jade,* "Truth(s)," the series' impressionistic use of flashbacks pays off when 01 Boxer tells Charlie three versions of the truth about himself . . . no one of which is completely a lie. On another show, the flashbacks might be too jarring.
- On *The West Wing,* "25," the president's daughter has been kidnapped, and because he feels he can no longer make clear decisions, he must decide whether to invoke the Twenty-fifth

Amendment and turn over power to the other party. No other show tells stories about the highest levels of the American republic.

- Every episode of *The Amazing Race* takes its couples to places we haven't seen before and makes them jump through hoops we haven't seen before. No other show mixes travelogue with competition in quite the same way.

Any way your show's template is distinctive should give you a way to make an episode that belongs only to that show, and not to any other. It's your job to figure out what is most refreshing and distinctive about the show when you come up with springboards for it.

In rare cases, an episode can play against the show's template. Stung by criticism that his whole show was based on witty banter—which was indeed part of the joy of watching *Buffy*—showrunner Joss Whedon wrote an episode, "Hush," in which all the people of Sunnydale lose their voices. *Star Trek: Deep Space Nine* broke the mold with "Far Beyond the Stars," in which the core cast actors are science-fiction writers in the 1950s, and Avery Brooks plays Benny Russell, a science-fiction writer *imagining* a space station called Deep Space Nine in the distant future where, impossibly, a black man could be captain. *Moonlighting* won an Emmy with "Atomic Shakespeare," in which the cast reenacted a wild version of Shakespeare's *The Taming of the Shrew,* with Bruce Willis playing Petruchio and Cybill Shepherd playing Katharina. (The latter two episodes worked rather nicely because the characters' personalities remained the same; only their identities changed.)

These kinds of episodes are rare, obviously, because if you play against the template too often, the template ceases to exist. Your audience won't know what to expect, and they'll get confused. When they get confused, they get disappointed. You remember what happens when they get disappointed, right?

If you're writing a freelance script, you probably want to forget about playing against the show's template. You *can* play against the template in a spec script, because you're trying to stand out from the crowd. But it's far, far riskier than simply trying to nail the template. Not only do you have to know the show backwards and forwards, you're depending on your reader to know the show backwards and forwards too, so they can appreciate your genius. In fact, you're depending on the story editor or network exec who's reading your script to allow the possibility that you're a genius, rather than just assuming that you don't know the template, and moving on to the next spec in her tottering stack.

If you're writing on staff, you are welcome to propose a template-breaking show to the showrunner. If your idea is clever enough, maybe he'll even write it himself . . . and make a note to keep you around.

How to Come Up with Great Springboards

How do you come up with great springboards?

Writers are often asked, "Where do you get your ideas?" They shrug off this question as if it's ridiculous. "Filene's Basement," they say, or "I have a small golden bird that sings to me in my sleep."

Novelists can get away with waiting for inspiration, if their mortgage isn't crippling. TV writers know that inspiration is not dependable enough when you've got a new script due every Friday. So, they have tools they can use when inspiration is stuck like a Maserati in a mudslide.

Keep a Story File. Many writers keep extensive ones. Any time a story idea comes to you, write it down. It will come in handy, if not on one show, then on another. James Nadler told me about a story he'd originated for *Big Wolf on Campus*. They rejected it. He wrote another version of it for *The Zack Files,* but the story was killed. He wrote yet another version—same concept, different characters, different situation—for *Seriously Weird*. That one got on the air.

If story ideas don't regularly occur to you, you may not be getting enough input. Read newspapers. Read thought-provoking nonfiction, such as Jared Diamond's *Guns, Germs, and Steel,* or Malcolm Gladwell's *Blink*. Reading *indiscriminately* is often better than reading discriminately, because ideas are more likely to come to you when you're reading outside of your usual interests—there's room for your brain to breathe. (If this sounds like an excuse to procrastinate . . . then it's worth the price of this book, isn't it?)

Steal from What Is Going on Around You. A few years back, for example, researchers defrosted some victims of the 1918 Spanish flu epidemic that killed more people than World War I. They'd been buried in permafrost; the researchers wanted to see what was so particularly virulent about that flu strain. It was in the science sections of all the major papers. How can you pitch that as an *ER* episode? As a *CSI*? As an *X-Files*?

For *Medium,* Melinda Hsu regularly turns to books about unsolved murders and crime websites like Court TV's (www.courttv.com). She's looking for an inspiringly lurid crime. From there it's a matter of finding something that gives Alison, the heroine, a stake in the crime.

For *Judging Amy,* Paul Guyot consulted "real-life stories of the juvenile justice system, not necessarily just for the courtroom cases on the show, but, for instance, we'd hear or read about a particular story and then decide on interesting or dramatic ways that it might affect the characters' personal lives."

And Jordan Craig, writing the brilliant cartoon *The Untalkative Bunny*: "The mean emu was taken from real life. My wife was reading the paper—an emu had escaped from a zoo—it pecked someone—so we wanted to put it into the show."

Steal from Your Own Life. What's the weirdest, most stressful thing that's happened to you lately? Ever? What's bugging you right now? How could you rework that as an episode springboard? Marc Abrams (*The Bernie Mac Show*):

> Try to pull a spec script from something that happened to you or a friend. That automatically invests you emotionally in the story, so you write it from a truer place.[1]

Chris Abbott (*Magnum, P.I.*):

> See the world. Because if all you're doing is watching TV and movies, you just recycle old ideas. And if you actually have a life, you can write about things that are actually happening.

Steal from the Audience's Life. If you know you're writing for a teen audience, stories about first love, zits, and even gender confusion (if you can get it past the censor) might work. You don't have to be writing for a show whose bread and butter are teen and tween stories, either. Even on *Star Trek: Enterprise* or *Desperate Housewives,* there's a "zit" story, if you can just figure out what it is.

Likewise, if you're writing for an adult audience, they're worried about promotions, respect at work, balancing work and home, their kids and their parents. What's the "respect at work" story for *Lost*? On the surface it's a show about people stranded on a desert island. But deeper down it's a show about people who've got unfinished business in their lives. Respect at work might be central to someone's unfinished business. Or, the story territory might be respect in the work they're now all involved in—staying alive.

Steal from Literature. Paul Guyot (*Judging Amy*):

> If the muse is out to lunch, then the tools I personally fall back on are other writers. People who originally inspired me to write. Maybe I'll flip through a book by Graham Greene or John Steinbeck, or a screenplay by Robert Benton or David Chase, or any of a number of other greats, depending on just what type of inspiration I'm searching for.

However, it's not a good idea to steal from the same genre of literature. Don't use a crime story for a crime drama unless you can afford to buy the screen rights for the story. It's not fair to the writer, and the odds are the story's been optioned by someone else, which may get you in trouble.

If you're not feeling inspired by the newspaper, the audience, or your own life, you can extract springboards from the show bible. As suggested above, a great episode challenges a core character's fears and weaknesses. So use that principle to generate ideas: *What would your lead most hate to do?* Okay, force him to do it. How does he deal? If your lead loves a girl, force him to be mean to her. If he's shy, force him to be exhibitionistic. If he's inarticulate, force him to lead a crowd. (By "force," I mean, of course, "give him a valid motivation he'd find it hard to resist.")

Put your lead through situations that are particularly awful for him or her because of the kind of person he or she is. Javier Grillo-Marxuach (*Charmed, Lost*):

> You just can't go wrong torturing your lead. . . . A lot of the time, series leads are glorified and nobody pokes fun of them. When you've got a character like Worf on *Star Trek: The Next Generation,* he wasn't the most interesting character until they figured out that they could use him as a straight man and poke fun at him all the time. They could have him [drink] prune juice and it would be funny. You could turn Prue [on *Charmed*] into a man and there'd be laughs galore.[2]

Challenge Your Character's Strengths. If your character is especially good at something, that can get him or her into trouble that no one else can.

In one of Melinda Hsu's *Medium* episodes, psychic Alison Dubois had to choose whether or not to get a murderer arrested—knowing that this murderer is a pilot who will save a plane full of people from crashing if he's not arrested. It's a hell of a moral quandary—and one only a psychic would ever have to deal with. Likewise, Sabrina's magical powers regularly get her into trouble on *Sabrina, the Teenage Witch,* as when she casts a spell to make a hip-hop diva easier to interview, and winds up switching bodies with her (*Sabrina, the Teenage Witch,* "Shift Happens").

Tempt Your Core Cast with Their Goals. Give a core cast member the chance to get what she's always wanted. Now deny it.

Give Dave a chance to sleep with Maddy—something he's done makes her feel romantic about him. Now give him an obstacle we wouldn't have expected—just as Dave is about to get himself invited to bed, he discovers that Maddy is mourning a death in her family, and he'd be taking advantage of her momentary weakness. Give Ross a chance to earn Rachel's respect. Give Lucy Ricardo a chance to really impress Ricky.

Fresh Opportunity + Fresh Obstacle = Fresh Story.

A familiar conflict in new packaging—that's practically a definition of a good television springboard.

Come Up with a Great Act Two or Three Out. I'll explain about act outs shortly, but in essence, find a really nasty jam to put the hero in. Then work backward to figure out how the hero got there, and work forward to see what he does about it. In *Firefly's* "War Stories," the act three out is that Mal, the show's central character, is dead. Dead, you see? How did he get dead? How does he get out of being dead?

Find a Great Ending and Work Backward from There. Another *Firefly* episode starts with its ending—Mal stranded naked in the desert, thinking "*That* went well . . ."—and then flashes back to "72 hours earlier . . ."

Consider Silly Ideas. When you're brainstorming springboards in the writing room, writers will toss out ridiculous and/or obscene story ideas to let off steam. Some of these contain the seed for a good idea. Studio execs are fond of saying, "Here's the bad version." It sometimes sounds fatuous, but don't be afraid to throw out a bad idea and then tinker with it to see if there is a good version of it.

Steal Plot Elements. From old books, movies, and even TV shows. Leila Basen (*Mental Block, Emily of the New Moon, Neverending Story*): "I look at TV Tome [www.tv.com] and see what the episode's about. Once you've filtered that through your brain, it's not going to be the same story anymore." Chris Abbott, too:

> I almost hate to say it but I'll always go back to classic novels or classic movies. Read a lot, watch a lot—it's important to watch TV to learn the craft. But also go to plays, go to movies, go to opera. . . . You can always go back to Shakespeare. What is the element of conflict, what is the area of conflict and what is the hero's flaw, what does he need to learn? Take basic concepts. Don't take the plot, otherwise you're just coloring in the lines. And some people call it plagiarizing. . . . [Laughing] We used to call it "homage."

This is not the same as stealing the entire plot of another TV show. See below.

What Makes a *Bad* Story Idea

What sort of springboards should you rule out? In increasing order of awfulness, here are some no-nos:

Episodes That Could Be Done Equally Well on Any of a Dozen Other Shows. A series is only as distinctive as the stories it tells. Every story should answer the question, Why are we watching *this* show? Larry David, talking about *Seinfeld:* "We were very determined to try and do ideas that not only had not been done before but that no one else could do."[3]

In their book *Successful TV Writing,* veteran showrunners Lee Goldberg and William Rabkin talk about the first few episodes of *Baywatch*. They had a hostage drama, they had characters coming out of their core cast's past, they had a crime story—none of which particularly required a show about lifeguards. Then they came up with the idea of two characters being trapped in the back of an armored car at the bottom of the bay. Not the most sophisticated idea, but at least *it could only be done on Baywatch*.

Once creator Aaron Sorkin left *West Wing,* the show began running episodes with story lines like "Leo has a heart attack" and "At Donna's bedside while she recuperates from surgery, Colin questions Josh about his personal relationship with Donna." Any show's cast can have health problems, right? So any time you've got two characters suffering from health problems in the same season, you've run out of inspiration.

Any cop show can spotlight a murder, but on a *CSI* show the solution has to hinge on a clever forensics investigation. A *CSI* episode that relies on one of the investigators tricking a suspect into blowing his story, *Columbo*-style, or a crazy hunch, is a weak CSI episode.

If you're pitching a springboard for a science-fiction series, the story should be one that revolves around a science-fictional element—some scientific fact or technology we don't have in our own time. A *Babylon 5* episode that is nothing more than glorified workplace politics that *happens* to take place on a space station is a bad *B5* episode.

Like all rules, this one, too, can be broken when you know what you're doing. In Joss Whedon's famous *Buffy* episode "The Body," Buffy's mom dies—for no supernatural reason at all. Any drama show can have a character drop dead. But how Buffy and her friends deal with this intrusion of ordinary death into their world, when they deal with extraordinary death every night, makes the show exceptional—reminding us how supernatural, ultimately, death is. Buffy duking it out with a vampire in the hospital morgue seems almost an afterthought.

When a show itself is less distinctive, having a story line that can't be on any other show may not be entirely possible. Many *Homicide* springboards could be *NYPD Blue* springboards. To the greatest degree possible, you need to find the twist that makes that springboard as particular to the show as possible. It can depend on the world the show lives in—New York, for example, was hit on 9/11, Baltimore wasn't. It can depend on the show's particular core cast and their flaws. *NYPD Blue* centers on a detective who's a recovering alcoholic, *Homicide* doesn't. It can simply depend on the "rules of engagement" a show has. *NYPD Blue*'s cops regularly browbeat confessions out of their suspect, *Homicide*'s don't.

Worse than an episode that could be on another show is an episode that *has been* on another show, unless you've got a new twist.

> *Crafty TV Writing*: What makes a bad spec?
> Tom Chehak: Any story I did ten years ago.

Stealing Entire Plots from Other TV Shows. Yes, you can sometimes find a twist that justifies the steal. But c'mon, come up with something fresh. A stolen story line tells the reader that you have no imagination.

If this means you have to watch a lot of television to know

what's been done, well, you should be watching a lot of television. In the writing room it's easy to spot a "used" springboard. There are three to eight writers there, plus a couple of assistants. If it's been on the air, someone's probably seen it. If you're writing on your own, though, you'll have to know or guess whether a plotline is something that's been done to death, or it's something new. Your guess is probably pretty good, though.

For example, if your plot is that a core character's brother shows up, and he's still trouble, you can guess it's been done on dozens of shows. (Sorry, Josh Schwartz.) Someone's old girlfriend showing up: ditto. (Sorry, Josh Schwartz.) Unless you've got a brand-new twist or perspective, try to come up with something fresher. On *Northern Exposure,* someone's brother showed up—and he was *black*.

Whereas, say, when you've got a story line like, "President Ford comes to town and Eric and his friends plan to streak at the rally," you can feel fairly safe that it hasn't been overdone (*That '70s Show,* "Streaking"). In other words, you probably *know* when you have a tired old story springboard that's been done. If you're still not sure, ask your friends. One nice thing about writing for TV is that everyone watches TV, and everyone feels comfortable talking about it.

Sometimes when you're staffing a show, the network will kill a script at the last minute, and everybody has to come up with a new story *now*. In that situation you may have to fall back on story ideas that aren't truly distinctive. To be honest, at that point you're all probably frantically thinking of episode ideas from other shows that you can poach and ways you can twist them so you can live with yourself afterward. As a rule of thumb, even *in extremis,* don't poach anything from this or last season. Steal from at least three or four years ago. And be aware that if you're stealing from *Rebecca* (or other classic movies or TV), some people in the audience are going to be thinking, "They're not going to do *Rebecca,* are they?"*

Remember, the audience may not remember exactly where they saw that story line before, but they know you stole it. It's just too forced and threadbare, and doesn't look like life. It looks like other TV. And at least one of your fellow writers will know where you saw it, and mock you in public.

If you're pitching a freelance script, a used story line will just irritate the story editors. The reason they're hiring freelancers in the first place is to bring new ideas.

If you're speccing a script, you really have no excuse. If you think it might have been on television anywhere, any time, come up with something more original. You should give yourself a solid week to come up with a truly kickass springboard. If you can't come up with something original in a week, you're in the wrong business.

An Episode with No Emotional Heart. People watch television to be caught up in a story emotionally, whether it's to laugh, cry, wince, or be scared for a character's sake. A good episode takes the audience through an experience that moves them. To move the audience, the protagonist has to be moved by what he or she is going through; if he doesn't care, we won't, either. Anthony Zuiker (*CSI*):

> There needs to be an emotional connection to the story that you want to tell; you can't just hide the ball cleverly. In our best episodes, characters have emotional attachments to something in the case, like the murder of a child or something that resonates from their own experience.[4]

This coming from the creator of one of the coldest, most cerebral dramas on the air, whose central character keeps bugs for

---

*Especially if, as *The O.C.* did, and *Medium* didn't, you call the woman from the past "Rebecca."

pets. Yet we know that Grissom cares deeply about finding out the truth, and we care about the victims of the lurid crimes he's investigating. To make us care, make sure the character cares.

Betray a Character. This one's really bad. We watch television to see characters we care about go through their lives. The more we watch the show, the more they seem like real people to us. We get to know their quirks, their fears, their hopes, and their past. They become part of our extended family. If you get these characters *wrong,* the audience (or the reader) is going to be mad at you. They're going to feel as if you've lied about a member of their family.

Homer Simpson can get into virtually any sort of foolishness, but he'd never commit adultery; he's not really sexual at all. Tony Soprano does cheat on his wife, but he'd never rat to the feds. Gil Grissom doesn't let emotion sway his mind from the facts. Andy Sipowicz would never take a bribe. Superman would never let someone die to save his own life. If you have a character violate the core of his personality, the audience will feel it doesn't know the character anymore. They will stop watching the show.

Simply failing to get the characters *right* makes a bad episode, but getting them positively *wrong* is a killer.

An Episode That Resolves a Central Conflict of the Show. This is the most dangerous thing you can do on TV. Once a central conflict is resolved in a show, further episodes may be crippled. In *Moonlighting,* Dave and Maddy fought like cats and dogs; their sexual tension drove the show. Many viewers felt the show died when Dave and Maddy finally gave in to their sexual tension and slept with each other.

A spec script or freelance pitch that resolves the central conflict of the show will earn immediate, permanent rejection. Of the writer. Whoever's reading it will be appalled: "What are you *thinking*?"

Sometimes a show's central conflict wears out its welcome over time. *The X-Files* was a show about a skeptic and a believer chasing after an elaborate government conspiracy to hide evidence of alien infiltration. But the hints had to add up to something sooner or later; and the more the audience knew, the more the show began to go from enigmatic to preposterous. Either showrunner Chris Carter and his staff couldn't figure out how to retool the show, or they were tired of writing it after seven seasons, so they pulled the plug.

Likewise, in the first few seasons of *Sex and the City,* Carrie Bradshaw kept looking for love. The central question of the show is announced in the pilot: Is romance dead? But as the show went on, creator Darren Star faced a choice. Either allow Carrie Bradshaw to find true romance on her terms—which would have killed the show's central conflict—or have Carrie keep finding fault with it—which eventually made it look as if she didn't really *want* it. (Not to mention that a thirty-three-year-old single girl going to parties every night is a hot chiquita, but a forty-year-old single woman—or man—going to parties every night is kinda pathetic.) For a show to last more than seven years, its central conflict may have to evolve.

A show may resolve its central conflict if everyone agrees that the show is "not working" and it needs to be retooled. Then the showrunner will write the episode that retools the show himself (after strenuous consultation with the network), and this episode will create a *new* central conflict to take over from the old one.

Mixing and Matching

For most shows, you'll need more than one great springboard.

Back in the Jurassic, shows told only one story per episode. Lucy had one harebrained scheme per episode on *I Love Lucy*. Crockett and Tubbs dealt with one case per episode on *Miami Vice*. These days, most shows tell multiple stories. *Friends* typically told three stories. *Sex and the City* told four.

The most prominent story in an episode—starring the lead

character if there is one—is called the A story. The lesser stories are called B and C stories. A B story is still a substantial story; a C story is slight. Writers might say that an episode with a big story and two inconsequential secondary stories has an "A story and two C stories." An episode with two fairly substantial stories of about equal prominence might be said to have "two B stories." A series of moments or gags that connect but don't really add up to a proper story—some delivery guys who keep trying to deliver a crate of jelly beans at the most inconvenient possible times—is called a *runner*.

On staff, you typically plot the A stories out much further into the future than the B and C stories, which get moved around from episode to episode for all sorts of real-world reasons.

If your show is a sitcom, all your stories will be comic. But if it's a drama, you may want to vary their style. If your A story is action-filled, the B story might want to be thoughtful. If your A story is serious, your B story may want to be comic. If your A story is restricted to one or two locations, you may want a B story that jumps from place to place, so the whole episode doesn't feel claustrophobic. That way you can vary the pitch, pace, and rhythm of the episode by cutting between different kinds of stories.

Be careful, though. If your A story is *too* serious, a really goofy B story may seem inappropriate. You can't really team up a wrenching tale of childhood abuse with a clever story about an odd but weird ice-cream truck guy. (At least, not on American broadcast TV.) But then, if your story is so deep you can't team it up with anything lighter, maybe you should ease up, eh?

Themed Shows

On some shows, all the stories in an episode are related by a theme—a different one for each episode. Some shows make the theme explicit. For example, in *Sex and the City,* Carrie Bradshaw types out the episode's question on her computer screen somewhere in the story. Other shows may be less obvious, and ask the audience to figure out what the episode's theme is.

If you pay attention, you may notice that many nonthemed shows also like to have themed episodes from time to time. The British show *Coupling* often joins its stories by a theme. In "The Man with Two Legs," Jeff tells a stupid lie that gets him in trouble; so does Sally. In "The Melty Man Cometh," everyone is looking for reassurance. Another show might have an episode in which various different core cast members are dealing with their exes, or an episode in which all embarrass themselves in different kinds of situations, or one where all the stories are about parental loss in different ways.

What's neat about a themed show is it can show different perspectives on the same story: one character tries to make up with his or her ex and fails, the other tries differently and succeeds. If juxtaposing the two story lines says something more about the theme, it's worth doing. If you're just making the same point twice, it may be no more than stunt plotting.

3

WRITING THE SCRIPT

Movies don't *really* have acts. "Three-act structure" is *a way of looking at* a movie's story. In the first act, you get the hero up a tree. In the second act, he tries to get down the tree but winds up farther up the tree. In the third act he falls out of the tree. The audience doesn't much think about where the acts begin or end, and if the writer's smart, he uses them only as a way of crystallizing what he thinks is wrong with his script when something's not working.

TV really does have acts. Every ten minutes or so, we cut to a commercial. That's an *act break*. The flow of narrative stops dead. The audience is distracted by commercials and promos. They get up to get stuff from the refrigerator, or return telephone calls. They channel-surf to see what else is playing.

Sometimes they don't come back.

If they don't come back, they may not tune in next week.

A television show lives in fear of its audience abandoning it.

A movie audience is captive. They've already paid their money. They've bought their tickets. They've bought their popcorn. They're sitting in the dark, with all those knees to climb over if they want to sneak into the next theater.

When TV viewers click over from your show to, say, *Battlebots*, your network loses money. With the exception of pay cable such as HBO, TV supports itself by selling eyeballs. The more eyeballs watching a show, the more the network can charge advertisers for airing commercials on that show.

It also matters how rich those eyeballs are and how likely they are to spend their money. A show like *The West Wing* can survive with a smaller audience than *American Idol* because the former's audience is better educated and wealthier.

Television shows spend a lot of effort making sure that you don't click over to another show. They do it with *teasers, tags*, and *act outs*.

Teasers and Tags

The *teaser* is the first segment on the show. It's intended to pull you in. It often sets up the A story. On a murder mystery, it often shows the murder, or the detectives arriving at the murder scene. On *Six Feet Under,* a show about a family of undertakers, it shows someone becoming that episode's corpse. The teaser isn't required to have anything to do with the A story, though. It can be any quirky, scary, funny, or dramatic moment that reminds you why you like this show, if you're a fan, or promises that you will like it, if you're not one yet.

The *tag* is the last segment on the show. It's where you tie up the episode's loose ends. It can be a goofy afterthought that shows the characters returned to equilibrium after they've been through all the stress of the episode. A classic *Star Trek* episode would put Captain Kirk, Bones, and Spock through some kind of adventure; the tag would have them all safely back on the bridge, with Kirk and McCoy teasing Spock about what just happened. It can also be the emotional resolution to a story that had a big climactic action resolution in the last act; it reveals how the core cast *feels* about what happened. The tag is also where you can establish the next threat the cast will face, or reveal that this episode's threat has not been fully dealt with. No matter what, the ultimate point of a tag is to get the audience to tune in again next week.

Not all shows separate their tag from their last act with a commercial; in that case your tag is both your Act Four out and your episode out. Most shows do have a separate teaser, followed by the main title sequence and then usually a commercial. But whether or not the commercials are there, you still need to "tease" the audience to get them into the show, and tag them on the way out so they'll come back.

Act Outs

In between the teaser and the tag are the acts. Half-hour comedies have two or, more commonly, three acts. One-hour dramas have four acts. The last thing that happens before the commercial—whatever the act "goes out on"—is called the *act out*. It is supposed to be an event so compelling that you absolutely must stay tuned to find out what happens next.

An act out is typically a cliffhanger, a situation where the outcome is up in the air. The jeopardy or stakes can be physical, emotional, or moral. Will he pull the trigger? Will the rope break? Will she kiss him? Will he betray her to the police? If the audience wants to find out how the situation turned out, they're going to have to leave the remote alone.

You don't want to depend on bogus jeopardy for your cliffhangers. We're aware we're watching a TV show. So even if the hero is in deadly personal danger, we know at some level that he's not going to be killed. Jack Bauer or Andy Sipowicz or Sydney Bristow is not going to die. They're series regulars. If you were really going to kill one of them off, you'd have run a promo about it: "One of our cast is going to die tonight!" So don't expect the audience to get their panties in a knot if you threaten their lives. Larry David, talking about *Seinfeld:* "You'll notice we never did any shows where two of the characters stopped talking to each other, because you knew they would eventually make up."[1]

We might stay tuned to see *how* your hero is going to get out of this pickle, and on *Alias,* act outs often do depend on putting Sydney Bristow in mortal danger, so we can see how she talks or fights her way out of the jam she's in. But it can be more intense to put someone the hero cares about in personal danger, instead of him, because we *don't* know that *that character* won't be killed. Crockett and Tubbs are always going to survive an episode of *Miami Vice*. Crockett's new girlfriend might not. Likewise, if Ross on *Friends* gets a job offer to be an archaeologist in Kathmandu, the audience won't feel much jeopardy. We all know they're not going to shoot the next season in Kathmandu. But if he's dating a recurring character who's got a job offer in Kathmandu, the job offer is a real threat because the story could legitimately go both ways.

A bogus cliffhanger, especially if it's one that winds up in the promos for the episode, is sometimes called "schmuck bait," because only a schmuck would be lured by it.[2]

An act out doesn't have to be the obvious cliffhanger that you've been building toward. An entire act can be about "Will she tell him the truth?" and the act out is—yes, she tells him the truth. But this works because the resolution raises new questions. The emotional resolution puts you in a whole new ball game. How are things going to be *now*? How will the story progress? How will the characters deal?

Sometimes these questions are implicit in the resolution. When a husband tells his wife he's been cheating, we don't need the show to remind us to wonder what she's going to do. Sometimes, though, you need to get the consequences going before you go out on the act. If the decision is that Sydney Bristow has to break into a maximum security prison, you might want to hold the act out until she's staring at its electrified fences and concrete walls—and then go out on that image, and the question it raises in our minds, "How the hell is she going to get in *there*???" Shelley Eriksen (*Show Me Yours*):

> I tend to, in the tried and true way, go with the cliffhanger. Unless you can twist it in some way. If the decision surprises you, you can go out on it: Oh my God they're gonna do X, what's gonna happen? I would never have them choose something that's not a surprise and then go out on the act right there. If you have to go with the decision that's expected, then either go out on the cliffhanger or have the decision and *immediately* plant them right into the difficulty it puts them into.

The last act, of course, resolves the episode's story. Unless the episode is the first of a two-parter—"To be continued . . ."—the last act out is not typically a cliffhanger. There you want to leave the audience with a satisfied feeling so they'll tune in again.

When you're plotting an episode, *the act outs are nearly as important as the acts themselves*. As our showrunner on *Charlie Jade,* Bob Wertheimer, said, "We make our money on teasers, tags, and outs." And showrunner James Nadler says that the worst thing a spec script can have is "bad act breaks."

That means that when you build the plot for an episode, nail the act outs as soon as you can—right after the showrunner and network approve the episode's story springboards.

Breaking the story down into teasers, tags, acts, and act outs is called *breaking story;* the document you are working up is a *breakdown*. It tells, story line by story line, what happens in each act and how you're ending each act. You're not weaving the story lines together yet; you're not even including every step each story will take. You're just going story by story, act by act, sketching what will happen. (See the sample breakdown in Appendix 5.)

There is a basic formula for the acts and act outs for four-act one-hour drama. The formula applies best to single-story drama where a single protagonist has a single problem per show. The more multilayered the show is, the less the formula applies. Use it more to understand the form than as a template for writing your episode.

The teaser, or first or second scene of Act One, will typically establish the episode's driving question: the problem the hero must solve. The rest of Act One shows the hero trying plan A: the most direct solution to the problem. The Act One out often shows the hero that the easy fix is not going to work; or it shows us that the hero is in more jeopardy than he thought.

Act Two will develop the story further in the same direction, but the Act Two out often takes the story in a sharply new direction. (In the old action adventure shows, such as *Magnum, P.I.,* the Act Two out left the hero in maximum physical jeopardy. The Act Three out showed the hero that he was all wrong and now he has to change everything and fix it. Stories are told faster now, so the "hero is all wrong" moment has moved up to the Act Two out.)

Act Three has the hero pursuing the new direction, but the Act Three out often leaves him in the worst jeopardy he's been in so far. It doesn't have to be physical jeopardy—moral or emotional jeopardy is fine. The point is to put the hero at maximum risk.

Act Four shows him resolving his jeopardy and solving the problem, with the main conflict wrapped up by the Act Four out.

To expand on the old "get your hero up a tree" paradigm, the basic structure of a four-act hour drama could be:

TEASER:	A fabulous treasure is stolen by unknown thieves.
ACT ONE:	The hero learns about the treasure. He finds the thieves in their hideout. But (act out) the treasure isn't there.
ACT TWO:	The hero learns that the treasure is hidden in a tree, but (act out) discovers he's got the wrong tree.
ACT THREE:	The hero climbs up the right tree but (act out) the tree catches fire.
ACT FOUR:	The hero grabs the treasure and makes his way down the burning tree.
TAG:	We learn (though the hero might not) that the treasure is really a deadly weapon. . . .

This is simplistic and formulaic, of course. But there's a lot to be said for using the formula. Much good television, some of it groundbreaking in other ways, fits neatly into the above formula. Much of the rest plays off the audience's expectations that the episode will fit in. And whenever good writers go completely off the formula, they are almost always playing against it in some clever way, not just ignoring it.

Typically, at the top of each act there are a few lines of dialogue to recap where we are, for audience members who've clicked over from another show, or who weren't paying enough attention.

Pay cable series do not cut to commercials. This puts the choice to use act outs in the hands of the writers. They may choose to ignore act breaks. *Sopranos* scripts are written without act breaks.

They may also ignore program length if they like. *Sex and the City* episodes are not all equally long on cable or on the DVD. However, experienced writers generally write with act outs somewhere in the back of their minds because they're used to it. This helps later when the show is recut to a standard length and aired in syndication or overseas. When *Sex and the City* airs in Canada, or in syndication, it has commercials. If the writers have not been careful to write possible act outs, then the act outs the editors pick when they have to break to a commercial may not be very strong.

As I'm writing this, many U.S. broadcast networks, led by ABC, are moving to a *five*-act structure, which gives them more places to put commercials. *House* and *Lost* have a teaser plus five acts; essentially the tag has become a full act. The challenge for the writer is to find five act outs instead of four. That may mean more "soft" act outs—reflective character moments rather than turning the story on its head. It may also mean going out on the B or C story at least once.

Comedy Structure

Comedy comes in two formats, two act and three act. Two acts are typical for a traditional three-camera sitcom with long, talky scenes on a few sets, though sitcoms are often three acts now. Single-camera half-hour shows are almost always three acts.

While single-camera versus three-camera format is a network decision, not a screenwriting one, it does affect the writing. With three camera, you can't rely on cinematography to help the story. Your scenes will tend to be longer, more dialogue-driven set pieces. You're depending more on the actor's delivering an effective performance; you won't be spending as much time crafting one in editing. With three cameras going all at once, an actor can't give a "big" performance for a wide shot and then a more intense, subtle performance for a tight shot.

You can easily tell whether you're watching a three-camera show. The lighting is flat, with few shadows. We never see the whole room—the "fourth wall" is reserved for the cameras. There are few camera moves beyond the occasional smash zoom for effect. There are few tight close-ups. You almost never see canted angles or crane shots.

Single-camera format allows you to do more with camera and editing than three-camera format. That gives you the latitude to compress more plot into the same 22 minutes.

Everybody Loves Raymond, Friends, Cheers, and *All in the Family* are all three camera; the format was invented on *I Love Lucy*. *Arrested Development, Coupling, Scrubs,* and my show, *Naked Josh*, are single camera.

The basic formula for half-hour is:

ACT ONE: Establish the problems your heroes are going to deal with. What a mess!

ACT TWO: The heroes try to solve the problems but only complicate matters. Now we're wondering how they're ever going to get out of this.

ACT THREE: The heroes ingeniously solve their problems and end up where they started.

Two-act is the same but even more boiled down:

ACT ONE: Establish the problems your heroes are going to deal with. What a mess!

ACT TWO: The hero confronts his or her problems and resolves them.

Finding Act Outs

It can be awkward to find act outs in a story. Sometimes a story for a one-hour (four-act) show will have three natural act outs.

You will need to manufacture a fourth, by introducing a mystery, a cliffhanger, or a great emotional moment. You can't just go out on nothing. What if you have four natural act outs, but they all occur in the second half of the story as you see it? You may need to get into the story later or speed up the first half so that your first great act out comes at the end of the first act.

Commonly, the act outs belong to the A story. But they don't have to, and a smashing act out in the B story early on can save you when your A story is just slowly building.

You have some leeway in placing your act outs. If your average act length is eight minutes and change, you can have a nine-minute act or a seven-minute act. But a ten-minute act is pushing it, and a six-minute act is a problem. If you can't get the act outs to behave, you sometimes have to junk an otherwise perfectly good story. (Yes, they're that important.)

When you're writing for an established show, whether it's for a spec or a freelance script, it's a good idea to watch episodes of the show carefully. Stop at the end of each act. Write down what happened, overall, in the act. What was the act out? Was it a cliffhanger or was something resolved? Did it involve physical or emotional jeopardy? Where did you think the story was heading? Where did you think the audience thought the story was heading?

Try to get a sense of how many scenes there are per act, how much story the episodes get through in an act, and *how stories are told* in this show.

Breaking Story

On a show, the writing staff usually breaks story together. *Breaking story* is the process of turning springboards into the bones of a story. The term refers to finding the "breaks" or act outs of a story, though many writers relish the aggressive nuance. You have to break the story before it breaks you. (People say things like "We need to beat this story about the head and shoulders some more" and "I finally cracked the spine of the story" and "I think we just need to take this story around back and beat it to death.")

Imagine a conference room or office lounge with a big white board, a coffee table, chairs, and a couch or two. Imagine three to eight writers in the room, one of them pacing, one standing by the whiteboard with a dry-erase marker, and the rest of them sprawled on the furniture and the floor in poses normally appropriate only for teenagers. This is the *writing room* or just *the room.* It is usually the conference room nearest to the writers' offices. The writing room can also be anywhere the show's writers assemble to brainstorm story: someone's personal office, the coffee shop downstairs, or even the closest Chinese restaurant.

There are, frankly, very few things more fun than breaking story with a bunch of writers in the room. It is scary and stressful and there are interpersonal explosions, and together the bunch of you create something that no one alone could have done, and battle the monsters of confusion, cost, and cliché on the behalf of the audience. It feels very much like being in the cast of a television show you like, where everyone is amazingly witty, the stakes are high, and the deadline is rushing closer.

The point of a well-run writing room is that anyone can have an idea, and everybody will, but only the best idea will survive. When you're breaking story, the story has to convince everyone in the room. It's easy for you to write a story that convinces yourself, but only a really good story will convince a roomful of experienced story editors.

If you're writing a spec or a freelance script, it's still helpful to run your story by other writers, or even friends. The key thing is to *tell the story out loud*. People tend to be much less critical of anything printed on a page than they are about things said out loud. When you tell your story out loud, they'll feel free to interrupt, asking for clarification when your story is confusing, pointing out plotholes, and offering improvements. If it's on the page, they're going to give it the benefit of the doubt. You don't want the benefit of the doubt—you want a bulletproof story.

Time Compression

Try to compress your action stories so they take place in as little time as is plausible. Surprisingly often, this is no more than two days and a night. The shorter the episode's time line, the more urgent everything seems. If your hero's on the run all night, it's much scarier than if he's on the run over the course of a week. If he's on the run for a week, and we only see a few chase scenes, that means the rest of the time he's not doing anything scary. He's getting some sleep, changing his clothes, shaving, calling his parents for advice, taking meetings, and watching the telly.

ER episodes take place over a day and a night and a day. *Hill Street Blues* episodes take place over the course of a single day. *24* episodes take place over the course of a single hour. This kind of compression "forces you to throw out the extraneous stuff," says James Nadler. No one has time to buy groceries, and if a character fights with her husband, it's an urgent fight, not one that can wait for a more opportune time.

Character-based stories seem to work best if their time line is shorter than a week, but here again, the more compression the better. Three days is better than a week, if the story will plausibly work within three days; twenty-four hours is even better.

As a side benefit, the fewer days in which the story takes place, the happier the wardrobe department is. Every new day is a new change of clothes. For many shows, this is visually a distraction. (For *Sex and the City* and *Alias,* on the other hand, it's an opportunity for kicky new outfits.) For the continuity person, clothes are another damn thing to keep track of. Also, if you're shooting different days' material in the same place, it means everyone has to take a break while the actors change.

You may run across an old rule of thumb that "you can only sleep during commercials." The idea was that you had to go out on the same day the act began with; the next day could only begin after the commercials. But audiences are more sophisticated now. While this rule may help clarity, many writers feel that this is outdated dogma.

Weaving Stories Together—The Beat Sheet

A *beat* is a the smallest unit of storytelling. It is a piece of the story in which *something happens.** It could be something dramatic:

```
INT. BLUES'S HOUSE--DAY

Blues comes home to find Charlie there waiting
for her. He apologizes for standing her up
the other day--but he can't explain. There
were "things he needed to do." Blues blows up
at him. She's sick of him being so mysterious.
She tells him to get the hell out of her
house.
```

Or it could be action:

```
EXT. BLUES'S HOUSE--DAY

Charlie leaves Blues's house--and is ambushed
by Shikari. Only a lucky accident saves his
life.
```

*The term "beat" in dialogue, indicating a momentary pause, has nothing to do with the "beat" of story structure.

Both of these examples are also single scenes. A scene is continuous action in a single place. A scene continues until you cut away to a new scene in a new setting. However, a beat can take place over several scenes:

```
EXT. HIGHWAY / STREET / WATERFRONT--NIGHT

Starsky and Hutch chase the bad guys, finally
cornering them on a dock.
```

Note that though this is formatted as if it were a single scene, "HIGHWAY/STREET/WATERFRONT" is not a location. It's several locations. This beat will turn into many scenes in the step outline:

```
EXT. HIGHWAY--NIGHT

Starsky and Hutch chase the bad guys through
crazy traffic until the bad guys bail off the
freeway . . .

EXT. STREET--NIGHT

Starsky and Hutch play dodgeball with cars,
driving through an alleyway market, totaling
it, as they chase the bad guys, till they end
up on the . . .

EXT. WATERFRONT--NIGHT

Our heroes finally corner the bad guys on a
dock.
```

The script might break this down further into more scenes, especially if the story editor writing the episode goes to the actual physical locations and tailors the action for that place.

Likewise, several beats can take place in the same setting:

```
EXT. BEACH PARTY--NIGHT

Alex brings some THUGS to confront Ryan, but
winds up reconciling with Marissa . . . and
breaking up with her. Meanwhile . . .
```

```
EXT. BEACH PARTY--NIGHT
Seth tells Summer he thinks he did the right
thing after all. She reluctantly admits he
may be right.
```

A *beat sheet* is the entire episode told beat by beat. A breakdown keeps the A, B, and C stories separate, to make it clearer whether they're working or not. A beat sheet weaves the stories together in the order you intend them to appear in the episode.

A half-hour beat sheet could be three to six pages long, single-spaced; a one-hour beat sheet could be six to fifteen pages long. But there is no required number of pages. A beat sheet is as long as it needs to be to tell the story efficiently.

The A, B, and C stories should be balanced so that no single act is too heavy with one particular story line. Generally, the A story has more beats than the B story, which has more than the C story. So, in an hour drama, the A story might have three to four beats per act, the B story might have two, and the C story only one. How many beats there are depends on the pace of the storytelling. A talky drama like *Gilmore Girls* might have fewer beats per act than a high-pitch high-speed thriller like *24*. In general the pace of storytelling and dialogue has been speeding up. The scenes in *Miami Vice* now seem draggy—long and long-winded. The scenes in 1951's original *Dragnet* seem draggy beyond belief.

The point of writing a beat sheet first is to allow you to get a clear sense of the way the story will flow. It's hard to read a thirty-page half-hour script, hold it all in your head at once, and get a sense whether it's going to work as an episode. With a three- or four- or even eight-page beat sheet, it's much easier.

The beats should be written as clearly and simply as possible. This is a document for you. You're not trying to sell the story to an outsider; you're just trying to grasp the story all at once. (But see the section "Treatments," below.)

Typically, a beat sheet doesn't contain much dialogue. It might have a few lines here and there if they are exceptionally clever, or if they crystallize a dialogue scene, but in general save the dialogue and detailed action description for the pages. If your beat sheet is too detailed, it defeats the purpose of recounting the story in broad strokes.

In your beat sheet, try to make sure each scene raises a question—whether an emotional or a plot question, whether implicit or explicit—that a later scene answers. That's what pulls the audience through the story.

You should know, at a minimum, who's in the scene and where it takes place. You should know what each character wants going into the scene, and what the conflict is. You should know what twists happen, and where the characters are going to end up. All of these may very well change when you actually sit down to write the script. But if you don't know these things, you're just *"hand waving,"* writing scene descriptions that read well on the page but postpone the hard thinking till the draft.

No Hand Waving, Please

Try to solve as many story problems as possible in the beat sheet. Story problems rarely go away by themselves while you're *writing pages,* actually writing the rough draft screenplay.* Anything that's a problem in the beat sheet will stay a problem, but now you've wasted work figuring out and writing scenes that may need to be discarded, or at least heavily rewritten.

*No one uses the term "teleplay" outside of legal documents and, possibly, Nate 'n' Al's in Beverly Hills, where the writers are older than the waitresses, and the waitresses can remember World War II.

There are accomplished writers who like to leave their beat sheets rough so there's something to be worked out as they go to pages. This probably feels more fun and alive. Some even claim to write without a beat sheet. Writers who can write well by the seat of their pants—David E. Kelley, for example—have probably internalized one-hour drama structure in general and their show in particular so well that they no longer need to work from an outline. However, even among Olympians, this approach can easily lead to first drafts that require massive page-one rewrites when the story doesn't work. You hear about the episodes that the great genius wrote on the plane from New York to L.A. You don't hear about the episodes that the great genius abandoned somewhere over the Grand Canyon and had to use the AirFone to place a panicked call to his supervising producer.

Having a beat sheet that seems to work does not guarantee that the script will work. Some story problems only become apparent once you write the script. For example, you may find that you have accidentally written the story from the wrong emotional point of view, or that it's a secondary character who has the interesting emotional decision, rather than a core cast member. While experienced story editors sometimes catch these mistakes at the beat sheet level, they may not surface until someone has written the script and it doesn't quite work. Ironically, the better you are as a prose writer, the harder it is to tell when your story isn't working. A good prose stylist can make a dog of a story sound wonderful, at least until it becomes a script and starts howling.

As with breakdowns, or any story anywhere, the best way to make sure the beats work is to run through them out loud with someone else. That's exactly what the story editors often do. First they'll work out the beats—called *beating out the story*. Then someone will stand up at the big whiteboard in the writer's room and run through the beats out loud and see if everyone in the room finds them convincing.

The Most Powerful Screenwriting Tool in the World

I'd like to take a moment here to stress that *the most powerful single tool* in screenwriting of any kind is *telling your story out loud*. Preferably without notes. You can sometimes see what's wrong with a story when it's sitting on the page. But when a story is fixed in print on paper or on your computer screen it becomes more concrete and harder to alter.

When you tell a story out loud, it is a fluid, living thing. You will naturally add to it, making it richer. You will also be able to tell instantly what doesn't work. Some of the things you say will sound boring. Sometimes you won't be able to remember what happens next. That's because the story logic doesn't flow smoothly enough. When a beat or sequence is boring on the page, your eye naturally skims. When you're telling a story out loud, you can't avoid how boring the boring sections are. You may come up with something more interesting on the spot, but at a minimum you'll know you have to replace what you've got.

Telling a story out loud, off the top of your head, without notes, is scary. It requires way more effort than reading prose on a page. As a culture we've fallen out of the habit of telling stories out loud. But it is the most natural thing in the world. You actually know how to do it. You used to tell stories, back when you were small and had to explain how it was the cat that jumped up on the shelf and extracted the cookies from the cookie jar.

Remember how you're not supposed to shoot off your mouth until you know what you're going to say? In storytelling, that is wrong, wrong, wrong. Whether you are writing a TV episode, a screenplay, a novel, an essay, a presentation, or a speech, there is *nothing* as effective in streamlining, enriching, and generally beating a story into shape as winging the whole thing front to back off the top of your head.

After all, what do you have to lose? You're not driving a car. You can't hurt anyone. If you get your story wrapped around a tree, you can always untangle it and get it back on the road again with a few leaps of imagination.

Mix It Up

As you weave the beats of the various stories together, you need to take into account not just story logic, but rhythm. All the stories should be building in intensity as the episode unspools. But you don't want to just cut from one high-pitch sequence to another. After a while that gets tiresome. Instead, cut from a high-pitch sequence in the A story to a dramatic beat in the B story. Cut from a serious scene in the A story to a comic beat in the B story. (If you have a truly heavy beat in the A story, you probably don't want to cut to a comic beat. But if you have a truly heavy beat, it's probably your act out. Somehow the audience minds cutting from tragedy to comedy more than it minds cutting to a tampon commercial.) That's why it's good to match an action A story to a dramatic B story and vice versa: as the stories intensify, the dramatic story will be full of heavy, slow dramatic beats while the action story will be full of fast-paced action beats—perfect for cutting back and forth.

What makes this difficult is that your A, B, and C stories need to keep pace with one another. If all the events in your A story are taking place within a few minutes of one another, and the events in the B story start in the morning, last through the day, and finish at sunset, you're going to have trouble cutting back and forth. You can't, for example, have Jack say something in your A story, cut to a two-minute scene in the B story, and then come back to Jill's reaction of shock at what Jack just said. She's had two minutes to get over her shock.

The best solution is to choose or craft your B story so it has more or less the same time line as the A story. If that's not possible, you can help yourself a little by having the longer story bookend the shorter story. If your A story takes all day, and your B story takes an hour, you can start the A story, cut back and forth between the A and B stories over the course of the one hour where they're both going on, and then finish the A story.

You can also sometimes fudge the issue by removing the signposts that indicate what time it is. Tell both stories during the vague black hours between midnight and six A.M., when no one's on the street and no stores are open. If the stories are compelling enough, the audience may not notice that, upon reflection, one story probably takes place within an hour and the other probably takes six hours from beginning to end.

What you can't do is move into night in your A story, and then cut back to the B story still in daylight. The audience will assume that any time you cut from day to night to day, it's now the *next* day.

The Rule of One

Early TV shows had only an A story. Then shows developed multiple story lines. But scenes still clearly belonged to either the A story or the B story. Now, in the most sophisticated shows, especially in complicated serial dramas such as *The Sopranos,* several stories can be going on in the same scene. Just as in real life, a character who wants one thing bumps into a character who has an entirely different agenda. Naturally, their agendas conflict.

Nonetheless, keep your stories clear. In any given story, for any given character, one dramatic thing is going on at a time. Each story has one protagonist. The protagonist has one goal, opportunity, or problem. He faces one obstacle or principal antagonist. He stands to gain one thing (stakes). He stands to lose one thing (jeopardy). These story elements can change over the course of the episode. He can defeat one obstacle only to come up against another one. He can lose what he was trying to gain, but discover there's something else he can gain. But at any one moment we're only dealing with one of each.

A guy can come over to a girl's house because he wants to kiss her, or because he wants her friendly advice, but not both at the same time. A hero can be in danger because his brakes have been severed, or because his steering wheel has been sabotaged, but not both. Otherwise it gets confusing. Nobody tells the legend of the knight who went questing for the Holy Grail and/or the Sacred Place Setting.

Often this is a matter of managing what the audience and the hero know. In the fourth season of *24,* Jack Bauer has to deal with several main terrorist schemes: a plot to kidnap the secretary of defense, a plot to blow up nuclear reactors, a plot to shoot down the president, and a plot to fire off nuclear missiles. But in any given episode, we only know about one of these plots. It's not until one is defeated that the storytellers warn us about the next one. That keeps the jeopardy clear. (Arguably, the fact that the season is about four things in a row, instead of one thing slowly revealed, is a sign of desperation in the story department.) On TV, two bombs are *less* scary than one bomb. But a small bomb that is meant to be found, thus hiding the bigger bomb, is scarier still.

You can also give a character two goals if they are at different levels: text and subtext, conscious and unconscious. A guy can come over to a girl's house to ask for her advice about a woman he's supposed to marry *but really* because he wants to know if the girl loves him. A knight can go questing for the Sacred Place

Setting *but really* he's only trying to redeem his honor after he ran away from battle. The protagonist of a story should need only one thing, but nothing prevents him from asking for other things, so long as we, the audience, are clear that they are not what he really needs.

The exception to the Rule of One is the Rule of Three. The hero might not need one thing, he might need three. The first thing is easy to get. The second thing is harder to get. The last thing he doesn't get at all, or he gets it, but sets off the alarms.

For some reason, two things don't work, and neither do four. It's a rule of comedy that two jokes merely cancel each other out.[3] Three things somehow become one, even if you're not Catholic.

Tracking Expectations

If you're doing your job right, the audience is not passively watching the story unfold. They're caught up in the story and second-guessing you at every turn.

It's important to track what the audience *knows* and what they *expect*. Remember, your audience watches even more TV than you do. After all, while you're reading this book, they're watching television. While you write, they watch television. While you cook, they watch television. When you set something up, they're likely to notice the setup and expect a payoff down the road. If you drop a hint, they'll pick it up.

It's important to track what the audience *knows*, first of all, because you never want to waste time repeating anything they know. (Nothing more boring than having Jack give Jill a recap of his adventures when we could fill Jill in ourselves.) If we've seen something happen, but a character doesn't know about it, don't have another character tell her about it onscreen—find a way to have that conversation happen offscreen. Often you can have the two of them start a conversation about the event and then cut away, or cut to a shot of the two of them behind a window or a glass door so we can see the conversation continuing and we can fill in the rest.

It's important to track what the audience *expects* because that's what creates suspense. They're trying to figure out where the story is going. They're rooting for the hero to win and they're worried the hero may be in danger.

You can expect the audience to be fairly quick on the uptake. If you set something up, they'll probably guess it's a setup. If you so much as have a character explain how a jet engine works, they're going to be alert to the likelihood that how a jet engine works will figure in the plot later. (Giving this sort of technical explanation in advance, so that a plot twist or a bit of comic business won't come out of nowhere, is sometimes called *laying pipe*. You have to lay the pipe before you turn on the faucet.)

On *CSI*'s "The Dove Commission," a woman in a red dress is murdered at a dance. One of the first characters to be interviewed by the forensics guys is another woman in another red dress, who then drops out of the story. There's some really helpful guy who really wants to help the investigators. Guess what? Yep, you guessed it. The really helpful guy did it. And he hadn't meant to kill the woman in the red dress. He'd meant to kill the other woman in the other red dress.

The audience knows you don't see two red dresses by accident on a TV show. They see two red dresses, and they're going to guess there was some sort of mixup between the two dresses.

How do you deal with that? First of all, you have to decide whether you *want* to tip off the audience. After all, in a mystery, the audience *likes* to figure it out for themselves and get a little ahead of the investigators. So long as you're not too blatant with that other red dress, the audience members who figure things out in advance will be tickled pink, and the ones who miss the clue will feel amused that a second red dress was waved in front of their faces and they didn't get it.

I think a lot of people like to get ahead of poor Jack Bauer on *24*. Every time he goes somewhere, he calls for backup. Lots of it. Except when he's going to get jumped. So if he goes somewhere dangerous without backup, you know he's going to get jumped. He, apparently, doesn't. (Silly boy. You'd think he'd learn.)

On shows like *America's Next Top Model* and *American Idol,* the contestants are often a mix of the gorgeous or gifted and the homely or talentless. Each group of models in *America's Next Top Model* has maybe two real models and a bunch of civilians. That's so the audience can guess who's going to win, and then feel smart when they're right. If there were ten real models it would be more of a competition—but it would be too hard to guess who's going to win. These shows are as much about satisfying expectations as about real competition.

That's one kind of storytelling. It's comforting—we know what's going to happen. But it's not particularly involving. Knowing more than the hero is a little alienating. If we were looking at the world through the hero's eyes, we'd feel more for what he's going through.

If you'd rather we experience the story from the hero's point of view, be careful not to let us get ahead of him. Don't offer the audience clues in advance. Procedurals like *NYPD Blue* give you the information the moment the detectives beat it out of their suspects. So you never see the clues until they do. Or, offer ambiguous clues. *Medium* is about Alison Dubois trying to figure out what her precognitive dreams *mean,* so while we get the clues when she does, we, too, don't know what they mean, exactly.

Other detective shows give the audience the clues but don't *hang a sign* (or a red dress) on them. If a viewer is brilliant (or jaded, or a TV writer herself), she may see the twist coming, but they're expecting she won't. Be careful trying to write this way: the audience will sniff out any but the most subtle setups.

But perhaps the most interesting way to use the audience's expectations is to use it *against* them. Let them see the second red dress, let them assume that's what you're telling them, and then pull the red dress out from under them—the solution has nothing to do with the two red dresses. The best magicians keep your eyes on one thing while they're working their sleight of hand elsewhere. The most surprising storytellers give you the clues to figure out where the story is going but lead you astray by giving you false clues on top of the real ones. Chris Abbott (*Magnum, P.I.*):

> My favorite writers always know what the audience expects and then completely turn a corner on them. I like to leave hints so some people can figure it out. Especially when I'm writing mysteries. Then I leave big red herrings everywhere [so they ignore the hints]. I try to mix it up as much as I can.
>
> But you have to do it in a way that isn't cheating. Everything they see has to be true, but it can also be looked at in another way. Look at *The Usual Suspects, Sixth Sense.* The same facts, but with different meanings. The story has to be emotionally compelling before the twist and then after the twist as well. It has to work at both levels.

Sometimes a setup is so obvious that you have to address the audience's expectations. For example, the audience has seen people lie and get nailed for it so often on TV that if we see a character tell a lie, we assume there will be consquences. In a comedy, we're expecting wacky hijinks as the lie spins out of control. In a drama, we're expecting the character will get busted for it.

In a case where we've seen the story played out too many times, you need to come up with a new twist *and* you need to hint to the audience that you're not going down the old familiar path. Otherwise the audience may change the channel before you get to the twist.

In *Everwood*'s "Need to Know," Ephraim lies to his girlfriend Amy, claiming he's sick, so he can skip a date with her and go see his *ex*-girlfriend's band. This is such a classic setup, it practically *telegraphs* to the audience that Ephraim will get caught. Now we're just waiting for the other shoe to drop. Interestingly, Ephraim *doesn't* get caught. He gets in trouble because he *tells* Amy later; the story is his guilt. But the twist is spoiled because it's not clear that the ending is in play. A simple *couplet* (one character's single line of dialogue followed by another character's one-line response) could have *taken the curse off* the setup:

```
                    EPHRAIM
     I'll get caught.

                    BRIGHT
     You won't get caught. People lie all the
     time.
```

And they get away with it, too, in real life, all the time. Just not on TV.

If you carefully track what the audience is expecting, you can choose either to fulfill their expectations or to surprise them. Either can work. A good surprise is always fun. But it's over in a moment. Suspense lasts. If the audience suspects where you're heading, but isn't sure you're going there, they'll be in suspense until you reveal the outcome. So long as you get where you're going in an entertaining way, the audience won't mind a bit if the results are something they expected.

Whether a show usually fulfills the audience's expectations or goes for the surprise twist is often part of the template. Moira Kirland (*Medium*):

> Our best shows are when we completely subvert the audience's expectations, and we do that consciously. For example, in "Coming Soon," Alison has a dream that there's a threatening man in her house. Then she sees the man from her dream. He's a witness to a crime, a Good Samaritan doing his civic duty. Apparently a nice guy. But when she shakes his hand she's sure he's a serial killer. And the audience is thinking: this is the one where Alison has to convince everyone he's a serial killer, and no one will believe her, and he'll kidnap her and she'll have to escape. But the way we play it out, in Act Three she realizes all her visions are of events taking place in the future. He hasn't started killing yet. So in Act Four, all she can do is find the girl who will be his first victim and say, "You're gonna meet this guy. Don't get in the car with him. If he tries to get you to do it, fight him." And that's all she can do.

In this case they're subverting two expectations: one, that the killer will kidnap Alison, and two, that Alison will be able to stop the serial killer. Neither happens. Moira Kirland again:

> What we try to do is to set up the paradigm and then alter it. In *Desperate Housewives* and *Lost,* you go, "I think I know where that's going." But you're wrong. And that's more satisfying. It's always satisfying to be surprised.
>
> There are fewer shows now like *Murder, She Wrote* or *Touched by an Angel* that allow you to see clearly where we're going. But sometimes you want that. A nice quiet hour of unchallenging TV. It's like macaroni and cheese. It's not that exciting, but you know what it's going to be, and that's comforting. *Law & Order* I enjoy but I'm not surprised. You know the first person they interview is not the killer. You get the template. Or they have guest stars. On this one show, the

fiancée was Kelly Martin. Of course she did it. She's got to play her big thing. You're not going to have Kelly Martin on the show and she didn't do it. Sometimes you don't want to work that hard. It's a cool medium, not a hot one. It does everything for you.

Treatments

If you're writing on staff or as a freelancer, your beat sheet has to be approved by the showrunner. Before the network approves it, you'll probably have to turn it into a *treatment.* A treatment looks like a fleshed-out beat sheet. The beat sheet is there to help the writer write the script. Everyone reading the beat sheet already knows the story, more or less. The treatment is written for people who don't know the story yet.

Therein lies the danger. Treatments, it turns out, are hard to read. I don't know why. Possibly because they tend to maximize plot and minimize character and atmosphere. It is very hard to convey the flavor of a scene in a treatment without going to hand waving, so they tend to read rather dry. Practically every time I've seen a treatment go to someone who's unfamiliar with the story, it gets a confused reaction, no matter how clear the writers thought it was. I've also seen the network reject a script on the grounds that they didn't like the story—but they'd read and approved the treatment!

There are two ways you can deal with this. The first is to expand on anything in the treatment that could be at all unclear. Don't just write what happens. Write what the point of what happens is, and how the characters feel about what happens. Explain how the story fits into the overall character arc. Do your best to sell *why* you want to tell this particular story. (I call this "subtitles for the nuance-impaired.")

But much better, don't depend on a cold read. If at all possible, pitch the story to the network exec in person or at least over the phone *before* you send the treatment in. Once the network exec has had a chance to ask all her questions, and you've answered them, rewrite the treatment so it answers her questions *again*. Only *then* send her text on the page.

Going to Pages—the Script

Once the treatment is approved by the network, the writer starts writing pages. Up till now the entire writers' room might have been working on the episode, but now it's up to one writer (or writing team) to turn the beat sheet or treatment into pages of dialogue and action.

Now it's up to you to get the scenes right, nail the voices of the characters, and reproduce the overall tone of the show. In theory, this is the "easy" part, which really means, I suspect, that it comes naturally to experienced TV writers and they don't really know how to talk about it.

If you're writing on spec or freelancing, now would be a good time to reread some of the scripts from the show. If you're a freelancer, you can get as many scripts as you like from your story editor.

Watch an episode with the sound off. Get a sense for how visual the show is.

Listen to an episode with the picture off. Focus on the voices. "Ideally," John Rogers (*Cosby, Global Frequency*) reminds me, "you should be able to cross out all the characters' names in a script, and the dialogue is so distinctive you can still tell who's saying what." If you listen to the character's voices without the distraction of visuals, you'll get a better sense of how they express themselves.

As you're writing each scene, it's a good idea to remind yourself:

1. What does each character want?
2. How will he try to get it from the other character, in a way that reveals their personalities?
3. Why doesn't the other character want to give it to him?
4. How will the other character deny it to him in a way that reveals their personalities?
5. What is this scene supposed to do for the story as a whole?

Your job is to make (1), (2), (3), and (4) work for (5). Characters have to be honestly motivated, so you often have to keep screwing around with their motivations until you can get *them* to want to do the things *you* want them to do.

Movies flow—one scene segues smoothly into another. *TV pulses*. You want to come into a scene with a bang if possible. On the way out, you either want your scenes to *pop*—to end with a bang, or to *flow*—to cut so smoothly into the next scene that the roller coaster of your plot never slows down.

Comedy scenes almost always pop. They typically end with a *button,* an extra neat line or pair of lines that propel you out of the scene into the next. The exception is when the segue itself is the joke, as in a "flip cut," about which more later.

Dramatic scenes can pop when you want to make a moment of some revelation the audience needs to absorb. Either it's information you want to *hang a lantern on,* or it's an emotional moment—something left hanging or something powerfully resolved—that you want the audience to feel deeply. After a scene pops is one of the best times to cut to another story line. If you're staying in the same story line, you more often want your scenes to flow.

It's a basic principle of editing that you want to get into a scene as late as possible and out as soon as possible. (There's a whole section devoted to this in *Crafty Screenwriting.*) This will help propel the story along.

This doesn't mean that you can just cut in to the scene as the dramatic conclusion is happening. We want to see how the characters got to that conclusion. But we don't need to see the chitchat that happens before the characters get into their argument—unless, of course, it's tense, argumentative chitchat that has the argument as subtext. It's perfectly legitimate to start in mid-argument, so long as your characters still haven't got to the meat of whatever they're really angry about.

Deciding what's the bone (the conclusion), what's the meat (the argument), and what's the fat and gristle (chitchat before, aftermath after) is often just a matter of trimming—until you realize you've trimmed too much and you have to put some dialogue back.

On the way out of your scene, don't linger too long on the emotional aftermath. Use the emotional force of the scene's conclusion to bounce the audience into the next scene. Instead of hanging around showing how the characters feel about the conclusion, show how they feel about it by their actions in the next scene.

Sometimes you'll realize as you're writing that you can just drop a scene. You've got a scene of Joe working himself up to asking Sally on a date, another of Sally turning him down, another of Joe berating himself with, "What was I thinking?" You might realize you can just cut from Joe working himself up to Joe already having been cut down. If you realize a scene isn't necessary, don't write it, lose it.

Often the hardest thing about writing a scene is finding the best way into it. You know what the scene is supposed to do from the beat sheet, but you just can't seem to get it going.

A strong segue is always nice, whether it's physical—Joe slams out of one room, cut to Sally slamming into another—or emotional—Joe decides he's finally going to ask Sally on a date, cut to the aftermath of her turning him down, "What was I thinking???"

The sheer emotional momentum will carry you into the next scene.

When that doesn't work, four more ways to get into a scene when it's not coming naturally are:

1. Start writing at the earliest possible point.
2. Write it backward.
3. Set the action at odds with the drama.
4. Write a scene as a battle between you and the characters.

Writing at the earliest possible point is simply to start with the character getting out of the car, going up the steps, knocking on the door, saying hello, until inevitably the characters do what you wanted them to do. Then just go back and cut everything you don't need.

Writing it backward means writing the conclusion, and then writing whatever you need to see before that to *earn* that conclusion. Writing backward like this is never fun, but once you've got a rough draft of the scene you can massage it for flow later.

Often **setting the action against the drama** is just the catalyst you need. If the scene is a breakup, where the characters are liable to start shouting at each other, you might set it in a library where they can't yell, and force them to carry a bag so big it takes both of them to carry it, so they have to cooperate. If one character is supposed to declare love to another, force him to do it in an elevator filled with fighting children; show us that if he waits for the elevator to get to his floor it will be too late. That could give you enough friction to get the scene going. Comedic and dramatic counterpoint is always good for a scene. It's also how life truly does seem to happen, while you're making other plans. Shelley Eriksen:

> What's the most ridiculous thing they could be doing right now? For example, we had a scene set in a restaurant about Kate telling David that Ben is leaving. David looks on Ben as a sexual

> rival. So this is good news for him. We couldn't afford the restaurant. I had to rewrite the scene, set it somewhere else . . . so they're having oral sex while she tells him. It's a free location. . . . What's an action they could be *doing* that works against the information? That's a good way to get it started.

A tricky way to get a compact scene is to **treat the scene as a battle** between you, the writer, who wants to get the scene to the conclusion you need, and the characters, whose job it is to slow you down. You know where you need the scene to go, but they have conflicting motives. They don't want it to get there. Allow them to wrestle with you for control of the scene. Eventually you'll win, but be fair and let them have their say for a while.

Leila Basen (*Mental Block, Emily of the New Moon*) points out that you can use almost any line to unblock a scene.

> I had a couple of old Woody Allen scripts, and I'd steal a line from a scene, and one of the characters would come in saying that line, and the scene would go from there. Later I'd cut the line. But you can often start a scene with any line, and then let it go from there.

When you're writing your scenes, depending on the show, you may want to try to keep the personnel down. Production managers love *two-handers:* two people talking in a room, with no one else involved in the conversation. It's easy to shoot two people talking. A few wide shots, some over-the-shoulder shots, and some closeups, and you're done. Adding a third character can easily add half again as many shots. Even if the new character is saying little, the production unit will have to shoot his reactions to everything. A third character makes choreographing the scene more challenging. On lower-budget shows, save multiple-character scenes for where they will have the most impact.

On high-budget shows—any prime-time network drama, for

example—the budget allows multiple-character scenes. There, it's more a question of how you keep more than three characters involved in a scene. So long as two characters disagree, it's easy as pie to write a scene between them. The more characters you put in the scene, the harder it is for everyone to have a distinct point of view. If someone's in a scene, you have to serve them. You can't have core cast sitting around while the other kids play. You have to give them something to say, business to do, some way of demonstrating how they feel. If they don't have dialogue, give the actors some way for their characters to show their attitude. Otherwise they'll make up stuff on the set, and you may not like what they come up with.

Try to Write Physically. Even if you're not writing an action scene, give the characters something to do while the scene is happening. In the *Murphy Brown* pilot, during Murphy's entire first meeting with Miles Silverberg in her office, she's rounding up all the cartons of cigarettes she's stashed throughout the office and dumping them in a trash bin. Bill Persky and John Markus of *The Cosby Show*:

PERSKY: Most action written by situation comedy writers is: She's pouring coffee. There isn't enough. She starts to make another pot of coffee. . . . That's not good enough.

MARKUS: That's what the director will give you on the stage.

PERSKY: [. . .] But better that somebody spilled jelly—a jar of jelly—on the floor and you're trying to get the jelly up and you're talking—

MARKUS: And people are coming over—

PERSKY: —and people are coming in and stepping in the jelly—because that's what happens in life.[4]

Ideally, the physical action should be something that's an obstacle to what the character is trying to do emotionally. If Jack is coming over to break up with Jill, and Jill is contending with spilled jam, or a kid with a skinned knee, it ratchets up the pitch of the dialogue a few notches.

Don't be afraid to get clever with your dialogue. TV is more compressed than movies; it's also more stylized. TV scenes often end with a button. The button is sometimes an *echo*—a line we've heard before earlier in the episode—or a *callback*—a line we've heard before but now it's given a fresh and often ironic meaning. Callbacks and buttons are not easy to use in the movies because movie dialogue is usually more realistic; it has to be, with the characters thirty-feet high on a screen in a dark room. On TV, the audience accepts stylization in dialogue so long as it expresses character and makes the scene snap. They know we're fighting for their attention.

In the finished product, your acts need to be roughly equal in length. You have some leeway. On *Psi Factor,* for example, "Our third acts were usually a bit short," says James Nadler. Your page count may vary much more. The movie ratio of one page of script to one minute of screen time doesn't apply to TV. A "TV hour" is 40 minutes—the rest of the hour is commercials, promos, and the main title sequence. But hour scripts are much longer than 40 pages. A typical script for a one-hour show is 55 pages. A *West Wing* script might be 67 pages, while *Gilmore Girls* scripts can run 75 or more pages. That's partly because people talk more, and faster, on TV; and partly because the production is less likely to spend money on long, spectacular shots without dialogue when the spectacle is going to end up on a small screen in a room full of distractions.

Some pages will run longer than others onscreen. A moody dialogue scene will play more slowly than a snappy dialogue scene. An action scene will play longer or shorter depending on how much detail you've written on the page. If you've been sketchy, a quarter page might take a minute, while if you've really tried to grab your reader's mind's eye, a page could take half a minute.

At some point, if you're in production, the script coordinator will *time* the script. Script timing is guesstimating how long each scene will play in the completed episode. There's a craft to this. She has to know the style of writing in the episodes, as well as the show's shooting and editing style. It's risky because if the episode times long, you'll have to cut pages, and if it times short, you'll need to expand it. If she's wrong, you may shoot pages you don't need—expensive—or come up short in the edit—disastrous.

If you're speccing a script, timing is academic. The acts should feel roughly equal in length. If you're freelancing, do the guesstimate yourself. Read the script and see the action and dialogue in your mind's eye, with a stopwatch handy. Write down how long the scenes took, and add up the timings.

If your acts are wildly out of balance, you'll need to rejigger the scene order, or the act outs, so that they're roughly in tune with one another. Acts that are 10, 8, 11, and 11 minutes long might fly, but acts that are 10, 6, 13, and 11 will not do. You may be able to move some scenes in the B story from Act Three to Act Two, for example. Or you may be able to find a scene early in Act Three that can work as an alternate Act Two out, thus lengthening Act Two and shortening Act Three.

In production, you'll have a specific page count you're trying to hit. You can overshoot it a little, but don't write short. It costs money to shoot each additional page, but it's worse to come up short. An episode that's too long can always be trimmed, but if it's too short, the editors will have to scam additional footage from somewhere to make up the time. Delivering a TV episode that isn't the exact correct length for the network's needs is simply not an option. You can't have dead airtime on television, and if the episode is too long, the network is hardly going to cut valuable commercials to make up the time. After all, from the network's point of view, the episode is only there to get people to *watch* the commercials.

Dialogue

Dialogue does two things:

1. It's how characters get what they want from each other.
2. It reveals what characters are thinking and feeling.

Well-wrought dialogue does neither of these things directly. People are rarely straightforward. They don't get very far in life when they are. Dialogue where the characters speak exactly what's on their minds is called "on the nose":

```
                    COLUMBO
     Did you murder your ex-wife and that
     waiter?
```

Real people—and realistic television characters—don't blurt out what's on their minds. They don't ask directly for what they want, if they even know what they want. They manipulate and insinuate, either unconsciously or intentionally:

```
                    COLUMBO
     Oh, uh, Mr. Simpson, I've been wonder-
     ing . . . do you know where I could buy
     some gloves . . . ?
```

They talk at cross-purposes. They respond to what they think they heard, which is often what they were scared of hearing, or what they wanted to hear. Two people can be talking about two entirely different things but think they're in the same conversation.

Aside from being more like real life, elliptical dialogue makes for stronger writing because while the characters are *not* saying exactly what's on their minds, what they *are* saying tells us all about who they are. The trick to great dialogue is making it clear to the audience what's going on while at the same time allowing the characters to reveal who they are by speaking *un*clearly to each other. *How* a character deflects criticism, or criticizes, or changes the subject, is what makes him or her a character.

When the audience has to involve themselves in the conversation to make sense of it—so long as it isn't so muddy that they're left out in the cold—they'll be pulled into the world of your story. They'll feel more like they're watching real life and less like they're watching pixels on a screen. The act of making sense of unclear dialogue is what pulls them in. After all, a present isn't really a present unless you have to unwrap it.

Especially when your world is unrealistic—whether you're writing for talking unicorns or evil robots from space—you want to give the characters their own distinct, revelatory way of speaking. The more they feel like real, individual people, the more we'll be drawn into the story.

A supposed test for dialogue is if you can erase all the character names on the page and still leave the reader able to follow who's saying what. This is a little overboard, though. After all, the actors are going to give the dialogue their own voices. A great actor makes your dialogue her own—gives it her own intonation and rhythms—until it sounds as if she's coming up with it on the spot. There are a hundred ways to say "Yuh?" So while "Yuh?" may not be distinctive on the page, it will be distinctive when the actor says it; and sometimes, "Yuh?" is just what the character would say.

On the other hand, if you can get hold of a show's scripts, it's a good exercise to do exactly that: erase the character names, and see if you can tell who's saying what. See how the characters' voices come through. What makes each character's voice distinctive? On a sitcom, you should be able to distinguish the characters pretty easily. On a character-based drama the differences will be more subtle. On a dry procedural like *CSI,* of course, the character's personality may barely pierce the jargon. But some characters will be more laconic than others, and some will be more negative than others. You can spot a classic Gil Grissom line, for example, by the complete *lack* of personality.

Brilliant dialogue, no matter how classic for the character, should never slow the story down. Anthony Zuiker (*CSI*):

> Dialogue is the Christmas lights on a story. . . . The story is the backbone of your script. If everyone is so flavorful that you begin to show off in the writing, rather than sticking to the spine of the story, that stays fun for the audience for about four minutes.[5]

Beyond the way the characters themselves talk, many shows have their own style of dialogue. *Buffy the Vampire Slayer* created its own quippy pseudo-slang that eventually made its way into the high schools we were meant to think it came out of. *Dawson's Creek*'s high school students were famous for talking like thirty-year-olds who'd been through years of therapy, and were intentionally written that way. *The West Wing* and *Sports Night* share Aaron Sorkin's trademark high-speed tennis-ball dialogue, while *Gilmore Girls* has even faster dialogue, as well as a strange habit of treating all the punch lines as throwaways.

If you're writing for a show with stylized dialogue, don't be afraid to go a little too far in making it snap. If it's not real enough, it throws the audience out of the experience. But if it's too mundane it loses its snap. It's less work for a story editor or showrunner to tone it down than to punch it up. Stylized dialogue *should* be fun to write and fun to hear. The audience will forgive you for stretching realism a bit. They won't forgive you for being boring.

Read all your dialogue out loud. This is an absolute must. Lines that read fine on the page can be impossible to say out loud.

Have friends read your dialogue to you, too. You'll probably find that some lines are unsayable, some are not as graceful as you thought, and many are completely unnecessary.

(As Harrison Ford once supposedly told George Lucas, "You can write this stuff, George, but you sure as hell can't say it." Only he didn't say "stuff.")

Action

In movie writing, it's a rule that you should only write what you can see or hear. Don't direct the camera. Don't talk about how the room smells, or what the character's backstory is. If it's not in dialogue we won't hear it; if it's not in the action, we won't see it. So why write it?

TV writers break this rule in two significant ways.

One, TV writers often do put camera direction in. Partly this is because they *can*. The showrunner *hired* the director. If the director wants to get hired to direct another episode of this show, he better pay attention to how the showrunner wants the scene shot.

Even if you are not the showrunner, you may occasionally put in a camera direction to make clear how the scene is supposed to be shot. If you're looking for a grand crane pull-away, you need to say so, because the production manager needs to have a crane available that day on the set. If you're tight on someone's face in shadow, the set dresser may not need to dress the entire set. The actor may not even need pants. Writers put in more direction on TV scripts because the preproduction process is so much more rushed than in the movies. Often the departments will have no more than a week of solid preproduction. That's very little time to ponder and confer and storyboard a fifty-five-page script. If production needs to know something, it's a good idea to `WRITE IT`

IN ALL CAPS in the script, so the crew is less likely to miss it. This includes camera moves, where they are important to telling the story: HE IS IN SILHOUETTE, WE DO NOT SEE HIS FACE.

Second, TV writers often put what the characters are thinking into the action description. This works as a kind of shorthand:

```
                    JACK
      Hey, I called the other night . . .

   Oh, my God. He knows! Jill tries to cover:

                    JILL
      Yeah, I accidentally kicked the plug
      out. I'm such a klutz.
```

If the actor knows what the character is thinking, he can act it. The alternative would be for you to go into way too much depth of detail about what we see:

```
                    JACK
      Hey, I called the other night.

   Jill shrugs, maybe a little nervously. She
   forces a self-deprecating grin.

                    JILL
      Yeah, I accidentally kicked the plug
      out . . .
```

And even then, the reader may not get it, the director may miss the point, and the actor may just be confused.

Aside from making for snappier writing, telling us what the character is thinking also puts the reader more into the character's point of view. The episode will read better. You have to be careful with this tool, though, and never use it for evil. Someone can act "Oh my God, he knows!" Someone can act "Oh, great. I've put my foot in it, haven't I?" Someone can even act, "Isn't that just like a man?" These are all shorthand for distinct emotional reactions—specific flavors of alarm, embarrassment, and disdain. But no one can act a thought:

```
The hematologist said the exact same thing!
```

Sure, the actors won't complain. Actors can have an exaggerated sense of how much information their acting can communicate. A few actually do seem to convey what they're thinking, but most can only convey what they're feeling. It's up to you to make sure you're writing something that's actable. If not, you have to take the thought out of action description and move it into dialogue so the audience can hear it:

```
                    JILL
The hematologist said the exact same
thing!
```

Staff writers will sometimes even put editorial comments into scripts, "hanging a sign" (or a lantern) on the episode theme or other nuance that might go unnoticed in a quick read. The justification for it is the same as earlier. People don't always read TV scripts as carefully as they should. There's no time. If you don't want to get a phone call from a confused network exec, you occasionally put in:

Yes, this *is* an extraordinary coincidence;
that's the point.

Subtitles for the nuance-impaired are legitimate when the episode, if properly shot and edited, will easily communicate something that the script may not get across. Producers and executives are used to reading dialogue, but editing, for example, doesn't read well. If you want a montage to make a certain point, you're going to have to tell us what that point is:

```
MONTAGE

of every moment Cordelia's made a fool
of herself.
```

Be careful writing directly to the reader this way. It's slightly naughty. It may be justified when you're on staff, but it's risky in a freelance script, and very risky in a spec. Use it only when you're sure of what you're doing.

And now, the moment you've all been waiting for . . .

When you finish your first draft, go to lunch. When you come back, the rewriting begins . . .

▪ PART TWO ▪

THE WRITER'S TOOLKIT

4

BAD WRITING AND HOW TO FIX IT (OR AT LEAST GET AWAY WITH IT)

Writing is rewriting.

There may be a few writers in the world whose first drafts are shootable, but they're rare, and most of the ones who claim it are fibbing. Either their scripts go through many extra drafts after their "shootable" first draft or there are many "rough" drafts before the one they choose to call the "first." For almost every writer, a first draft has parts that work and parts that don't, experiments that failed, tone that's off, dialogue that seems a little forced, and so on.

You can try to write a perfect first draft, by writing slowly and carefully. But it's not worth it. You'll come up with ideas as you write later acts that will require a rewrite of earlier scenes. Some scenes in your outline just won't work on the page. You may not realize that until you can read the whole script through.

Most important, TV is not a personal medium, unlike books and even the movies. What you're going for and what the show needs are almost never exactly the same, *even when it's your own show*. You need to read your own completed first draft before you can get a sense of your episode as a whole, and see how it matches and does not match the show you're writing.

Most professional TV writers blast through the first draft and then go back and revise. For me, writing the first draft is the least difficult part of writing a script. Going from nothing to a springboard to a breakdown to a beat sheet is twice as hard as going from a beat sheet to a first draft script. Rewriting the first draft script into something shootable is also twice as hard. Therefore, to me, writing the first draft is about one-fifth of the job. (This is ironic because under the rules of both the U.S. and Canadian Writers Guilds, the writer who writes the first draft gets the credit and the episode writing fee.)

Writing is rewriting.

When Is Your Draft Done?

How *much* rewriting you need to do depends on what you're hired to do. Staff writers should try to be as *efficient* as possible; freelancers and spec writers should try to write as *well* as possible.

If you're staffing a show, then you try to make the episodes as good as you can make them in the time that you have. You write your first draft, read it, polish it, fix any gaping flaws, and make it as good as you *reasonably* can without comments. Then turn it in. You get notes. You address the notes. You turn it in again. Lather, rinse, repeat, until your showrunner or head writer takes the script away from you for her pass. You move on to the next one. You're always going to be working on one script or another, and if any script is perfect, it's a bloody miracle. Chris Abbott:

> I always turn in my first draft. It depends on how much you trust the people who're going to read it. Personally, I think if you think you're close you ought to turn it in and start to get

notes. People can write the same script endlessly . . . that way they can fail without feeling badly. It's never going to be perfect. You're not painting the Mona Lisa.

I mean, do turn in a finished script. Don't turn it in with "chase scene here" or "research pending"—and I've seen scripts like that. You want it to be the best it can be but don't get hung up on it. For one thing, what you may think of as a flaw, someone else may find wonderful—and what you think is the best thing in the script may be the problem.

If you are the head writer or showrunner supervising the writer, then it's a management question: How much more can this writer do on this script before she stops making it better, and just start making it different (or even worse)? Even the most brilliant writers can burn out on a script. Only time will restore perspective. And there is never enough time.

As a freelancer, you have more time, but the standards for your work are higher. Shows hire freelancers to take the pressure off, so you want to carry as much of the load as you can. You may want to do several passes before you turn anything in and get comments. This is less efficient for you, but it's more efficient for the show staff, and they're not paying you by the week anyway.

You should turn in the most polished, brilliant, shootable script you possibly can. Do all the research you need to do, ask all the questions you can think of, but don't turn anything in until it's as good as you can make it on your own. By the second draft your script is supposed to be as good as you can reasonably make it, so that when the story editors take it over, all they have to do is tweak a few things that you couldn't possibly have known were "off" and wait for the network to approve it. If you do your job right, no one will even think of asking you to do another pass on your script without getting paid to do so—a sort of "nondraft draft"—because you'll have done everything a freelancer could. If they want you to do more, they're just going to have to hire you on staff. After all, a freelance script is essentially an audition piece for getting hired on staff.

If you're writing a spec script, then you have more time but less help, and the standards are much higher. But the questions are similar. The deadline you're up against is staffing season (about which more later). Your spec needs to be as close to brilliant as you can make it, but time is of the essence. If you get your brilliant script to an agent too late for her to sign you for this staffing season, you've blown it. If you already have an agent, if you get your brilliant script to him too late for him to send out, you've also blown it. A reasonably good spec in the hands of an agent in March (pre–staffing season) is useful; a great spec delivered in June (post–staffing season) is not much help. In television, the best is the enemy of the good.

You have to manage yourself. At a certain point you'll probably realize that you can't make the script any better. Different is not always better. Sometimes it's just different. There are a million directions in which you can take any given script, and new directions often seem more promising than the path you've gone down. You've lost your perspective. That's the point at which you need to set your script aside for a time. But there is no time. So you get perspective by showing it to trusted friends. When your trusted friends have run out of intelligent comments, you show it to your agent. When your agent has run out of comments—or at least comments that you feel capable of addressing—then it's time to send your script off to producers and network executives.

It's always a battle between perfecting a script and actually getting it out. Never show a work in progress to anyone who can hire you or get you a job. That includes your agent. But scripts are never perfect; and at some point you've done all you can and you have to send them on their merry way into the world. Kind of like children.

You don't send your child out before she's ready for the world. But at some point your child is not a child anymore. John Rogers (*Cosby, Global Frequency*):

> If you're taking a year to write your spec, snap the f*** out of it. You won't get a year to write on the show. Practice at the same speed as production—two to four weeks. If you complain that "Hey, I can't write a good spec in that time," then write more until you can. You're not just pimping your art, you're asking somebody to fork over thousands of dollars to employ you and hundreds of thousands of dollars to shoot what you write. You must bring the A game.[1]

That may be a bit harsh, but no one asked you to be a TV writer, eh? If you take a year to write your spec, you have no business writing TV. And anyway, by then events on the show you're speccing may have rendered your plot obsolete.

Contracts and Drafts

Under the rules of the WGA (Writers Guild of America) and the WGC (Writers Guild of Canada), a freelancer is hired to write two drafts and a polish. According to Guild rules, the first draft is whatever you deliver to the producer, no matter how rough or how polished it is. You get notes, you rewrite, you deliver a second draft. The "polish" is supposed to be no more than a cleanup pass to tighten and improve dialogue; you're not supposed to be introducing new scenes, let alone new characters or new subplots.

In features, producers will often try to turn that polish into a rewrite if a rewrite is called for. They will also try to convince you that your first draft is not a first draft at all, but a "rough" draft, and that your second draft is therefore a first draft. That's okay.

It's a producer's job to try to get people to do more work for less money; it's an agent's job to say, "Ch'Yeah, right. Dream on, babe." The difference between a mature producer and an immature one is how he reacts when your agent reminds him of the Guild rules he knows all too well, as she sends him an invoice for the second draft.

Remember, as you're considering whether to insist on your contractual payments or be a "nice guy," that every time you flout your Guild agreement, you're undercutting all your fellow writers. If a few writers write under scale, then everyone winds up having to write under scale, and then we're all screwed. I once spent a summer writing a show in South Africa, where there is no writers' union. The talent pool is not very deep there. Why? Because producers pay as little as they can. We were getting Guild scale on a Guild contract, but the local writers were getting a few thousand bucks an episode. It doesn't pay for someone to become a screenwriter there. You might as well become a novelist. Although producers don't realize it, Guild agreements help them in the long run, by drawing a decent-sized group of talented, skilled writers to the business and holding them there. I would never have spent ten years paying my dues if all there was at the end of the rainbow was a mess of pottage. I don't even like pottage.

Taking Criticism

It's hard to hear that the script you've slaved over for so long is less than brilliant. One of the skills that successful writers in any medium develop is the ability to listen to and really *hear* criticism. Paul Guyot (*Judging Amy*):

> There was a writer on a show I worked on once who was so in love with his own words that he would call us all together and

> read scenes or dialogue that he had just written. Of course, you can imagine how this guy was at taking notes. He would be willing to ruin a scene or entire episode in order to preserve what he felt was "golden words."

That kind of behavior is excellent for a pompous character in a sitcom. For a writer writing a sitcom, not so much. You have to be willing to throw away any and all of your golden words if someone gives you a better idea.

If you're writing a spec, it's up to you to realize what's a better idea and what's not. If you've got comments from friends, then the usual rules of feedback apply. Assume that any criticism is true, but don't feel you have to take any suggestion of how to correct the flaw. Readers are usually much better at telling you that there's a problem than pinpointing where the problem really lies, and almost nobody but a professional writer will reliably give you the right solution.

How do you get feedback on your script? If you're in show business, lots of people will be willing to read your script. If you don't know anyone, what do you do?

I'd recommend seeking out intelligent fans and writers on the Net. Fans are better than other aspiring writers because they don't want to take over your episode and won't be offended if you don't rewrite it the way they would.

Most popular shows have fan sites. Fan sites often have forums where people post critiques of the latest episodes. Many shows have their own fan newsgroups, for instance, rec.tv.buffy. Many also have Television Without Pity (www.televisionwithoutpity.com/) forums. See whose comments you think are insightful. Write to those fans, compliment them, and ask if they'd be willing to read your spec script. They'll probably be thrilled.

You can also check out writing websites and see if other writers at your level are interested in forming an online writing group to read and critique one another's stuff.

If you are lucky enough to have comments from a professional TV writer, then take them seriously. Take them so seriously that even if you think they're absolutely wrong you do the changes anyway. Do them with all the heart and soul you're capable of. If the results are bad, then, and only then, should you decide to go another way. You'll probably see why the comments are right long before you're through.

Sure, discuss the comments first, if there's anything you don't understand. But then, take them.

There is one exception to this rule. Even with feedback from a professional writer, you are entitled to ignore any advice that amounts to "I would have written it differently." Listen to the professional writer's take, consider it seriously. But ultimately, the spec has to be the kind of story *you* love to write, because you're selling your own unique perspective and style. If it feels wrong to you, *and you can't figure out how to make it feel right to you,* then you won't do a good job with it. Go with what you're sure of.

Don't ask more than one professional at a time for comments. You're going to rewrite based on the first person's comments, aren't you? So why do you need two sets of comments? Getting the same comments twice just wastes one professional's expensive time. Getting different comments will just confuse you. Either way, you've burned a favor for nothing. If you're taking the comments seriously—reworking the script, not just patching holes—then you should only need one set of notes. Once you've done one set of notes, your script is now better, and you can ask your second contact for notes, knowing she'll be more impressed with it.

If you're freelancing a script for a show, then you have a story editor assigned to you. Do what they tell you to do! The point of the exercise is to get hired again. If you do what the story editor tells you, and the results don't work, then it's his fault, he'll know it, he'll fix it, and you'll both have a pleasant experience. If you do something different, then the story editor is likely to hate whatever you did, rewrite it his way anyway, and never hire you again.

If you're a story editor and the comments are coming from the showrunner, then the same thing goes, only now you have a full-time job to lose.

Don't fight with people who are going to rewrite you. Ask for clarifications. Point out problems. Argue, try to persuade, but never fight. They have the last word. If they don't like what you've done, they will simply rewrite your script the way they asked you to in the first place. In TV, you have to be willing to throw away your brilliant ideas and words in favor of someone else's dumb idea, if he or she outranks you.

You are not there to write great TV. You are there to make your showrunner's life easier. The two may in fact be the same, or they may not. Your showrunner probably has a better idea than you do which way to go. If the showrunner wants you to take your desert island episode and set it in an elevator at midnight, that's what you do. The mark of a great TV writer is that she'll figure out why setting it in an elevator is actually brilliant, and deliver the episode that proves it.

Words are cheap. Television is expensive. It's not your show. You're not running it, and you're not paying for it. If you want to keep your words exactly the way you wrote them, write a novel. Blog. Write a play. When you're a playwright, and the actor or director asks to change a line, you are entitled to say no, and that's that. *Television is not a medium of personal expression.* If you can bring your own brilliance to someone else's expression, then you'll keep working.

The Flavors of Bad Writing

Bad writing comes in many flavors. There is not much to say about dialogue that lacks the spark of life, or contributes nothing to revealing the character, or just doesn't snap—what can you say about weak tea? Action sequences that lack invention—well, if it's boring you as you write it, it's probably boring everyone else, too. Pacing that doesn't build, characters that don't behave the way any plausible person would behave in their situation, or behave out of character—these problems should be obvious, right?

But there are ways that scripts can tank that are less obvious.

Pulling vs. Pushing

The key to telling a good story, whether it's in front of a campfire or onscreen, is drawing your audience into the story. When your audience is fully involved in the story, they're giving life to your characters. They're filling in everything that happens *between* the moments you're showing onscreen. They're anticipating what will happen next. They're rooting for what they hope will happen, or rooting against what they fear will happen.

Pushing is giving the audience more story than they can absorb. If you're pushing story at them, you're not *pulling* them into the story. You pull them in by giving them reasons to want more story than you've given them so far.

It's the difference between a lecture and a conversation. A lecture may carry more sheer information than a conversation, but you often carry away more information from a conversation, because you're actively engaged in it. More important, you carry away more of an emotional reaction to a conversation. That's why no oration is complete without some call-and-response. If there's no way to participate in the story, it's hard to care about what happens.

In a classic detective story, you want to pull the audience into the story by setting up questions that the audience will adopt as their own. Once they have questions, the detective finds the answers. You never provide an answer until you've set up the question properly; so the audience is there with the detective, trying to solve the puzzle. If the detective (or the camera) is uncovering clues faster than the audience can ask questions, the audience is reduced to a passenger, and they're thinking, "Wake me when we get there."

If you pull them, they'll pull themselves in. If you push them, they'll push themselves out.

The same is true for an emotional story. We want the question before we get the answer. Will Ross dare to kiss Rachel? Will Rachel slap him if he does? If we don't know what's in play—what to hope for or fear—then when it happens, we have no stake in the outcome.

In a drama, you want the audience to be rooting for the main character to get somewhere emotionally. They should feel the dramatic tension and want it released. If the drama gets resolved faster than tension builds, you're just pushing dramatic events at the audience.

Pushing usually becomes obvious only after you've written a first draft. Some of this is just pacing. In a horror movie, we all love the moment when the character pauses outside the haunted house, wondering whether to go in or not. That's the moment we're screaming, "Don't go in the house!" If you show the character getting out of the car and then cut to the moment when he actually opens the front door—if you lose the moment of deciding—the story is the same, but you're pushing the story at the audience. It's the pause that makes the moment.

Let your scenes breathe. Give your characters time to wonder, and ponder, and pause. Give them time to absorb the emotional shocks, which is also the time for us to start to wonder how they'll react. Don't move on to the next beat before you've given the characters, and the audience, time to absorb this one.

Sometimes when a scene feels too slow the real problem is the opposite. You're going too *fast*. You're not letting the viewer absorb the emotion of the scene. So they're less invested in it. Since they don't care, they're bored. They want you to move on to something more interesting. The scene feels slow. But if you *slow* the scene down and let it breathe, it feels richer and deeper, and the audience isn't so anxious to get going. They're happy to stay in the scene. It feels as though it's at the right pace.

Slowing the pace down can be a little difficult when you've set a clock on the action. Who has time to stop and chat when a bomb is going to explode? If the stakes are the destruction of the world, when is there time for the hero to pause and be human?

Screenwriters usually fudge the issue, and we're glad they do. There are tearful reunions in every thriller, even when every second counts. Soldiers in no-man's-land will stop to embrace their dying buddy, while bullets are whistling and they ought to be diving for cover. Even in *24,* where every minute is accounted for, and millions of lives are literally at stake, the characters take time to indulge in their emotions.

Better than fudging the issue, trap your characters somewhere for a bit. If they're in a car driving to a destination, they have time to talk and emote because they're doing all they can already. If they're caught in a cage or an elevator, and they cannot possibly get out until someone comes for them, they can take a moment and catch up emotionally: cry, or rage, or reconcile, or accuse. They also have time if they are hiding. Then they have to emote quietly, which may be even more effective.

Or, hold back that crucial bit of information that will send them off on their life-or-death mission until they've had their dramatic scene. The audience can know that the characters have run out of time, but don't let the characters figure it out until they've had a chance to absorb the emotional impact of the events they've been through already.

The audience can know more than the hero. That automatically establishes a nice tension. The audience wants to tell the hero what he doesn't know—"Watch out, he's got a knife!"—and that draws them into the story. But *the hero must never know substantively more than the audience.* If there's something the hero knows that we need to know in order to appreciate the predicament he's in, then tell us as soon as possible, and certainly before the predicament becomes urgent. We can be involved in the story if the hero doesn't know what's going on—like him, we're going to be involved in the process of figuring it out. But we can't be involved in the story if he knows what's going on and we don't.

In African dance music, the drummers drum everything but the beat; they let the audience fill it in for themselves with their feet. Leave room for the audience to participate in the story. Detective stories are all about the questions, not the outcome. Once the outcome comes out, the story is over, after all. Dramatic stories are all about the struggle, not the resolution. Don't resolve your dramatic issues until you're ready to pose new dramatic issues. There should always be something to pull the viewer into the story.

Geography

Try to give your episode a sense of place. Every show is set somewhere, whether it's *Friends,* which is set in a mythical New York of big, affordable apartments, or *Lost,* which takes place on Gilligan's Island. The flavor of the place should permeate your episode. James Nadler (*PSI Factor*):

> One weekend I read three *West Wing* specs . . . but I'd written one, too, so I was particularly aware of what I wanted the show to do. None of them had a feel for Washington, D.C., and its geography. . . . All the specs felt like they were taking place on

the back lot of a studio. You have to capture the city a show's in. A *Sex and the City* that doesn't feel like New York just makes me irritated.

It's true: *Sex and the City* has such a well-developed sense of place that New York is practically a character in the show. In the finale, Carrie has less trouble leaving Big than she has leaving New York.

The same geographical location may be a different place in different shows. *Sex and the City*'s New York is not the same as *NYPD Blue*'s New York. Be sure you're writing for the right New York. Carrie Bradshaw's streets glisten with romance; Andy Sipowicz's streets drip with pain.

Some shows, particularly sitcoms, don't worry too much about a sense of place. *Everybody Loves Raymond* could take place in any suburb (and probably does). But no one will mind if you are more specific. Even in a cartoon, a sense of place grounds the show. *The Untalkative Bunny* takes place in Ottawa, not Your City; even the cartoon backgrounds are based on actual reference photographs. Your scripts should have the telltale details that ground your show in a specific place, whether it's a real one or a fictional one. You can't have too much of a sense of place.

What does a high-powered restaurant in Washington, D.C., look like? You can easily find out what the top restaurants in D.C. are. Many of them will have websites with pictures. Is it a sleek and shiny modern restaurant? Is it a classic Georgian-style restaurant with drapes and antique chairs and paintings of George Washington?

If you have a character stealing a painting from the Hermitage Museum in Moscow (not that you should, unless you're writing *Alias*), give a few telling details that show us what the Hermitage looks and feels like. Go to their website. Show us the canals, the huge wide plaza with its statue, the Louis XIV architecture.

If your show is set on a space station, write in the details, even if only in passing. Does the space station have vending machines? What do people do with their dirty laundry? That's what grounds the show in human reality and makes it more than an allegory.

The better the sense of place in your episode, the more real the episode feels, the easier the audience will find it to believe in the fictional parts of the story.

Suspension of Disbelief

TV is a constructed reality. The audience knows that, so they're willing to suspend their disbelief. But they'll only suspend so much. The more you have characters behaving in ways that don't match their reality—the more *plotholes* you have—the less invested they'll be in the characters and the story. But because you're trying to entertain, you often have to choose between a more entertaining story with plotholes and a more accurate story without them. Which do you choose?

The audience is there to be entertained; if they wanted accuracy, they wouldn't be watching television, whether fiction or "reality" or Fox News. They will tolerate unreal situations as long as they're more entertaining than real ones. When you're fudging your facts *without* being clever and entertaining, they'll click to the next channel. But when you come up with something fun, they'll forgive you for the shortcuts you took to get there. Chris Abbott:

> I'd rather surprise an audience than be logical. You can't be so illogical you throw the audience out, but if you can find the thinnest, tiniest strand of logic—too much logic is the murderer of good scripts. Scripts are like dreams. You kinda go into a dream state. You don't care about logic so long as you're not pulled out of the scene.

> Like that Al Pacino movie about Alaska, where he couldn't sleep because the sun is up all the time—*Insomnia*. Right away from the beginning of the film you know it's wrong. I've been up in that area of the world and they have blackout drapes everywhere—it's dark enough to sleep. So the whole premise of the movie falls apart.
>
> You can't have a plothole just because it's convenient to the writer. That irritates the audience. There are certain logical steps you have to take. Then you can open it up. If you ground it in reality in the beginning, then you can take liberties later on.

The degree to which the audience expects to have to suspend their disbelief is part of the tone of a show. When people are shot, how much pain are they in? How seriously do people take guns being pointed at them? A show like *Alias* expects the audience to suspend a fair amount of disbelief. The bad guys ambush Sydney Bristow in a parking garage and there's a big shootout. Why don't they just sneak into her apartment and shoot her when she comes in? The audience doesn't care, because the parking garage shootout is more fun. The *Alias* audience is looking for exciting shootouts, so they'll suspend their disbelief when doing so gets them one.

In *CSI* we're expected to believe that a small team of forensics experts handles everything from collecting evidence (actually done by evidence techs) to laboratory work (actually done by specialized lab techs). Watching the real process of forensics would mean watching dozens of different specialists at work. We'd rather follow a few characters. So we'll suspend our disbelief.

The audience will suspend their disbelief when it will buy them the kind of story they want to see; and they'll do it when it's part of the tone of the show. In a "realistic" cop show like *Homicide* your cops wouldn't do their own forensics. If they started doing their own DNA analysis, the show would lose its audience. But the cops can go talk to the forensics guys, though in real life it would be a phone call or some results e-mailed to them. Who wants to watch a phone call when you can watch a cop in a morgue? In a "realistic" cop show, your cops are handling a few exciting cases, when really they'd have a case docket of dozens of homicides, most of them run of the mill. We're still expected to suspend our disbelief, but in a less extravagant fashion.

On the other hand, the more extravagant a show is overall, the more the audience is willing to suspend its disbelief in the particulars. If you can swallow that Sydney Bristow is a superspy and a college student at the same time, then you should have no trouble swallowing that the mysterious ancient manuscript she's chasing after is worth killing people for. If the show stays true to itself, and the results are entertaining, we're cool with it.

The audience won't suspend disbelief when they feel you've been lazy and the story you came up with isn't as good as it would have been if you'd obeyed the constructed reality of your show. If you establish that the villain has a high-security laboratory, you better show the hero engaging in some amazingly clever and strenuous behavior to get in and out of it. You better show the hero in some jeopardy when he does it, or the audience will feel you've copped out.

Beware the "idiot stick." When the plot depends on a normally intelligent character utterly failing to figure out something obvious, he's said to be carrying the idiot stick. (Hank Azaria is said to have coined the term on *Herman's Head* when he would ask the writers unhappily, "Who's carrying the idiot ball now?" But "idiot stick" sounds better.) Don't force your character to be dim-witted unless he's a dim-witted character. The audience may go along with it, but they won't be committed to the story you're telling.

Remember, it's *storytelling*. The audience wants a good story. If it gets a good story it will forgive a lot. If not, not.

It's like comedy. If the audience is laughing, they'll put up with almost any amount of unrealistic behavior. If they're frowning, you're hosed.

It's hard to avoid all plotholes. Sooner or later, you wind up painting yourself into a corner. When you do that in a movie script, you can go back and rewrite the whole damn thing. In TV, you've already shot some episodes. You may have established something that gets you in trouble later on. Say the villains know where the hero lives. Why don't they just post a sniper on the roof and put a bullet in his head next time he walks out his door? You may have to choose between a lot of "shoe leather" (tedious scene-work intended solely to set something up) every time he walks out his door or ignoring the plothole.

A solution might be to establish that the hero's blinds are always down and he exits the place through a secret underground tunnel. But then some director goes and opens the blinds because the lighting will look better. Directors don't know the season arc, nor do they necessarily care. They just know the show they're directing. So they're always making decisions that make their episode cooler at the potential expense of the season logic. And now you're stuck. Do you have the hero move to a new apartment? You can't, that would mean even more shoe leather and junking the very expensive studio set that was budgeted to last the whole season. What do you do?

One solution is to live with the glitch. Try not to draw attention to it. Stop having scenes in which the villains are discussing finding your hero. You try not to open that can o' worms. And you hope the audience is willing to suspend their disbelief.

A better solution (in general) is to *address* the problem and give a *character* reason why things are happening the way they are. Addressing the problem means simply calling attention to it, rather than glossing it over. Have one of the villains raise the very issue you think your audience is going to ask: "Why don't we just put a sniper on the roof and put a bullet in his head?"

The answer can tell us something about the chief villain. Maybe he thinks he's clever: "Because we've bugged his apartment and I want him to lead us to the people he's working for." Maybe he's legalistic, and wants the hero arrested, not shot. Maybe he's prideful, and rejects the suggestion just because it came from someone else. Maybe he's sentimental, and wants to seduce the hero over to his own side rather than killing him. Any of these can work; all of them tell us something about the chief villain's character that the logical explanation does not.

It's not that you can't have characters make dumb, illogical decisions. In real life, people do things that seem unmotivated or illogical all the time, often because they're not thinking clearly. We're human. But the mistakes we make reveal who we are.

Just as with other plotholes, if you need the hero to make a dumb mistake, give him an emotional reason why he's making the mistake. Maybe his pride is in the way. Maybe his generosity of spirit. In a thriller, the reason is often that the hero has run out of time to ponder his decision and needs to go with his gut. In a comedy, maybe it's his stinginess. If he makes a dumb mistake for a good character reason, we'll stay invested in the episode. If it's just so you can get him where you want to get him, we'll feel betrayed.

The corollary to this is: when your character *avoids* making a dumb mistake, especially one that TV characters are prone to making in general (e.g., go into a haunted house), *make a moment of it*. Have them debate making the dumb mistake, and then do something cleverer. That way the audience can enjoy your cleverness and the fact that you respect them too much to have your character do lame, unbelievable things. This can be just a tiny moment onscreen when we know what the character's considering doing. But it should be there.

Then, of course, your character's cleverness gets him into even worse trouble . . .

Offscreen Story

Q. How much can happen offscreen?
A. Nothing important.

The basic rule is that anything important to the story has to happen onscreen. If someone's in danger, we need to see him or her threatened, and we need to see him or her escape the danger. We don't need to see every threatening incident, but we need to see one; and we don't need to see every escape, but we need to see one. (See "The Rule of One" in Chapter 3.) If the protagonist has an important decision to make, that decision should happen onscreen. Part of why we're watching, after all, is to see the character make that decision. Do it offscreen and you're cheating your audience. You're only telling half the story; or, to put it another way, you're not telling the story, you're only telling us *about* the story.

Characters can do inconsequential things offscreen. They can eat, sleep, work, and go to the little boy's room offscreen.

It's surprising how much "important" action can turn out to be inconsequential. Many story beats turn out to be unnecessary; in the editing process, you cut them, and the story is no worse, and sometimes it's better. Paul Guyot:

> A lot more can happen offscreen than most writers think. Just take editing. Usually there's anywhere from eight to as much as twenty minutes cut out of a one-hour episode before it hits the air. Does the story still work without all that other stuff that the writer originally thought *had* to go into the script? Usually it's even better.

These cuts are scenes that survived the entire rewriting process, went to the production floor, and got shot at great expense. But cut them in editing and—surprise!—you don't miss 'em.

Still, characters should not do anything critical to the show or the story offscreen. The key is "*important to the show.*" If it's a mystery show, they should not discover clues offscreen. If it's a drama, they should not argue or work things out offscreen. If it's a medical show, they shouldn't find out important medical clues or perform crucial medical procedures offscreen.

A character on a family drama shouldn't get married offscreen. But a character on a thriller could. If Jack Bauer's daughter goes off to college between seasons of *24,* that's fine. The story is about counterterrorism. The first incarnation of *Cheers* ended up with Sam rich, and buying a yacht. Second incarnation starts with Sam back in the bar having lost his yacht. *Cheers* is not about buying or sinking yachts, it's about a bunch of friendly barflies. We could have seen the yacht sink, but what does that have to do with the story?

What if the important turning points of your story can't be put onscreen? What if they would cost too much, or aren't appropriate for television? Then it's not a story you can tell on TV. If your episode hinges on events that can't be put on TV, you're writing the wrong story.

This is true whether the offscreen moment is between scenes, between acts, between episodes, or between seasons. Very little story can happen offscreen, even when time has elapsed. Characters generally pick up their story where their story left off. If Ross is dating Charlie the paleontologist at the end of one season, in the spring, he's still dating her at the beginning of the next, in the fall—even if he drops her by the end of the first episode.

Your story can have unshootable events as background. *China Beach* takes place during the Vietnam War. On a TV budget you can't afford battles, you can only afford the occasional helicopter and a half-dozen badly wounded guys. But you could have a story set during the Tet Offensive, when all hell broke loose for the unprepared Americans—if that story was about half a dozen badly wounded guys coming to China Beach and dealing with their sudden feeling that we were losing the war. You could even have a story about half a dozen badly wounded guys trying to fight off a small group of Viet Cong.

You can have unshootable events in the middle of the story if the point of the story is not how those events turn out, but how those events are set in motion by the characters' decisions, or how the characters feel about those events. If the president orders a missile strike in *The West Wing,* we don't need to see the missile strike, because the story is how the president makes his decision, and then how he feels about the outcome.

TV is like theater in that it is more about people's reactions to big events than about the big events themselves. A movie may show us a battle; TV might show us the characters hiding from the battle, or coming into a bar after the battle's over, or coming home to open up a bar after the war's over.

Sometimes you have to deal with offscreen events that need to be handled onscreen. Sometimes an actor stomps off the show when you won't raise his salary. Unless the actor is willing or contractually obliged to participate in his character's demise, you may have to do this offscreen. Your actor may actually die, as happened tragically on *Eight Simple Rules for Dating My Teenage Daughter* and *15/Love* and many other shows.

You can usually get away with an important offscreen event if you show the immediate emotional aftermath. *15/Love* had the actors' characters die offscreen, and then showed the surviving characters dealing with their shock and sorrow in a "very special episode." But the story is really about their shock and sorrow, not about the death itself.

Occasionally, it's *better* to have something crucial happen offscreen. Some events are wrong for the tone of a show. On *Friends,* Chandler is supposed to have kissed a transvestite. Ross ribbing him about it is funny. But it might have been too embarrassing for the audience to see it onscreen. When the subject matter of a detective show is too horrific—child abuse or torture—we probably don't want to see that onscreen, either, even if it's a show that normally shows the crime.

And, of course, if what happened at a crucial point in the story is supposed to be a *mystery,* then it *better* happen offscreen.

Go-Tos

Of course the go-to joke is: "Libraries? In Mississippi???"

—JON STEWART, *The Daily Show*

A *go-to* is an easy, or lazy, way to get something done dramatically.

A classic go-to might occur when you need the hero to know something that's going on in the wide world. He turns on the television—and wouldn't you know it, there's a news report about the very thing you needed him to know! Or, he buys some gum from a newsstand—and there's his face on the cover of the *Post*!

You typically use an expositional go-to when you need the hero to know information that, honestly, he could pick up in any number of boring ways but you just don't want to waste time on the shoe leather of how he learns it. TV is a constructed reality. The audience understands that the instant TV news report stands in for the hero turning on the TV and watching two hours of summer reruns before a news report comes on. They accept that, on TV, television sets play nothing but relevant news reports. And they're happy to get on with the story. Still, you're not impressing them. And the less you seem to care about them, the less they're going to care about your show.

For a trivial piece of *expo* (exposition), the audience will forgive you if you *take the curse off* your go-to. For example, the hero doesn't turn on the TV set—he notices a battery-powered TV set being stolen by a rioter, so that the news he needs is running past him, not just sitting still in a TV store. Instead of buying the paper, have him buy fish and chips, and notice the news wrapping the fish, or use the paper to light a fire. The cleverer you can make the exposition, the more the audience will forgive you for the go-to. As long as they feel you care, they'll care.

But if the information is something that the plot hangs on—something that the hero couldn't learn in three hours of watching TV—then you're going to have to build a sequence where the hero learns it. Otherwise no amount of cleverness will take the curse off the go-to.

A go-to doesn't have to be expositional. It may also be the all-too-predictable payoff to an obvious setup. In the *Jack and Bobby* pilot, Bobby steals his mother's marijuana to ingratiate himself with some bullies who are hanging out with his ex–best friend. This is such an ill-conceived plan that it's obvious the screenwriters are planning for Bobby to get in trouble for it. The go-to is for Bobby to get ratted out by the bullies.

Tragically, that's what happens.

That's bad plotting.

As we've discussed, the audience does not always want a surprise outcome. But the audience always wants a surprise path *to* that outcome. If they can see where you're going and how you're going to get there, then they don't need to watch your episode, do they? It's like solving a crossword puzzle that someone's already penciled in.

Sure, the audience may even be willing to watch an episode *again*. But they'll do that only when *how* you get to your outcome is so witty, or so moving, that it pleases them a second time.

The problem with a go-to in a plot is that the audience can see how you're getting there.

The solution is to take advantage of the go-to. Use the audience's expectation against them, and go in *another* direction. In the *Jack and Bobby* example, if Bobby's going to get ratted out, have it be by the now-jealous ex–best friend, not the bullies. Or, better, he gets along with everyone, but the pot makes his asthma flare up. Or he doesn't get in trouble with the bullies or the authorities—but with his brother. Or he doesn't smoke (because of his asthma) and he realizes that people are really boring when they're stoned. Or he witnesses a crime, but because he's smoking pot he can't reveal he was there, or he's not an acceptable witness and the bad guy gets away with it.

Obviously, on network television you're never going to have Bobby smoke pot as a *story point* and nothing bad happens at all. Not because TV has a responsibility not to encourage bad behavior, though I think it does, but because if a story point has no consequences, you don't have a story, you only have a series of unconnected incidents. And the consequences should be something we didn't expect.

If you're using the first plot turn that comes into your head, odds are the audience is going to think of it, too. That's lazy plotting. You should be able to come up with four or five better solutions if you try.

Sometimes, as with plotholes, you just can't avoid a go-to. Sometimes you're out of time. Sometimes the go-to is so logical for your protagonist that avoiding it would make him behave illogically, or worse, out of character. In that case you probably want to try to get past the go-to as fast as possible. Don't spend time on it. The audience is already expecting the plot to go in this direction, so show as little of the go-to plot sequence as possible. The audience will fill in the gaps.

You Only Need to Show What the Audience Can't Figure Out for Themselves. If I show you a large chain attached to a big, broken leather dog collar in a backyard, and a postman getting out of his truck, then I can cut straight to the postman in shredded clothes, covered in dirt. You don't even need to see the dog, let alone the attack. In the *Jack and Bobby* example, you could probably cut from Bobby offering to bring pot to Bobby sitting in the principal's office. We can figure out the rest. If the story is familiar enough, you can just start it, finish it, and jump ahead to the interesting parts of your story. The audience will fill in the rest.

Point of View

One subtle mistake writers can make is writing the scene from the wrong point of view. Sometimes a day player—a minor speaking part—can be so much fun to write that you find yourself putting the spotlight on her. In a comedy script, she gets all the jokes. In a drama, she gets the big emotional meltdown.

In comedy, John Rogers says, this is called "sucking on the day player crack pipe":

> This comes about because, well, TV's a frikkin' grind. . . . You know every trick, every rhythm of the actors. . . . You know the lines they can hit, the jokes they don't know how to do, you know their parameters.
>
> Now, along comes the day player. A new character who you can do ANYTHING with . . . The actor himself has all these neat new little rhythms, they're happy to get the job so they really sell the lines, it's all fresh and shiny, and if the person is

> actually GOOD, well then, all bets are off. It's FUN to write for a good day player, and you can write the big funny for them, they're there to service the plot and comedy, not the other way around, you're pitching jokes and situations you've never tried before and you're all laughing and when's the last time you all LAUGHED so hard in the writer's room, you write them bigger and bigger, and you just can't stop—
>
> You're sucking on the day player crack pipe. Put it down, and step away. Otherwise, you will have your star standing there with his thumb up his ass while the day player gets alllll the laughs. And that is not a happy day for anyone.[2]

Remember Whose Story It Is. Check through your script to make sure that each scene is written from the emotional point of view of the character whose story it is. Of course, you can give emotional fireworks to the murder victim's mother. But the scene isn't about the mother. It's about *your cop hero trying to get some information* from her while she's melting down on camera.

In every law show, the witnesses get great scenes. But the shows aren't about the witnesses. They're about the hero lawyers who *use* the witnesses to *get what they want*. Don't forget that. Yes, the witness gets the big emotional meltdown—but the lawyer gets the big moral decision whether to indict her, too.

Not only will staying in your hero's point of view keep your audience engaged in his story, it will also add a nice layer to the scene. How does your lawyer hero *feel* about what the witness is going through? What does her testimony *do* to him in his story?

On the flip side, imagining the scene from the day player's perspective is a really useful tool to keep your script honest and inventive. John Rogers again:

> Switch gears. Sit down, and pretend that, say, a huge actor has just been hired to play the OTHER role in the scene, and your job is to make the role more interesting to play. Or put yourself

> in as [the secondary character]. Make [the hero] the asshole who's interfering with what YOU want. Now, [your character] has an agenda, has a drive, and will make [the hero's] life that much harder. Now, you have conflict. You have a SCENE. Maybe [the hero] will have to work a little harder, be a little more interesting to beat you. And maybe you've created a character, found another voice in the script or story you weren't anticipating.

But after you've written the scene from the day player's perspective, getting all that interesting dialogue and all those monkey wrenches thrown in the hero's clever plan, you have to go and rewrite the scene from the hero's perspective. It is, after all, called *Magnum, P.I.*, not *The Show About People Who Give Magnum, P.I., a Tough Time.*

Communicating Without Dialogue

Sometimes upon rereading your dialogue you may realize that it's not communicating as much as you hoped. When I write dialogue, I try to act what the characters are saying; I play the part. It's a good way to get the dialogue going, and to make sure the moments are flowing organically from one to another. The problem is that, just because you're organically *feeling* what the character is feeling doesn't mean that you're *communicating* it to the audience.

You can write the feeling into the action description (the "blacks"), but that's an inelegant way to get the result. (In computer science, we'd call it a "kludge.") Also, it may not get the result you want. If an actor doesn't feel the scene from the dialogue, he may ignore the blacks and play the whole thing shallowly.

The solution in most cases is to find an off-the-nose way for the characters to express themselves. Without the characters actually saying what they're saying, have them imply it. Feeling often comes through better in elliptical dialogue than in on-the-nose dialogue.

But what do you when your main character is one of those laconic characters we love so much—one of those guys who doesn't like to talk about himself, or a woman with a secret she does not want to reveal even to herself? If there's another character to whom your laconic hero opens up—an old buddy, his wife, his son—then you're good to go. But some characters are simply not that introspective. They're not open even to themselves. Or, God forbid, your character is a teenager, and too embarrassed to open up to anybody, and barely speaks anyway ("Nothing." "Whatever."). What do you do?

In some shows, this character has already been thoughtfully equipped with voice-over. Angela in *My So-Called Life*, Meredith in *Grey's Anatomy*, Mary Alice in *Desperate Housewives*—all of these have no one with whom they can really communicate their innermost thoughts. Angela's a teenager who's too embarrassed, Meredith is a new intern who can't trust her competitive fellow interns, and Mary Alice is dead. Fortunately for the audience, who'd otherwise watch Angela go around looking bewildered all episode long, we get direct insight into her mind through her voice-over.

Don't let anyone tell you voice-overs are bad writing. They're a perfectly valid tool for storytelling. Some Emmy Award–winning writers use them. Hell, Shakespeare did it. Who do you think Hamlet's talking to? His bodkin?

When used to communicate what can't be communicated otherwise, voice-overs are just as valid as flashbacks—or any other deprecated storytelling tool that has proved its usefulness too many times to need defending from film school teachers. But there is this prejudice against them. James Nadler:

> I hate voice-over, unless it's an ironic v.o. *Desperate Housewives* gets away with it because it's a dead woman giving the voice-

> over, and it's ironic. My rule of thumb is that I'll try to write the story without a voice-over, and only if it fails to get the character's inner workings across will I go to a voice-over.

However, unless the show's template has already introduced a voice-over, it's risky to do one yourself in a freelance episode, and a bad idea to introduce it in a spec script. Remember, you're trying to nail the template, and if the showrunner wanted a voice-over, he'd already have one. If you're on staff, you can propose an episode with a voice-over. If the showrunner likes your pitch for it, you may get to write a mold-breaking episode. That's one of the many fun things about working on staff. But don't count on it.

One rarely used technique for getting past a character's inability to communicate is "breaking the fourth wall," that is, speaking directly to camera. Some shows do this theatrically: *Malcolm in the Middle*'s protagonist soliloquizes to the audience. Some motivate the soliloquy: *Trailer Park Boys* is a mockumentary series where borderline inarticulate characters address the camera as if they're speaking to an interviewer. You *definitely* don't want to break the fourth wall unless the technique is part of the show's template.

Lacking a voice-over and respecting the fourth wall, you can still get across what the character is thinking *without the character ever telling anyone directly.*

One way is to give the character someone who knows him well. Even if the guarded, laconic hero won't open up to his girlfriend, his girlfriend may still get where he's at. She can simply tell the hero what she thinks is going on. "You're not really mad about the job," she can say, "you're mad because your dad died!"

For bonus points, this can develop into a cross-conversation where your hero is also voicing his girlfriend's unspoken issues. Just because a character won't talk about himself doesn't mean he can't be articulate for someone else.

A more subtle technique is to have the protagonist run into

someone who's got the same problem he has. Then as the hero talks to the day player about the day player's supposed problem, we gradually realize he's really talking about himself, even if he doesn't realize it. Your character is feeling crippled with guilt? Have the character talk to someone else who's crippled with guilt. Your hero is paralyzed by depression? Have him give some depressed gal a pep talk. As he talks her out of her depression, he talks himself out of his depression. Your hero did something he regrets? You get the idea.

By the way, if you write this sort of scene on staff, you may want to make sure that you give the actor (and the network exec) subtitles for the nuance-impaired. Put it in the action description:

```
Yes, he's talking about himself here. But he
doesn't realize it.
```

If you're writing a spec, though, you can't hang a sign on how clever you are. So be a little subtler:

```
He looks off, realizing something. Shakes
his head ironically.
```

If none of these techniques works, you can hope the episode's music saves you. Music can do a lot to amplify a character's emotion and the tone of the scene. But music is not as powerful in TV as in the movies. In the movies the audience isn't hearing any other sounds. The dishwasher is not going, the baby is not gurgling happily. If you're depending on music to carry the emotion, you haven't done your job. Rethink how to convey the meaning, and rewrite the scenes that need to do it.

5

BRINGING THE FUNNY

> Analyzing humor is like dissecting a frog. Few people are interested, and it's bad for the frog's health.
>
> —E. B. WHITE

Comedy is harder to write than drama. In principle all you have to do is make the audience laugh. If they're laughing, you're good. But it's hard to sustain laughter without a story. A comedy series or comic drama needs everything drama needs—a central character, goal/problem/opportunity, obstacles/antagonist, stakes, and jeopardy—*and* it needs to be funny.

That's one reason, incidentally, why comedy staffs tend to be larger than drama staffs. A staff of five can comfortably write a one-hour drama. Sitcoms can have twenty people on staff. Some highly paid writers do nothing more than pitch a few brilliant jokes for each script.

What's So Funny?

As Aristotle said, "Comedy is tragedy that happens to your mother-in-law."[1]

By laughing, we can step back from a negative situation and get perspective on it. If the situation is happening to a fictional character, laughter allows us to shed some of our identification with the characters and experience relief—don't hurt *me*, God, hurt *him*! If a situation *is* happening to us, laughing allows us to get some perspective on it. We laugh at the part we can't do anything about so we can focus on the part we can do something about.

Laughter is how we avoid panicking.

Comedy is an essentially sadistic genre. If you *were* one of the Stooges, your life would be a never-ending hell of eye gouges, head whackings, and hair pullings. All comedy is based on a strong negative emotion, and each strong negative emotion has its own flavor of comedy:

- *Physical pain* without serious damage. Slapstick. *The Three Stooges*. More common in the movies than on TV: stunts are expensive to shoot.
- *Disgust*. Fart jokes. Slimy things on Nickelodeon. *South Park*. Grade-schoolers tend to find disgusting things funnier than adults do.
- *Embarrassment*. Characters get caught in humiliating situations, e.g., falling into a cream pie, getting caught in a lie, getting caught with their pants down. *I Love Lucy*. Much sitcom humor is embarrassment comedy.

Embarrassment comedy can also be embarrassing for the audience rather than the character. *Coupling* is funny because the characters say utterly atrocious things to one another. James Spader's sleazoid lawyer character on *Boston Legal* is funny because we expect him to apologize for his behavior, and he doesn't.

- *Frustration.* Characters try, and try, and try, and can't . . . get a date, get a job, get their jaws into that damn bird (*Road Runner, Sylvester & Tweety*), get away from their overbearing family (*Everybody Loves Raymond*).
- *Fear.* Especially fear of death. Absurdist humor like *Monty Python's Flying Circus*'s "Self-Defense Against Fresh Fruit" sketch. Situations so over-the-top awful you can't help but laugh.

In a comic plot or comic situation, you put your protagonist through one kind of hell or another; and then, usually, you bring him back to where he started, no better off or wiser than before.

Great Comic Premises

A great comic springboard often begins with a very familiar situation, then twists it, and carries the twist into the realm of absurdity. Characters deal with the same issues you and I deal with, but they take their reactions to ridiculous lengths. John Rogers (*Cosby, Global Frequency*):

> A great comedy springboard is to take a familiar thing and be revelatory about it. There was a *King of Queens* a buddy wrote. Kevin's under sedation, his appendix burst, his wife is by his bedside. And he utters another woman's name. Turns out he fantasizes about other women. That's a very familiar thing. Even when you're married, you have to accept your husband

> may not be fantasizing about you. Then Kevin tells her, "It's okay, because in my fantasies, you're dead." She's not too pleased with that. That turns into an entirely different thing. She starts giving him acceptable fantasies: "I'm out of town because my career is doing so well." She becomes invested in his fantasy life.
>
> In drama, it's stuff you're not familiar with. *Desperate Housewives*—nobody in real life has murdered a woman who was blackmailing them. *CSI,* etc., takes you someplace new. In comedy, you start with a common thing. Then give it some bizarre spin.

Drama is usually about high stakes: I'm worried because my neighbor may have buried someone under his swimming pool. Comedy is usually about characters treating small stakes as if they were big: I'm worried because my neighbor has a bigger television antenna than I do.

Plausible Surprise

At the heart of every comic situation is what Mark Farrell (*Corner Gas*) calls "plausible surprise." A character is in a situation the outcome of which we think we know; and something different and usually worse happens:

> There's a *Sylvester & Tweety* episode where he's chopping down the tree to get to Tweety Bird, and the cut is getting bigger and bigger, and you just know the tree is going to fall on Sylvester the next time he chops the tree, and he pulls the ax back—and the tree falls on him right away. We laugh because we're surprised. The outcome is plausible, and we're surprised.

As comedian and writer D. J. McCarthey notes, this is something like what a magician does, except that a magic trick gets oohs and aahs, and comedy gets laughs. You put the viewer's mind on train tracks, and then you derail him, and he laughs.

This suggests why so many gags are based on three similar incidents. A guy's walking on the street. He avoids walking under a ladder. He avoids stepping into an open manhole. And he gets hit by a truck. The first two incidents set up the pattern. The third is the payoff—the comic twist. Call this the "Duck-Duck-Goose Rule."

Comic situations can get quite implausible as they build. The trick is making sure that each step is plausible. As long as you get to the next step plausibly, and the audience is laughing, you can get the audience to swallow a basically implausible situation.

Funny Word Last

Comedians will tell you that the funny word goes on the end of the sentence. That often requires some rewriting.

More broadly, the joke goes at the end of the setup. The basic structure of a joke is: information, setup, punch line.

The joke is incomplete until the audience has all the information. You can't expect them to hold the joke in their heads until you show them why it's funny. The setup has to come first.

Constructing a joke is getting the audience careening down train tracks that you've laid, and then derailing their expectations. If you derail them first, not funny.

In drama, you can button a scene, or go with a smooth segue to the next scene. In comedy, you pretty much always button a scene. The only exception is if the segue itself is a punch line—a hello joke, a funny match cut, etc. (see "Squiggy," page 149).

Therefore a joke requires two things: *commitment,* which gets the train careening, and *juxtaposition,* which derails it.

Commitment

Nuance isn't funny. You want your audience's minds careening down the train tracks of one line of thought so you can derail them at high speed. If your scene is nuanced, they're not careening. If a character is angry, they should be hysterically angry. If they're feeling betrayed, they should feel the worst betrayal possible. If they step on a tack, they should be jumping up and down in pain, or moaning in suffering. Whatever your comedy scene entails, commit to it wholly.

Dramatic characters feel a lot but play down their reactions. A girl who's been rejected forever by the man she loves might quietly take his omelet away, wrap it up, and put it in the refrigerator. Comic characters feel less, but exaggerate their reactions. A girl who doesn't like that the man she loves called a secretary "cute" might throw scrambled eggs in his face.

Juxtaposition

Derailing your audience's expectations with a non sequitur isn't funny. You have to have a comic twist. That's the juxtaposition of two things that the audience doesn't expect to go together but have a point of reference that allows the writer to make a connection between them. What makes the juxtaposition funny is that it's not supposed to fit, but it kinda almost does.

As Kevin Bleyer (*Politically Incorrect*) says, "Much of comedy is contrasting two unlikely things and extending the metaphor beyond practicality."[2]

You can make a one-year-old laugh by putting a measuring cup on your head for a hat. She knows a measuring cup isn't a hat. But it sort of resembles a hat, so it's funny. Putting pasta on your head will not get nearly the same laugh, because pasta does not resemble a hat. Though it does resemble hair. If you don't want to try this experiment yourself, use contraceptives.

Wordplay is juxtaposition at the linguistic level. A pun is using a word's sound to juxtapose it with something it doesn't mean. As my grandpa Sam said after his friends locked him in a closet until he promised never to tell another pun: "But please o-pun the door."

The best juxtapositions, like the best metaphors, mean something. The odd juxtaposition sheds light on the original content. In metaphor, the "tenor" is the content; the "vehicle" is what the content is being compared to. In the best juxtapositions, whether metaphoric or comic, the vehicle tells you something about the tenor. My grandfather's wordplay didn't illuminate the phrase "open the door" in any way. That's why his friends threw him in Sheepshead Bay.

Puns are rarely funny onscreen. But one gag that often works is using familiar rhetoric in the wrong situation: the characters are talking about one thing, but the dialogue sounds as if coming from a different sort of scene. In *Friends*, "The One with the Breast Milk," Monica has gone shopping with Ross's new girlfriend, Julie, behind Rachel's back. Rachel feels betrayed.

```
                    MONICA
    And then, one thing led to another and,
    before I knew it, we were . . . shopping.

                    RACHEL
    Oh! Oh my God.

                    MONICA
    Honey, wait. We only did it once. It
    didn't mean anything to me.
```

```
                    RACHEL
    Yeah, right.

                    MONICA
    Really, Rachel, I was thinking of you
    the whole time. Look, I'm sorry, all
    right? I never meant for you to find out.
```

The content may be shopping, but the clichés the girls are using come from adultery. What makes the scene so telling is that for both Rachel and Monica, shopping is as passionate an activity as having sex, so Monica shopping with Julie is like cheating on Rachel with her. If it had been Joey who had spent time with Julie, Rachel would have had the same basic complaint—the same tenor—but without the comic twist—the vehicle.

Note that what makes this gag work is that the scene is *fully committed* to the adultery rhetoric. Courteney Cox and Jennifer Aniston play the scene all the way, Aniston behaving in every way like the betrayed lover, Cox apologizing and downplaying in just the embarrassed way a cheater might. If the scene only used one or two adultery clichés, or if Cox played the scene less guilty or Aniston less betrayed, it wouldn't be as funny.

Squiggy

Another typical joke is the "Squiggy," a.k.a. the "hello joke." It's when the answer to a rhetorical question is provided by another character's entrance:

```
                    LAVERNE
    What kind of degenerate freak would do
    that?

She opens the door. It's Squiggy.
```

```
                    SQUIGGY
      Hell-oo!
```

The commitment is in the first line, where we expect that the answer is "no one." The juxtaposition—and derailment—occurs when Squiggy shows up and we realize that yes, there actually *is* someone who'd do it. Ditto "the red dress," a.k.a. the *flip cut,* a.k.a. the *Gilligan cut,* when a character declares he'd never do something, and then you cut to him doing it:

```
                    GILLIGAN
      There's no way I'm putting on a red
      dress and dancing the samba.
                                        CUT TO:

   Gilligan, in the red dress, dancing the samba.
```

Gilligan commits to his position, and then is derailed, in the form of a comic juxtaposition: a goofy guy in a red dress.

Confusion

Another kind of juxtaposition is internal. A character thinks one thing is going on but another thing is going on.

For example, Ross is talking to Joey about a car; Joey thinks Ross is talking about a girl. Ross is saying perfectly reasonable things about the car, but Joey is increasingly appalled at what Ross is saying about the "girl." In "The One Where Estelle Dies," Joey has just found out that his agent Estelle has died. But Phoebe has been calling him, pretending to be Estelle to spare his feelings, and she doesn't know he knows about Estelle:

```
                    PHOEBE
              (in Estelle's voice)
      Joey, it's Estelle.
```

```
On Joey: shocked.

                    JOEY
     Estelle?

                    PHOEBE
     Yeah, I wanted to call and tell you that
     there's no hard feelings for firing me.

                    JOEY
     O-kay. I just, I can't believe you're
     calling me?

                    PHOEBE
     Well, I didn't think I should just drop
     by.

                    JOEY
     No, no, no!
                (terrified)
     Don't drop by, don't drop by!
```

Comedy Is in the Characters

A gag relies on the juxtaposition of two things we don't expect to go together. A comic character is someone who consistently reacts in a way we wouldn't normally expect.

There's a paradox there because how can characters consistently surprise us? The essence of a comic character is that they're over the top in a believable way. We believe them as human beings, yet they regularly surprise us by not behaving the way normal people would. Hence, consistent surprise.

Every stand-up comedian creates a comic persona for himself—a version of himself that exaggerates what's most unique about him to comic extremes. Woody Allen onstage is more broadly neurotic than the real Woody Allen. Rodney Dangerfield was more down-at-the-mouth. George Carlin is angrier than the real George Carlin. Carrot Top is goofier, and probably more annoying. The comic persona is the distilled essence of the real person—the essence of how they're *not normal.*

When you write comedy, you create comic personas for all your comic characters. A comic character is just a normal character taken to an extreme. Writers exaggerate the key characteristics to create a comic situation.

Jokes need to be based on the persona of the character involved in them. If your character is a klutz, the jokes should come out of pratfalls. We want to see Jerry Lewis bang his head, but Jack Benny banging his head isn't funny. Jerry Lewis being stingy isn't funny; Jack Benny being stingy is. We love watching comic characters because they are ridiculous in familiar ways. The laugh is in our familiarity with their flaws.

The more outlandish a comic character is, the easier it is to put them into a comic situation that plays to their flaws. South African comedy writer Dennis Venter (*Madam and Eve*):

> Take the established personality of the characters and put them into a situation that will make them as uncomfortable as hell. Don't put Will Truman [of *Will & Grace*] into a gay lawyers association dinner. Put him into a monster truck rally.

The less cartoonish the characters are, the more you shade into comic drama. Comedy is about the laughs: if a scene doesn't get laughs, it fails. Drama is about what it's like to be the characters, and the awkward, embarrassing situations in comic drama are there to give us insight into them. Not all scenes have to be funny, so long as most of them are.

The essence of any comic character is that she is a little ridiculous. We cannot completely sympathize with her. The moment we start really worrying about him, he stops being a fully comic character. That's why in a sitcom the peripheral characters are more purely comic; the lead characters are less ridiculous and more believable. We need to care about the leads.

As a show stays on the air, we sometimes start caring about the core cast so much that a comedy series starts to morph into a show that is part soap and part comedy. The more we cared about Ross and Rachel in *Friends* as the seasons progressed, the more the show became part romantic comedy (where we wanted the lovers to end up together) and the less it was a straight-out comedy. The same thing happened to Frasier and to Niles on *Frasier.* On *Seinfeld,* though, the writers never went too deep with the characters, and so we could continue to laugh at them throughout the run of the series. The Simpsons never stop being ridiculous, so *The Simpsons* has managed to stay purely funny for over a decade.

Likewise, comic characters can't become aware of how ridiculous they are. The moment comic characters get perspective on themselves, the comedy stops. Characters may be painfully aware of their own shortcomings—neurotic characters often cherish their neuroses—but they can't put it together and laugh or cry at how pathetic they are. Then we'd have to have sympathy for them.

Comedy Is in the Pauses, Too

Your basic comic payoff is a couplet:

> Ralph Kramden: says something grandiose
> Alice: cuts him down to size <laughter>

Both parts of the couplet can be funny:

Ross (frustrated): says something outrageous, embarrassing himself <laughter>
Rachel (unsurprised): cuts him down to size <laughter>

If you've really got your characters down, you can get a lot of mileage out of their reactions. The audience has a feeling for what the character's going to say—but what the character actually says is (plausibly) surprising, and therefore funny. As Chris Abbott puts it, "You never know what they're going to say, and then when they say it, you think, 'I *knew* he was gonna say that!'" *Everybody Loves Raymond* is brilliant at this:

Marie, Ray's mother: says something annoyingly outrageous <laughter>
Ray: does a slow burn <laughter>
Ray: makes a sarcastic comeback <laughter>

The audience is laughing before Raymond comes out with his retort. Now you've got three laughs instead of one or two. Another example is *Friends*, "The One with Two Parts, Part 2." The friends are throwing Phoebe a birthday party, but Joey is dating Phoebe's *twin sister*, Ursula:

```
                    JOEY
I'm takin' Ursula out tonight. It's her
birthday.

                    ROSS
Whoa-whoa-whoa. What about Phoebe's
birthday?

                    JOEY
When's that?

                    ROSS
Tonight.
```

```
                    JOEY
      Oh, man. What are the odds of that
      happening?

Ross and Chandler share a look. Joey
contemplates his ill fortune.

                    ROSS
      You take your time.

Joey thinks some more. Finally he gets it.

                  CHANDLER
      And there it is!
```

The comedy is all in Ross and Chandler—and the audience—being wayyyy ahead of Joey.

Don't Break the Frame

Any jokes that draw attention to the fact that you're watching a movie—whether in dialogue or in a character winking at the camera—will tend to yank the audience out of the picture. You can get away with this as a joke sometimes, but it tends to rob the other jokes of their funny.

Anything that draws attention to a joke being a *joke* will kill the funny. Nothing kills a joke better than starting it with, "Let me tell you the funniest thing . . ." That's because the audience can't be fully committed if you tell them in advance that they're going to be derailed. In *Friends,* Chandler's character is a jokester, but his jokes aren't funny. The laughter comes from the other characters reacting to his lame jokes. The joke is on him. He may be cracking a witticism, but we're laughing at his embarrassment, not at the wisecrack itself.

Joke on a Joke

Two jokes cancel each other out.

A guy in a dress is funny. A guy singing a witty song may be funny. A guy in a dress *and* singing a witty song is just disturbing. (British audiences differ on this point.)

If a joke is going on in the foreground, the background needs to be straight. If a joke is going on in the background, the characters in the foreground need to be straight. (Also, if the joke is in the background, the foreground characters can't be saying anything the audience needs to know.)

The reason you can't have two jokes at once is that you can't be fully committed to two setups at once. You can only build up steam on one train track.

Bric-a-brac

Don't make a joke for the sake of making a joke. Make sure your jokes build on one another. A joke has to have something to do with the other jokes in the scene. Otherwise it's clutter—bric-a-brac—and distracts from the scene's comic movement.

A *bit* is a series of jokes all arising from the same comic situation or story—the same basic juxtaposition. *Comedy builds, but only so long as you're on the same bit.* The longer you can stay on the same bit and keep them laughing, the harder they'll laugh.

A bric-a-brac joke may be funny, but it forces the audience into a new bit, stopping the momentum of the bit dead. You may get a laugh, but you're robbing the rest of the scene of its laughs.

Comedy writing staffs are always looking for the *topper*—the gag that tops the previous gag while staying in the same bit. The longer you can keep topping the previous joke, the funnier the bit gets. When you go into the next bit, you're going to have to spend some time setting it up. While you're setting it up, you're not bringing the funny. The beauty of a topper is it requires no additional setup. Milking a bit is efficient comedy.

Up and Back

If a bit is funny but doesn't advance character or plot, it's an *up and back*. You are, after all, telling a story here. While the bits themselves may kill, they also need to move the story forward. Otherwise you lose your overall pace and energy, and your episode becomes a series of skits. Skit comedy doesn't hold an audience the way a comic episode does. A comic episode can survive a dead bit because the plot is holding the audience. They still want to see what happens. They're invested in the outcome. A dead bit in a series of sketches may send the audience rooting around for the remote.

Keep Your Plots Simple. People watch comedy in order to laugh. Comedy plots exist only as a peg on which to hang the comic situations. The more plot you have, the fewer jokes there's room for in your twenty-two minutes. You need just enough plot to bring the funny. If you have a choice between milking a simple situation and complicating it in a clever way, milk it.

Don't Be Afraid to Use the Pauses. Remember, much of comedy is in the pauses.

The More Plot, the More Bits. The more bits, the shorter you're on each bit. Comedy builds, but only while you're on the same bit. Each time you go to a new bit, you need to give the audience a new setup. You lose your comic momentum.

It's Hard to Cut Plot in the Editing Room. If you run long and you have a simple plot, you can always trim a few slow bits, or even some jokes, to bring down the length. You'll still have plenty of jokes left. But if the plot is complicated, you're stuck. It's hard to cut plot points. If you have to get the story from A to D, it's hard to get rid of B and C. So you wind up cutting only gags and leaving the plot points. Now you have a drama, only one built on a ridiculous premise.

If You Keep Your Plots Simple, You Won't Burn Through So Many Bits. Every time you throw a new bit into your story, that's a bit you can't use in a later episode. For sheer self-preservation, hold on to your bits. Dennis Venter:

> I've seen too many newbie writers to the comedy genre trying to overcomplicate the plots. In comedy, plots are simple, characters are complex. It's how they react to the situation that brings the funny.[3]

Trivia

A joke can't depend on arcane knowledge. For example:

Q: What do you call the ruins of a Temple of Inanna?
A: A ho-tel.

This joke *kills* with Assyriologists.

You can get away with an arcane joke, though, if the meaning of the line is clear and you don't make a moment of it. *Gilmore Girls* often does throwaway pop culture references. If you get the joke, great; if not, you probably don't even know there was a joke there, so you don't feel left out.

If a joke depends on knowledge that's *too* widespread, be careful. Britney Spears is still a punch line, but once she does her inevitable *Playboy* spread, she stops being funny.

Moral: If a joke depends on knowledge, make sure it's mainstream, up-to-date knowledge that hasn't already been overused by the comic establishment.

Underwriting

One counterintuitive rule of comedy is that you can't write characters exactly the way they sound. Not in scripts actually intended to be performed. You need to leave a *gap* between how the line reads on the page and how it will come out sounding. If you write the way the character sounds, it'll be overkill. You need to leave room for the performance. According to Mark Farrell, actor/writer Brent Butt will often lower the pitch of his own lines when he does his pass on a *Corner Gas* script, writing them *down* instead of punching them *up,* so that his character doesn't come across too jokey. He knows he'll be adding the drollery back in his performance. Jacob Sager Weinstein (*Dennis Miller Live*):

> When we got freelance submissions, they sounded *too much* like [Dennis Miller's] comic persona. Anything he said on the air would seem even more sarcastic and smarter than the way it was written. So you had to underwrite so he wouldn't come off too harsh. If you wrote like he sounds, it would seem like he was parodying himself. So I learned to leave a gap between what I wrote and how he was going to say it, to let him fill it. . . . One of the biggest mistakes comedy writers can make is putting *too* much of the character's voice on the page.

This rule does *not* apply to specs, which are not intended to be performed. A spec is intended only to be read. The reader may read it carelessly, and the reader may not be as familiar with the characters and the show as you'd like. So in a spec, put the full snap into the line.

If you're freelancing, it's easy to check if you're under- or overwriting the jokes. Just ask your story editor.

As stand-up comics know, comedy is part joke and part delivery. Comics argue about whether the percentages are 30–70 or 20–80 percent, but the weight is on the performance. A mediocre comic will die onstage with great material. A great comic can pull through with mediocre material. Comics will tell you that many working stand-ups are not actually funny. They just *sound* funny, and people laugh.

This might explain why so many "like-a-jokes" get through. An American sitcom is expected to have three laughs a page. Even a writing staff of twenty can't write 22 episodes of a comedy and fill each page with real jokes. So they often resort to "like-a-jokes": gags that have the rhythm of a joke, and the sound of a joke, without actually being funny. Often like-a-jokes are placeholder jokes from an early draft for which no one has come up with a functioning replacement.

Learn to recognize like-a-jokes in your own writing, and do your best to replace them with real jokes before you send your script out into the world.

Overwriting

It takes many bad jokes to find a good one. Comedy writers will often use *placeholder jokes* to fill up a script while they're trying to get the story and the basic comic situations down. Then they'll go back in a *punch-up pass* and, they hope, replace the placeholder jokes with actual funny ones. On a sitcom, the entire writing staff will typically go through the script together in the writing room and pitch replacement jokes for *every gag in the script*. On shows with smaller writing staffs, the script might just get passed around from writer to writer.

As with all other rewrite situations, don't defend your jokes. If someone's offering a replacement line that you feel is offtrack, you can explain what you were *going for* and ask for help to get a joke that does what you wanted your joke to do. But if your fellow writers don't think your joke is funny, it's not. That's the beauty of comedy: if they're not laughing, *it's not funny*.

If you're writing on your own, it's much harder to be sure you're replacing a weak joke with a stronger joke. You still need to pitch yourself a dozen replacement gags for every gag you have in your script.

But you need to be careful not to toss out a good gag for a new one. One of the hardest things about writing comedy is that it depends on surprise for its effect. You'll read your comic writing over and over again, until all the surprise is gone. Any joke you've written will get less and less funny until you can't remember how you ever could have thought it was funny. It will seem like the stupidest, lamest joke in the world. You'll replace it with something new that seems funnier to you. The new joke may not actually be as funny. But you've lost your perspective. That's why so many comedy writers are partnered up.

If you're not in a partnership, you just need to develop what the best editors have: the ability to forget you've seen or heard something. Until you have, use time. Time gives you perspective. Write up your replacement gag pitches. But don't replace any of your jokes yet. Hide the script for a few days. Then read it again with your pitches handy. See if the new pitches are still funnier than the original joke. Only then should you swap out the old jokes for the new.

When many writers in a writing room pitch progressively unfunnier jokes for the same spot, it's a *joke spiral*—think of an airplane caught in a stall/spin. That's why some rooms enforce the concept of *first blurt:* the first funny joke pitch is the one that stays.

Learning to Be Funny

When you're a stand-up comedian, you know your jokes are funny. You've heard people laughing at them. Every time you tweak your joke, you can get feedback. Was it funnier this way? How about that way? But when you're writing comedy, you usually don't have that kind of feedback. You have the other writers' reactions. If you're working on a three-camera sitcom shot in front of a studio, after the first taping you can use the audience's reaction to help you rewrite for the second taping.

Unfortunately, as John Rogers points out, "studio audiences can actually hurt you. There's an intimacy to a live audience. You can manipulate that chemistry. Jokes are funny on their feet. They get an honest laugh." But the jokes may not be working for the audience watching the show on their television. They have not been helpfully warmed up by a comic beforehand. Comedy is like a flywheel, say the Zucker Brothers (*Airplane*): it is always easier to keep people laughing than to get people laughing. About all you can do is trust your comic craft, honed from watching people's reactions to your jokes and comic situations, to know what's actually funny and what's not.

Stand-up Comedy

Probably nothing is better training for comedy writing than doing stand-up comedy. You'll die onstage a million times, but you'll get an immediate gut sense of what's funny, and you'll learn how to work and rework a joke for maximum laughs.

There is no real obstacle to doing stand-up, other than fear. Looks are irrelevant to comedy. Drew Carey isn't a looker. Bill Cosby has a goofy face. Beauty may actually be an obstacle to a male comic: How many positively good-looking male comedians can you name?

You don't have to do stand-up. Many comedy writers don't. You may be shy. You may have no desire to get up onstage and humiliate yourself for years until you get the hang of it. You may be better at writing for other people than for yourself. If you're a man but your best characters are all women, stand-up may not work for you, unless you look good in a skirt.

Stand-up or no, though, what all good comedy writers need is firsthand experience in what makes audiences laugh. The only way to know for sure if a joke is funny is by trying it out on an audience. Since you don't always have an audience handy when you're writing TV, you have to develop a general sense of what brings the funny, and how to refine a joke so that it gets funnier. Noel Coward probably practiced at his parents' dinner parties. Doing improv in college is helpful. Being the small kid in the schoolyard is helpful, especially when you're going to school with future criminals. Lots of comedians seem to have graduated from the "I'm funny, don't hurt me" school of comedy.

Working on a live comedy show in any capacity will help—whether a taped TV show or live theater comedy—if you get to see how the jokes are refined from performance to performance. If nothing else, take a comedy writing workshop, and try out your material on your fellow writers.

PART THREE

WORKING IN TV LAND

6

PREPARING TO BE A TV WRITER

You want to write TV? Start *watching* TV.

TV watching is now your job. So tell everyone to get off your case. You have to watch TV to write TV.

Just like everybody else, TV writers have their favorite shows. They don't necessarily watch the most critically acclaimed shows. While many TV writers are fond of "groundbreaking" shows like *Six Feet Under* and *Nip/Tuck,* they also like reality TV. Tom Chehak watches *Curb Your Enthusiasm,* but also *American Idol* and *The Apprentice*. James Nadler watches *The West Wing* but also *The Starlet*. TV writers watch "reality" shows for the same reason as everyone else: for the compelling stories and the entertaining characters. A surprising number of drama writers watch *The Amazing Race,* perhaps because, as Moira Kirland (*Medium*) points out, it's about couples, which means they already have a relationship going in, and that relationship is going to get tested, just like in a fictional series.

TV writers also watch the competition. Many writers will watch at least a few episodes of the highest-rated new shows, whether the shows are their cup of tea or not. In a recent season, everyone checked out *Blind Justice* for about two minutes. The season before that, everyone watched at least a few *Lost* and *Desperate Housewives* episodes. Everybody watched *CSI* when it came out. Everyone checked out the first season of *24*. You need to be able to talk about the groundbreaking shows. For the past few years it's a rare meeting with network executives or producers where you didn't hear at least one mention of *The Sopranos*. But few writers keep watching shows they dislike. It's supposed to be entertainment, after all. James Nadler (*PSI Factor*):

> I'll dip in and watch everything just to get a sense of what the show is like, but unless it really catches me, that's it. I'll still watch old *Law & Order*s that I've seen twelve times before, because they're so beautifully structured, especially seasons three and four. I don't watch sitcoms, because I don't find them funny, but I'll watch most dramas at least once.

If you can afford it, get a TiVo or other digital video recorder so you can easily tape episodes and skip the commercials. You'll want to get the boxed set of DVDs of some shows. You can also rent lots of TV shows cheaply from services like Netflix (www.netflix.com) in the United States and Zip.Ca (www.zip.ca) in Canada. Since these services charge by the month, not by the DVD, the more you watch, the cheaper they are.

It's a good idea, if you haven't been an avid watcher of TV all your life, to check out old favorites. It's instructive to watch *Miami Vice* and *I Love Lucy* and *Dallas* and *The Honeymooners*. What still works? What seems dated? Many writing rooms regularly reference old *Simpsons* plots, possibly because *The Simpsons* has done almost every plot there is. (It's been said that the *Simpsons* writing room regularly references old *Rockford Files* plots.)

If you have a meeting coming up, watch the shows the person you're meeting has worked on. If you're meeting J. J. Abrams, don't just mention *Alias* and *Lost;* be able to talk knowledgeably about *Felicity.* This is a useful exercise before you ever get a meeting. What do all David E. Kelley shows have in common? How about Joss Whedon shows?

If you're meeting on a project, you also should be able to talk about shows in the same genre. If you're pitching for a police procedural, you should be familiar with *NYPD Blue, Homicide,* and *CSI.* If you're pitching a hospital show, you might want to know *ER, Scrubs, Grey's Anatomy,* and *St. Elsewhere.* Just because the exec you're meeting is under thirty doesn't mean she hasn't watched *Marcus Welby, M.D.* on DVD.

When you're just starting out, it's not enough to watch TV for passive enjoyment. Watch actively. Record the show on your VCR or TiVo. Stop the episode after each act out. Take a minute to analyze where the episode is now. Where has the story gone in this act? Was it a strong act out? What kind of act out was it—physical jeopardy, emotional bombshell, emotional cliffhanger? Where do you think the audience is expecting it to go? Where do *you* think it will go?

Write Down Your Conclusions. Just like the notes you took in college, you'll probably never reread what you wrote, but the act of writing it down forces you to crystallize your thoughts.

Take a Few Moments to Skim Through the Commercials. Write down what products the ads are for. According to the kinds of merchandise this show is pushing, who's the show's target audience?

Take a Few Minutes to Look at the Title Sequence. What does it say about the show? Sometimes the title sequence will tell you a lot. Is the show about a few characters, or a place? What tone is the title sequence trying to create?

Watch Three Episodes Back-to-Back. Does the template start to become clear?

You get to watch more TV now—but you can't watch TV to relax anymore!

Writing Partners

Do you need a writing partner?

Having a writing partner helps with some aspects of the job, and hurts with others. A good partnership can write much better than either writer can do alone. A bad partnership is like a bad marriage, with the added bonus of ruining your career.

Either way, you have to split the money. A partnership is treated as a single writer for all payments and credits. If the fee for a one-hour drama script is $30,000, you each get $15,000. Writing partners even have to split their weekly salaries as members of the writing staff.

A partnership can take any form you agree on. You can partner up on one project, or partner on all your projects. The partners can do equal work on everything, or one partner can do the heavy lifting on some projects and the other on others. So long as you both are clear on how it's supposed to work, anything that suits you both is fine.

Writing partnerships seem to work best when each writer brings something to the partnership that the other writer lacks. One partner is good with character; the other is good with plot. One is quick with ideas; the other is good at telling which ideas are good. One comes up with outrageous plot twists; the other has a great sense of what feels real. One has a knack for pitching jokes; the other creates great comic situations. Veteran showrunner Leila Basen (*Mental Block, Emily of the New Moon*) has partnered with David Preston for the past five years:

> He's a really good structure guy. I push, he reigns me in. You have to devise a working method, so that you're two parts of one brain.

It may therefore be a little hard to recognize the best candidate for a partnership. Most people prefer to be around people who think as they do, but someone who thinks unlike you may make a better partner in the long run.

A partnership can only work when both partners recognize the other's value. If the person who's good at spouting ideas at random takes credit for being the "creative" one, the person who's good at telling which ideas are worth developing is going to feel disrespected.

Both partners also have to trust that the other partner isn't simply using the partnership as a stepping-stone. As Leila Basen says, "You can't feel someone's trying to screw you."

If you meet someone you think you might work well with, it's definitely worth trying a partnership. Writing well requires the ability to have perspective on your own material; that's much easier when there are two of you. If a plot or a scene or a gag satisfies two professional writers, it's much more likely to be good than if there's only one writer sitting alone critiquing lines he just wrote.

It's very difficult to know what's funny on your own. That's why, in comedy, writing partnerships are very common, and can last a lifetime—literally. John Rogers (*Cosby, Global Frequency*):

> Saul Turtletaub (father of director Jon) and Bernie Orenstein had sort of taken me under their wing—having a stand-up around, rather than a film school grad, reminded them of the old days of writing. During a run-through, Saul turned to Bernie and asked, "Didn't we use that joke on *That Girl?*"
>
> Beat. "*You were on* That Girl*?*"
>
> We then did the math, and realized that Saul and Bernie had started their first writing job together one week before my birth. I was, literally, their career.[1]

A partnership can be motivating, too. You may not want to get out of bed in the morning, but if you've got a meeting with your partner, you will.

Writing partnerships all have different working methods. Some partners like to do the actual writing together: one partner at the keyboard, the other lying on the couch, or folding laundry, or what have you. Some just e-mail drafts back and forth. Car trips are handy for coming up with pitches. The rolling countryside helps loosen up your mind, it's easy to keep a conversation freewheeling, and sometimes you drive past something inspiring.

Every partnership needs rules for dealing with creative disagreements. Commonly, both writers agree that they won't send anything out unless both partners feel good about it—they each have veto power. Alternately, you can agree that each script will be assigned to one or the other partner to oversee, and that partner will have final say. Either arrangement can work as long as you agree in advance.

You need rules for revisions, too. What happens when the second partner cuts or rewrites something the first partner thought was working well? Can the first partner rewrite it back the way it was? Generally, the rule is that you should always come up with new stuff. If you don't like the revision, you can re-revise it, but you can't put your old stuff back in. Occasionally you'll trash something good this way, but almost never will you trash something so good you couldn't come up with something better.

It often takes longer for partners to get a draft out. A single writer can make a decision in moments. Writing partners have to talk things out. On the other hand, if the partnership is working, the draft will be better, and you may need to go through fewer drafts.

Writing in a partnership often feels more like work, but on the other hand, it can be less scary than writing on your own. You're on a tightrope, sure, but someone is helping you balance.

It is crucial to remember that *a partnership is a business arrangement*. For the sake of sanity, you probably want to restrict phone calls to, say, a twelve-hour window. Otherwise the partnership starts getting in the way of your personal life. Also, the kinds of things that partners may say to each other after 10 P.M., whether positive or negative, are often unhelpful to the partnership. (It should go without saying, but if your partnership starts *being* your personal life, one of them is likely to pay the price.)

It is really important to be clear on the terms of the arrangement. If one partner thinks you'rc supposed to do all your projects together and the other doesn't, the first one is going to feel betrayed. It's not a bad idea to put the terms down on paper, or in e-mails to each other, just so you have something to refer to later if there's confusion.

Also, be clear with your representation. If you write everything together, you can have one agent. Otherwise you need two agents, or there will be a conflict of interest.

If your partnership breaks up, try to separate the professional from the personal. No one in the business really wants to hear what a backstabbing prima donna or an arrogant hack your ex-partner is, any more than they want to hear the details of your divorce. Disrespecting your ex-partner in public just makes you look bad. Diss your ex-partner only to your close personal friends, and only after you've had enough drinks to make it seem funny.

Film Schools and Classes

Does it help to go to film school?

It can be helpful. I don't think it's necessary by any means. John Rogers: "Personally, almost every writer I know didn't go to film school; all their assistants did."

I got an M.F.A. from UCLA's School of Theater, Film and Television myself, and took screenwriting classes from professionals like Lew Hunter (*Fallen Angel*) and Sterling Silliphant (*In the*

Heat of the Night). But most of what I've learned about screenwriting has been from just writing, and listening to feedback from agents and development people, reading screenplays, and working for producers.

Screenwriting professors who've worked in the industry, who've spent time in the writing room, and who've made a living writing can have a lot to tell you. But film school, even in L.A., is often insulated from the real world in a way that makes it too easy for you to learn to write an abstractly "good" screenplay or TV script rather than one that gets produced or gets you a job. There can be a lot of emphasis on how to write something fresh and original and quirky, at the expense of what the biz really wants from you.

What a screenwriting program does best is:

- Give you feedback on your writing if you don't have a way to get it from working professionals.
- Give you time to learn something about screenwriting. Parents won't get on your case about not having a job if you're in film school.
- Introduce you to other baby screenwriters who can be helpful and supportive in your career. (Unless, of course, they just become rivals whose every success is a knife twisted in your guts.)
- Give you a platform to meet the industry, if you stand out from your fellow students.

Film school clearly helps some people. Josh Schwartz (*The O.C.*) first got attention by winning USC's Jack Nicholson Award. Word got around town; he got buzz. Of all the film schools, USC is probably the most hooked in to the business of show business. It is certainly the school most attuned to commercial filmmaking and television. UCLA and NYU are more indie-oriented. Doug Taylor (*The Atwood Stories*), writing about the

Canadian Film Centre, the Canadian government-supported equivalent of USC:

> The CFC can certainly open doors for its students as it makes a point of creating industry contacts for its filmmakers. People I've known who were especially successful at the CFC (i.e.: worked on short films that were really well received) often were able to get introductions to talent agents, producers, etc., sometimes even launching their careers.
>
> It seems like every year the Toronto gatekeepers are watching to see who the new wonder kids are at the CFC. You can actually get a buzz behind yourself on the basis of a short (tough to do on your own) because the CFC is so good at marketing their graduates.
>
> On the other hand, others I've known had less enthusiastic experiences. If the politics or preferences of the school don't happen to select you as their new darling, it can be an expensive way to spend a year or two, only to watch your co-students flourish.[2]

Replace "CFC" with "USC" and "Toronto" with "L.A." and you've probably got the 411 on USC.

One does hear rumors that many of the people selected as USC's darlings had big advantages going in. USC is where film and TV people send their kids. Will you get noticed over the daughter of the head of CBS? Maybe. Maybe not. The rumors may not even come out of logrolling—it may just be that showbiz kids know more going in, and know it more instinctively, and can take better advantage of the classes. You may learn more; they may leverage their knowledge better. Joss Whedon created his first show in his early thirties, but he's a third-generation television writer.

When you choose your film school, you're choosing which coast you want to work on. If you make friends in school in New York, they won't be able to help you much in L.A., and vice versa. So if you plan to work in TV and you want to go to film school, go to film school in L.A.

TV is a collaborative industry where writers hire other writers—unlike movies—so making friends, even ones at entry level, will eventually pay off when they get jobs. It may not help you much right away, though. While film school may be helpful to some people, a film school *degree* is practically useless in the industry. A film school credential is of no interest to the people hiring writers or even writers' assistants. I don't know anyone anywhere who ever got a writing gig because they had an M.F.A. A film school degree is only useful as a degree if you want to teach.

If you do want to go to film school, *the best time to go is after you know the business a little*. Don't waste your shot. Don't go when you just need a foot in the door. Get a foot in the door some other way. Go when you've been working in the business for at least three years. Go when you've read at least three hundred spec scripts. Go when you've already written at least three spec scripts of your own. Go when you know what your strengths and weaknesses are. Go, if at all, when you've hit a wall and you need a leg up over it. Once you know a few things, you'll be able to make the most of your professors' knowledge and the university's resources. You will impress your teachers, and *you'll* be the wunderkind.

The Free Alternative Film School

If you don't want to gamble three or four years and tens of thousands of dollars on film school, consider working in the industry first. While film school can insulate you from the real world, you may find it more useful to throw yourself into the real world instead. If you consider your first three years in the business to be school, not a job, then all sorts of opportunities open up that you might not consider if you were looking for a decently paying job.

If you want to know how to write for television, you need to immerse yourself in the world of working television writers. You need to know what screenplays get people jobs, and what don't. If you want to learn about wine, you have to drink great wine, mediocre wine, and bad wine. If you want to learn about TV writing, you need to read good TV scripts, and mediocre scripts, and bad scripts. Assuming you have a reasonably literate background, I'm not sure there's anything film school can teach you that you can't learn from reading a hundred professional-quality TV scripts *in the context of* people who are using those scripts to get jobs.

One of the most helpful things a beginning screenwriter can possibly do is to *work for a literary agent.* (In showbiz, a literary agent is one who handles screenplays and writers, as opposed to a "talent agent" who handles actors. An agent who handles books is called a "book agent.") Go to L.A. and get a job as an assistant to a lit agent. If you can't get a paid job, then offer to work as an unpaid intern. (Remember what I said about this being school, not a job?) Let me say this again: *There is probably no better way to learn how to write a TV script that will get you a job than to work for an agent who represents working TV writers.*

Work for free until you're worth paying money to. Lots of jobs open up when you're offering to work for nothing. Work as hard as you would work if you were getting overpaid. In far less time than it takes to get a film school degree—probably no more than six months in fact—you should be worth paying a salary to.

Read all the scripts that come in looking for representation. Most of them are trash. Read them diligently. Read all the spec scripts that the agent is representing. Most of these are trash, too, but more professional trash. Figure out what the difference is between represented trash and unrepresented trash.

Don't just read, think analytically. Figure out what each script is doing wrong, and how you'd fix it. (Whenever I see a movie with my writer friends, we usually "rewrite" the script in our heads afterward. *A Knight's Tale* turned out rather well after we fixed it.) Good scripts tend to hide how they're made. Bad scripts usually do some things well and other things badly. Bad scripts can teach you more than good scripts, if you put the work into reading them.

If you find an unrepresented script that knocks your socks off, let someone know. (Not that you'll be able to prevent yourself.)

Grab all the hot TV specs that are making the rounds in Hollywood. See what makes a spec jump off the stack. You can learn a good deal more about *professional* screenwriting at an agency than you will at film school, and it won't cost you a dime in tuition. And, as an added bonus, later on, when your own scripts are good enough to represent, you'll know some agents personally.

Work at more than one agency. Moving around often gets you promotions you wouldn't get otherwise, and you'll be exposed to different philosophies of what makes a script and a writer salable.

You can also do this as an unpaid intern in a production company, if you can't get a job at an agency. If you're still in college, there are also official student-only internships available at the networks and studios. UCLA, for example, has a section of the jobs office devoted to internships, many of them supervised by UCLA alumni. College internships are typically part-time, highly competitive, and provide course credit. They're lighter on the scut-work than informal, full-time internships you yourself create by volunteering.

If you get hired as an agent's assistant and you're put on the phones, you'll get to talk to network executives and development people. If you work for any of them, you'll get to talk to agents. You won't be having conversations, usually, but you'll get to know the people. You may get a sense of what they're saying to the person you're working for, and they may even think out loud at you, which is an education in itself.

You will make many more useful contacts at an agency than in a film school. Many people who are going to film school won't ever break in. *Everyone* you talk to at an agency has *already* broken in.

Any job at an agency is also a great way to hear about writer's assistant gigs that open up.

Seminars and Workshops

While you're working, go to every seminar and workshop you can *so long as it's taught by a professional.* David Milch (*Deadwood, NYPD Blue*) lectures from time to time, to anyone who wants to come hear him. Many showrunners are incredibly generous with their knowledge, as long as it doesn't involve being excessively generous with their time. Lee Goldberg (*Diagnosis Murder*):

> The real classroom, for me, was L.A. itself. Because the people who write, produce, and buy TV shows are here, you have many more chances to hear from them and meet them and learn from them. . . . Not a week goes by where some experienced writer/producer isn't sharing the secrets of his craft . . . somewhere in the city. There are regular seminars all the time at places like UCLA, WGA [Writers Guild of America], ATAS [Academy of Television Arts & Sciences], USC, the Museum of Broadcasting, AFI [American Film Institute], even the local Barnes & Noble.
>
> Equally important are the people you meet in the audience. Odds are you'll make some friends, some who are likely to become writer/producers or agents or industry execs someday and will form your inner circle of connections in the biz. It

happened to me that way. A lot of the people I work with today are people I sat with at Museum of Broadcasting seminars or in line for tapings of *Taxi* and *Soap*.[3]

DVDs

Some TV writers have kindly explained their thought processes as they wrote their shows. There are few interviews on the Net or in magazines worth reading, but there's a lot of fascinating commentary in television boxed sets. In particular, any time Joss Whedon comments on one of his own shows, you get a window into a master writer's perspective. Not only can he write, he knows how he's doing it. The boxed sets of *Buffy, Angel,* and *Firefly* are worth owning just so you can hear the commentary over and over.

Awards and Competitions

Awards can help your career, if they're real awards. I'm not sure that Scriptapalooza or Austin's Heart of Film will help you, or any award that advertises heavily. But anything that can get you noticed by agents is good. Melinda Hsu (*Medium*):

> On a whim I finally entered the Warner Bros. TV Writing Workshop competition and was picked as one of twelve or thirteen participants in January 2003. That gave me enough credibility so that agents started returning my calls.

Agent Liz Wise:

> There are only a few that we take seriously, like the Don and Gee Nicholl Fellowship in Screenwriting, etc. Winning a contest won't get you a job. But winning a contest may get you read,

which may get you a meeting, which may get you a pitch meeting, which may get you a job.

Fortunately, television seems to be less riddled with the scam competitions that riddle the spec feature script world—competitions that seem largely driven by the $50 entrance fees, rather than by a real desire of a production company, school, network, or studio to find talented people. As a rule of thumb, any contest or fellowship run by a studio, major production company, or network, by the Academy, or by one of the major film schools is legitimate. (See Appendix 2 for details on some of them.) The competition Melinda Hsu won, for example, was run by Warner Bros. Personally I am suspicious of any contest run by a website, or a magazine, or a company that makes screenwriting software, or an organization based outside of the major filmmaking cities (Los Angeles and New York in the United States, Montreal and Toronto in Canada). The exceptions are organizations affiliated with a major filmmaker (e.g., Sundance with Robert Redford, Project Greenlight, and Francis Coppola's American Zoetrope Screenplay Contest).

After all, the only real point of winning a contest is to get someone to read your spec. And *it is not that hard to get someone to read your spec.*

Fellowships are worth far more than awards. When you get a Disney Fellowship, you actually go to work at Disney for a year. They pay you a salary, but more important, you meet people, learn from them, and go to lunch with them. A contest can get your script in the door. A fellowship gets *you* in the door.

Yes, you'll have to sign over anything you write during the year. But that's what they're paying you for. And if you write anything on your own time—then you're probably not working hard enough. You're there to learn and impress, people, right? You shouldn't have any "my own time."

(To be cynical for a moment, no one can tell when a writer wrote something. So contracts that state that a company owns anything you write during a certain term are hard to enforce. A month after the expiration of the contract, you can send your agent the brilliant spec script you wrote in the, uh, past month.)

Government programs that exist to funnel money into culture are also worth a shot. They are thin on the ground in the United States, but all other Western nations have them. So long as you don't have to write uncommercial material to get cultural funding, there's no downside to applying for it. Not only is the money nice, but getting a screenwriting award from, say, Telefilm Canada tells any producer you're bringing your project to that the cultural Powers That Be are likely to support the project with production financing when you finish the screenplay.

The Spec Script

No one *needs* film school or writing awards, though. What you need are two great specs.

The front door to the television business is the spec script. A spec script is a sample episode for a TV series, almost always a current hit TV series. It's a "spec" script because it's written "on speculation," that is, no one's guaranteeing you anything for writing it.

When you write a spec script (often called just a "spec"), you are *not* writing it to sell it to the show of which it is an example. You're trying to prove that you know how to write someone else's show. It's one thing to make up your own show, or write an original feature. But can you watch a series, understand it, come up with a perfect couple of stories for it, and write a script that feels like a lost episode of this season of that show?

Again, you are *not* trying to sell it to the show itself. They already have their staff. They already have their preferred freelancers. The scripts are all assigned already. They don't want to read any more episodes of their own show, and they have a much more precise idea of what their show is or isn't than anyone watching it. *CSI* won't like your *CSI* spec. But *Law & Order* might. And *CSI* will read your *Law & Order*.

Agents will generally tell you to have two specs. One's a procedural, one's character-based. Even if you want to write procedurals, execs and showrunners want to read the character-based script to see what you can do when there are no dead bodies driving the story.

Some execs may look at a spec feature or a spec pilot, but when you're just starting out, you really have to prove that you can absorb the hidden rules of any show and write a script within them. You need to prove that you can catch the voices of characters who are not your own, and make them sing. The greater the difference between the two shows you're speccing, the more range you're showing. They want to know, can you write anything they give you?

Not every show is worth speccing. You may love *Trailer Park Boys* (a hysterical, faux-documentary comedy that's huge in Canada, eh?), but almost no one has seen it in the States. If they haven't seen it, they won't read your spec; they wouldn't be able to make sense of it if they did. The whole point of a spec is to demonstrate that you can nail the template for a show; if they haven't watched the show, they can't tell if you've nailed it.

You want to avoid freshman shows unless they're massive hits, because if the show isn't renewed, your spec is dead. *Firefly* was an awesome show, and probably fun to spec, but the moment the network pulled the plug, any *Firefly* spec was dead. "Never, ever spec a show that's struggling," says agent Liz Wise.

You also may want to avoid shows that have been successful so long that everyone is sick of reading their specs. Not everyone wants to read another *Law & Order* spec. Agent Jeff Alpern: "We usually think it is better to write a hot but established show. In other words, a show that has been on the air for two years or less."

But "if it's well written, the reader will be engaged," says Moira Kirland (*Medium*). And a truly brilliant spec keeps its value for a while. Liz Wise:

> Three to four years is the life span, but with a great spec you can usually squeeze out a bit more. It helps if the show is still on the air. A brilliant *X-Files* could last the entire run of the show, plus a few years afterward. This was because (a) a brilliant spec means it's not tied too closely into the particular arc of a particular season—instead it uses the rules and characters as a launching pad of inspiration; and (b) successful shows spawn copycats and have far-reaching influence, so tonally an *X-Files* could be a great spec years after *X-Files* was canceled, simply because other shows are trying to capture the *X-Files* vibe.
>
> A great spec is a great spec. They might sit on the shelf, but they're solid writing samples. The only real killer I've had is a client who wrote a drop-dead *Sports Night*. It was useless after only a year of cancellation, because tonally nothing was similar. And because the trend moved back to multicamera after single cam. Ironically, I just sent it out again for a couple of HBO shows like *Entourage*. It's so good it just kills me that I can't pull it out more.

Bear in mind, though, if your specs are all dated, it suggests you take an awfully long time to write a spec. That suggests you will take an awfully long time to write an episode for hire. Even when she's already working on a show, Melinda Hsu likes to write a new spec every season, making sure it's up-to-date on the latest story developments in that series, because then it's clear she can whip up something good in a few weeks. If it is too much effort to write a new spec every year—and that's not because you're already so busy with paid work that you don't have time to write for free—then you are in the wrong business.

If you have an agent, she'll tell you which shows you should spec, based on what shows are hot, what she sees as your strengths, and the kind of shows you want to work on. I'm a science-fiction and fantasy fan, so at one point my specs were a *Buffy* and an *X-Files*. I wouldn't spec two SF&F shows at the same time again, because it makes it hard to get on anything else. If you want to write in a certain genre, you want to spec one hot show in that genre and one mainstream character-based show. Agent Jeff Alpern:

> Assuming the writer wants to focus on SF, he or she should have an SF spec and a character-based show. Some SF shows look for writers who have character skills and you would want to be able to show that.

If you don't have an agent yet, you can still easily find out what shows people are speccing. Get the names of a couple of TV agents at the major agencies: CAA, ICM, William Morris, UTA. Don't bug the agents; just ask to talk to their assistants. Call early in the morning (before ten) or late in the afternoon (after five). Politely ask, "What shows are you recommending your clients spec this year?" They'll usually tell you.

Don't spec a show you don't like, even if it's hot. Not just because to spec it you're going to have to watch a lot of it, but because if you don't love the series, it will show in your writing. It is almost impossible to nail a show you don't like.

Pick a show that showcases your strengths. Your spec is most likely to get you on shows with a similar tone, structure, and demographic. If you're good at dry wit, spec a show with dry wit. It will get you on another show with dry wit before it gets you on a broad comedy. "For example," says Alpern, "if the hot show is *CSI,* but our writer concentrates on deep character, then we would suggest a more character-intensive show such as *Gilmore Girls*."

Before you start coming up with story springboards, revisit the show; only now, examine it with more concentration. You want to have the best possible sense of the show. You want to look at it from all angles and really absorb what makes it special, and how it delivers its goods.

- Record as many episodes as you can.
- Watch three episodes in a row. How do the episodes advance the overall story?
- Watch the same episode three times in a row. How does the episode tell its story?
- Check out the commercials. Who do advertisers think watches this show?
- Check out the title sequence. What does it tell you about the show's focus? Its tone?
- Read the fan sites on the Net. What do the fans seem to like about the show? (Don't trust this too much; people who populate fan sites are, after all, fanatics.)

Some writers go so far as to transcribe an episode themselves.[4] I've never done this, but it would give you a very hands-on feel for the show's dialogue style. Just bear in mind that how the dialogue comes out of the actor is not necessarily how it appears on the page. Writers program some of the delivery into the lines, but the actor adds his or her own style, and may do the line convincingly in a way that you'd be hard-pressed to capture on the page. When actors boast about how they ad-libbed some brilliant line, they're usually fibbing, but they can take a flatly written line and make it memorable ("I'll be back.")

Your spec script should be a perfect, typical episode of the series you're writing, with two exceptions:

1. Try to avoid stories that center on new characters. You want to demonstrate that you can write the core cast. The

episode where long-lost Aunt Millie shows up and turns everyone's life upside down is a great vehicle for whoever plays Aunt Millie, and a fun episode. But Aunt Millie isn't on the actual show. Putting the core cast in an interesting predicament makes a better spec, because you can spend more of the script showing how well you write them, rather than some character no one but you has ever imagined before.

2. Because it's not going on television, you can deal with slightly edgier material than the show does. You probably have a little more freedom to show homosexuality, for example. But be careful. You still have to keep the tone of the show. You probably wouldn't want to spec an *O.C.* episode involving incest because *The O.C.*, for all its angst, stays away from "ick factor" stories. If you are going to push the envelope, it should be in a direction that that show would naturally take if the network censors were all on holiday that week. You could, for example, do an incest story for an *Arrested Development* spec. (Or, you could have until they did an incest episode themselves, "Top Banana," earning "Worst Family Show of the Week" from a parental organization. Go team!)

Try to avoid any story line that will get dated, or violate the already-established chronology, e.g., episodes in which couples break up. Try to find a story line that would work equally well no matter where it appears along the show's time line.

You do hear about the occasional stunt spec. The writer who wrote a *Mary Tyler Moore* spec not long ago where Mary Richards came out as a lesbian. The writing team who specced an *I Love Lucy,* just to show they could nail it. The crossover *Sex and the City* episode where Carrie is dating one of Tony Soprano's wise guys.

I wouldn't recommend this unless you're at the top of your game. Yes, your spec will get pulled off the pile first. And if you nail a beloved old show, it's the sort of spec that people pass around for fun. But get this sort of thing even slightly wrong, and your spec is worthless. As Moira Kirland says, "A big move can backfire big."

If you do risk a crossover episode, you still have to nail the template of the show you're writing. You also have to nail how the show you're writing would see the characters of the other show. If Carrie Bradshaw is dating one of Tony's guys in a *Sex and the City* spec, then we have to see him the way *Sex and the City* would see him—not necessarily how *The Sopranos* sees him. Likewise, if it's a *Sopranos* spec, we have to see Carrie the way Carrie, the character, would come across in the *Sopranos* world. *The Sopranos* might not see her as an adorable, impulsive if indecisive girl; it might bust her for being a selfish, self-indulgent woman who's reckless with other people's hearts. Likewise, Tony Soprano on *Sex and the City* might just come across as a psychopath.

Although a stunt spec is risky, you still want your hook to be striking and memorable. "We know that readers read hundreds of scripts and most kind of blur into one another. If a spec has some catchy hook, then it may stand out better," says agent Jeff Alpern. Push the envelope on the show a little bit. If the show is gritty, you probably want to write an extra-gritty episode. If the show has crimes, your crime should be shocking. If the show has angst, your episode should be wrenching. You want readers to remember you, "Oh, yeah, sure, that was the one with the . . ."

Once you've written your spec, get as much feedback as you can. You want to polish it till it shines. Before showing my work to anyone in the business, I usually start with civilians. I want the people I know in the business to think my work is professional and polished, so I try never to show them anything less. Show your wife; show your boyfriend. Show your college buddies. Show your office buddies.

Show the members of your writing group, if you're lucky or clever enough to have one. (In a writing group, everyone shows unpolished work.)

Almost every television show has fan newsgroups on the Web. Note who seem to be the most intelligent and knowledgeable fans. E-mail them to ask if they'd be willing to give you feedback on a script. Most of them will feel flattered. The less well people know you, the more likely they are to tell you what they hate about your work.

As with all amateur feedback, the criticisms are more trustworthy than the suggestions. People are often right about what's wrong; they're usually wrong about how to fix it. It's up to you to decide what's the best way to fix things.

Try to avoid the impulse to defend your script from criticism. Don't explain to your reader (or yourself) why what you did is right and not wrong. It will render you deaf to the criticisms. The only outlet you should allow yourself is the script. Make it so good that those criticisms go away and people say, "I don't know. It reads just like a real episode. Can't you sell it to the show?" And then you can shrug sadly and say, "That's not how it works with spec scripts."

Don't feel bad about getting criticism. You'll always get more criticism than praise. You're writing TV, and most people know what a great TV episode is. If you don't measure up in some way, they'll tell you. You'll know you're getting to be a crafty writer when people tell you they don't think anything's wrong with your script, and you get frustrated because you know they're wrong. They must not be reading it carefully enough!

Take all the criticism to heart. If something's wrong, fix it. If there's something structurally wrong, rework and rewrite the entire script so that it's right, don't just gloss over it. Melinda Hsu:

> I usually won't let anyone, not even my agent or my close friends, read anything before the third draft. People will eagerly

> ask you if they can read a first draft or an early draft, but you have to say no, no matter how welcoming and supportive they sound—because they'll judge you by what they read. Usually you only get one shot with people, and while they're reading your first draft they're reading someone else's seventh draft and using the same standards to compare the two. Don't squander the opportunity to show someone your best work, even if it makes them wait a few more weeks to see it.

The standard for spec scripts is quite high. Your *CSI* spec is going into a pile of twenty other scripts in which there are four other *CSI* specs. The guy reading your script did his own *CSI* spec two years ago. You really have to write something great to get a meeting.

Spec Pilots as Samples

It is possible to spec a pilot episode for a show you've invented. "Some shows want to see original material," says Jeff Alpern, "and a spec pilot could serve that need." And many showrunners repeatedly say in public that they prefer to read pilots. Why not? They're bored with reading *CSI* specs. They've read hundreds, and even the best *CSI* spec is just another good episode of *CSI*. If they wanted to watch *CSI,* all they have to do is turn on their TiVo.

Reading a great pilot, on the other hand, is reading something fresh and new. It's like turning on the TV and catching an episode of a new show—one you'd like to start watching regularly. It demonstrates your chops in a way that mimicking another show's voice can't.

But. It is much harder to write a convincing pilot for a new show than it is to spec an episode of a current show. A pilot not only has to nail the template of the show, it has to create that template. It has to introduce the characters and create their voices. If I'm reading a spec *Alias,* I'm seeing Jennifer Garner in a tight dress. When I read your spec pilot (call it *A.K.A.*), I don't know who's in the tight dress. Jennifer Tilly? Roseanne Barr? In a spec episode you're writing for known characters. A loosely written line of dialogue will still get the actor's usual treatment. In a spec pilot you have to create the characters, and a loosely written line of dialogue will come off flat.

Moreover, it is simply hard to write a pilot that is also a good episode, because of all the extra burdens a pilot has to carry. A pilot has to create the template and tell us what we need to know about the characters while involving them in compelling action. Many pilots, even for successful series, make comparatively weak episodes. Often it's not till the second episode that a series really gets off the ground.

Most of the people who are successfully speccing pilots already have a track record. They have a few credits. They've got some good spec episode scripts. They've got an established agent. They've got reputations. Maybe they're already writer-producers. Whoever's reading their spec pilot already knows they can write his show; now he's trying to choose between them and someone else, and he wants to read something that will knock his socks off.

Though a great spec pilot will get you work as fast or faster than a great spec episode, it is much less likely that you'll write one. I wouldn't recommend a spec pilot as a sample until you are sure you've mastered your craft—until you've written, say, a dozen hours of actual television, or staffed a season of a show.

Screenwriting Software

Do you need a screenplay formatting program? No, but it makes writing screenplays slightly easier. Your script should read like a real script from the show you're writing for; it had better look like one.

If you're writing a spec script, you don't necessarily need a screenplay formatting program. After you've taken a look at a sample script from the show, you can define the styles on your word processor so that your formatting matches the real script. A quick once-over to deal with the few spots where dialogue breaks between pages, and you've got a properly formatted script.

Then why do most professional TV writers use a screenwriting program?

Software like Final Draft and Screenwriter exists primarily to speed up the formatting process. They come with script templates for different standard formats, so you can easily write in the standard Warner Bros. feature format, or NBC sitcom format, or ABC drama, or animation. (Single-camera comedies typically use drama format, but sitcom scripts are in an entirely different format than drama; so are animation scripts.) You can go from slugline to action to parenthetical in a keystroke or two, and the programs keep track of what character names and locations you've been using, so you only have to hit a few keys to return to `EXT. STATION HOUSE--NIGHT.`

There are the usual word-processing bells and whistles, such as dictionaries and thesauruses. There are also bells and whistles unique to screenwriting. Screenplay programs will turn your outline into index cards that you can move around onscreen, automatically making the changes in your outline. They also allow two writers to work on the same script file over the Internet. These functions can prove handy in certain circumstances.

Good screenwriting programs will let you automatically compare two different versions and mark the differences, in case someone has done revisions without marking them, or in case two different people have been revising a script at the same time.

The programs will even read your script out loud for you, but this is basically stunt programming. You really do need a human being to read your lines aloud to get anything out of them.

Basically these programs speed up the process of writing a screenplay about 5–10 percent. It's not a lot, but the programs are only a couple hundred bucks, often less on eBay. If you do a lot of screenwriting, 10 percent is a lot of time. You don't want to have to fuss with a naive word processor.

Where screenplay formatting programs really come into their own are during production. You need to be able to mark revised lines and revised pages. The script coordinator needs to be able to lock page breaks and page numbers, and print character sides for casting sessions. Regular word processors don't do that easily. Fortunately you don't need to do—or even know how to do—any of this yourself until you're working on a show, and then they'll buy you a copy of the right program.

Still, if you've got the money, you probably want one. The two most common programs are Final Draft (www.finaldraft.com) and Screenwriter (www.writebros.com). Final Draft is probably a little more common, but Screenwriter is catching up.

I've used Final Draft and Screenwriter, both on Mac. Either is good. I find Final Draft a little more intuitive. For a more detailed discussion of the two programs, see Appendix 3.

Final Draft and Screenwriter aren't the only game in town. Scriptware used to be common in Canada. Some writers are fond of Sophocles, which is less expensive. There are also Page 2 Stage and SceneWriter Pro.

You can also get templates for use with your word processing program to set up your styles properly for you. These are either cheap or free. You should be able to find some with a little poking around on the Net. There's a helpful rundown at www.online-communicator.com/swsoftin.html.

Any program or template is probably fine for writing a spec

script. Once you're writing for hire, after all, you'll have the money to upgrade.

Note that a file from one program won't necessarily work on another. Screenwriter can't read a Final Draft file or vice versa. You can save a Final Draft file to RTF and import that into Screenwriter, but you'll lose any revision information, pagination, scene numbering, dual dialogue, or other screenplay-specific information that RTF can't handle. That's because the companies won't release their file formats to each other. Grow up, guys. Play nice.

If you are e-mailing your script, it's best to save it as an Adobe Acrobat PDF first. Everyone can read a PDF. Don't rely on people having Final Draft or Screenwriter, though agencies generally will. With a PDF, you can't go wrong.

7

BREAKING IN

Okay. You've written two great spec scripts, one procedural, one character-driven. Now you need an agent. Agents who represent writers are called "literary" agents; you need a literary agent who works in TV. An agent who works in features can't help you much; nor can a lawyer. It is all but impossible to get hired onto a show without an agent, unless you have some kind of back door in.

Getting an Agent

With all agents, you need someone who's enthusiastic about you. There's a trade-off involved in how high level an agent is. If they're too low level, they can't get you in anywhere. If they're too high level, even if they're enthusiastic about you, they can't take the time with you that your career needs. They have more valuable clients they don't have to sell—they merely have to choose between offers and negotiate for them. You don't want the very hottest agent you can get who will still return your calls, because all she's doing is returning your calls, she's not beating the bushes looking for work for you.

To tell how effective your agent is, look for his or her name and the name of the agency in back issues of *Variety* and *The Hollywood Reporter*. They're available online, and you can often get a free trial offer that will serve you long enough to tell you what you need. The major agencies—CAA, ICM, Endeavor, UTA, William Morris—will come up a lot. Less well-known ones, such as Gersh, or Innovative, will come up now and then. If you can't find any references to an agent or agency you're interested in, it probably doesn't have much clout.

Also, consider how successful the agent seems to be. A rich agent is, by definition, making money for her clients. If an agent answers her own phone, that's not good. If she has an assistant, that's better. If you get a receptionist before you get to the assistant, you're dealing with someone who's making enough money for her clients that she can afford a couple levels of staff. If the agent's office phone is also her home phone, consider moving on.

Location means something. The major agencies are mostly in Beverly Hills. Some agents are in West Hollywood and Santa Monica, with a few in Manhattan. Canadian agents are mostly in Toronto. If an agent works in Tarzana, you have cause to doubt. An agent in San Francisco may have nice things to say about you, but can't take the meetings to say them in.

If you have a choice, you need an agent with enthusiasm *and* clout, but enthusiasm is more important. Enthusiasm—faith in you, greed at the prospect of all the dollars she can make off you, true passion about your talent—is what the people she's talking to on the phone will hear. An agent can't say, "This is the best writer I've had in years" about more than a few clients at a time.

If you have a choice between two agents, consider the following formula:

ENTHUSIASM x ENTHUSIASM x CLOUT

A really enthusiastic agent at a midlevel agency is better than a mildly interested agent at CAA. But any agent at CAA is better than a really enthusiastic agent no one's heard of.

Of course, you may not have a choice to make. You may have only one agent who's seriously interested. In that case, so long as he or she is a signatory with the Writers Guild, any agent is better than no agent.

If they're not a signatory with the Writers Guild, don't bother. Any agent who wants you to pay for screenplay critiques or script polishing services is not worth your time. Some legitimate but impoverished agencies want you to pay for script copies and/or postage, but the mainstream agencies don't expect you to pay for a thing. In fact, they take you out for lunch. TV's a good business for an agent. Once they put you on a show, they get 10 percent of your income from that show *as long as you're on the show*. One deal can mean five years of income for an agent.

The best way to get an agent is through a recommendation from someone in the biz, preferably someone with credits. Then you can say, e.g., "Darren Star suggested I contact you." If you have writer friends, they can ask their agents who else is looking for clients. (It's not cool to ask someone for an introduction to his or her own agent. If you sign with my agent, she's going to take some of her precious time to work for you instead of me, damn you.) Network execs, development people, and story editors can tell you who's sending them the freelance writing samples they like; those are the agents who are picking good writers and getting them work.

If you're out of the loop, you'll have to call the agencies and find out who might be looking for new clients. The Writers Guild website (www.wga.org) has a list of agencies. The *Hollywood Representation Directory* is more expensive (about $40), but lists individual agents at each agency. Get it from Amazon.com.

Find out who's in each agency's television division. Call one of the agents. Ask his assistant which other agent might be looking for clients. Also, assistants are all looking to move up, and some take on clients of their own. If it's a good agency, this might be worth a try, if you can't get a real agent of your very own.

Agents will sometimes "hip pocket" you. That means they're repping you, but the agency isn't. This is better than nothing, but if you're not getting action within six months, bail.

The WGA list actually specifies which agencies accept "unsolicited" scripts, meaning they're open to queries. Definitely hit these agencies, but try the other ones, too. All agencies have junior agents who are looking for hot new talent. The trick is finding out who they are, and making sure you don't sound clueless when you talk to them or their assistants.

If you sign with an agent, don't fret too much about the contract. Agency contracts are regulated by the State of California. An agent can't take more than 10 percent. There will be a clause stating that if your agent doesn't get you a bona fide offer in any four-month period, you can terminate the contract. I generally prefer a contract that can be terminated within a short period—you never know when an agent's going to lose interest—but in the beginning of your career you rarely have to worry about an agent holding on to you if you're not making money.

You do not need an entertainment lawyer. Television deals are standardized; your agent should be able to handle the boilerplate. Having the right manager can help, but until you're successful you are unlikely to be able to attract a really good manager.

Staffing Season

The best time to get an agent is in the annual lull in the staffing season. Television has a very specific annual rhythm. Most series start production around early July. That means they need to be fully staffed in June so they can get everybody up to speed and get enough scripts finished before production begins to survive to the end of their season. (Once production begins, you never get ahead, you just get more behind.) This means that during a frenetic few weeks from late March through early May, shows hire most of their staff. This is *staffing season.*

The groundwork for staffing season is laid early on. Story editors and showrunners are reading you in January and February, which means network execs are reading you around Christmas. That means you were polishing your specs with your agent all through the fall, which means you got your agent in the summer or early fall. Hence, the best time to get a TV agent to read your spec is in late June or July—after they've recovered from staffing season, but early enough for you to send out queries and get your script read.

Of course, if you're an established writer, that is, a proven commission earner, then any time of year outside of staffing season itself is a good time. Agents are almost always willing to sign you if all they've got to do is negotiate your deal. It's the hard work of breaking in a new writer that they'd really rather avoid.

If you don't have a job at the end of staffing season, odds are you're sitting this year out. A few windows open up later on. By August it becomes clear who's getting on whose nerves, and a few people get canned and people get hired to replace them. In November some shows that started with an initial order of 13 episodes get an additional "back nine" order. Naturally, they're already behind, so the network often springs for an additional staffer. You might also get a freelance script. But don't count on it. You're competing against veterans whose shows got canceled or who didn't get a job this year.

If your agent did not get you work in one season, evaluate if she's still right for you. Is she still passionate about you? Is he breaking his back to get you mid-season work—freelance scripts and gigs on mid-season replacement shows? Or has he lost faith? One sitcom writer wrote anonymously: "I let my agents undervalue me. I stayed when I knew they didn't believe in my ability. NEVER do that."[1]

However, *never* ditch an agent until you have another lined up. To be without an agent in television is to be a nonperson. Any Guild-signatory agent is better than no agent.

Different readers will want different samples. A network exec might be willing to read a spec feature as an original writing sample. A showrunner may not have time. Some will be willing to look at a spec pilot, to see how creative you can be. Others just want to see two scripts where you've nailed a show's template. Your agent will know who wants what and when.

L.A., the Big Nipple

The vast majority of television shows are written in L.A. Even many American shows that shoot in other cities are written in L.A. For example, many shows shoot in Vancouver, but the writing staff all live and work in sight of the Santa Monica Mountains.

By and large, breaking into American television means moving to L.A. (In Canada, it's Toronto, though some writing is done in

Montreal. In Britain, it's London.) Living in L.A. means you can take a meeting *that day*. It means you bump into people at parties, in restaurants, and at cafés—people who know someone who knows someone who can get you a meeting. It means you overhear what people are saying about the hot shows and the flops. L.A. has the biggest community of creative people working in TV and the movies in the world. No other city comes close.

Being in L.A. is also psychically draining and expensive. It is easy to get your hopes up and hard to get any concrete success. People can be shallow and like you only as long as they can use you. But that's showbiz. You did want to be in showbiz, right?

Can you get hired *before* you make the big move to L.A.? Agent Liz Wise:

> You can get staffed from out of town if you are brilliant and have a brilliant connected agent. But it's also just as likely you'll win the lottery. Never say never. But if you really want to get staffed you need to know people and have heat behind you. You need a friend who will get you a showrunner meeting, or who will bring you onto their show, or give you a script. If you're from elsewhere, you need to have produced/written/directed something people in this town will have heard of. If you want to just be one of the thousand competing in the trenches, then you have to be right here, in the trenches, ready for months of meetings all leading up to the right meeting with the right person. I'm not saying it can't be done by flying in from time to time, but it's rare. I've staffed someone that way, but boy is it a fluke.
>
> Let's say you were aiming for staffing this year. You would have spent last summer getting your specs in shape (one spec, one original). You would have spent the fall finding an agent who totally digs you (meaning you've flown here periodically to take meetings and do face-to-face). You'd work with your agent as the fall season unrolled watching what works and deciding what spec you're going to finish before Christmas. As fall

becomes Christmas, you and your specs would start to get introduced to executives and cable shows. Hopefully you start to get great feedback, and you get some momentum. You get some meetings, you rock in the room, and an executive sets you up with a meeting with the showrunner. So far you've flown in at least four times. You're getting serious heat, and people are loving meeting with you—you stay down, find a place, and hang out until you get a job. If you're not getting any love or any heat, staying down here may be pointless and expensive. So you head back home and write a new and better spec and start the process all over again.

Later on in your career, you may be able to move out of L.A. Unfortunately, you'll still have to be prepared to live away from home for months at a time, if you're on a show that's shooting on location, as many do. Chris Abbott (*Magnum, P.I.*) lives in Utah now, but began her career in L.A.:

> Sometimes people ask me, "Can I make it without moving to Hollywood?" I say, "Sure. You can make it wherever you live. But you can't make it as a Hollywood writer unless you're willing to come to Hollywood. 'Cause they aren't going to come to you."[2]
>
> You can't be in Utah early in a career. And if you're going to run a show you have to be in L.A. Though actually I could have lived anywhere. On *Magnum, P.I.*, I spent five years shooting in Hawaii. Then I was on a show in Florida with Burt Reynolds, then a show in North Carolina, then a show in Virginia. If you have enough of a reputation you can live anywhere. I moved up here because I hadn't been writing for episodic television so much.
>
> But as it turns out in the endless world of reinvention I live in, I got a call from daytime TV, so now I'm writing that. Everybody lives out of town and we do story conferences by telephone. We have Yahoo Messenger so we can write things to

> each other while we talk, but you need to be on the phone so you can hear people's voices.[3]

If you move out of town, be ready for your workload to fade to nothing unless you can keep in touch. As far as L.A. is concerned, if you're not coming to meetings, you're in Uganda. Paul Guyot (*Judging Amy*) writes, "I definitely noticed that my agents checked out on me once they learned I moved [away] for good."[4]

The Back Door

While you're trying to get hired off your specs, there are other ways in. One of the best back doors is getting work as a TV writer's assistant. You can observe a lot by looking, as Yogi Berra said, and there are few better ways to observe something than by assisting someone who's doing it. As a writer's assistant, you'll take notes as the writers break story in the room. You'll see those breakdowns become outlines, then writer's drafts, then production drafts, and you'll read everything. You'll see the writers deal with production notes from everyone, and listen in as they gripe and try to come up with solutions.

Moreover, people hire people they know, and if you're their assistant, they know *you*. On a TV show, if your writing is at all in the ballpark, the writers will eventually throw you a script if they can. I'm not sure I can phrase it better than Lee Goldberg (*Diagnosis Murder*):

> The pay is crap ($500 a week), the hours are hell (9 A.M. to as late as, well, 9 A.M.), and the work is menial (answering phones, running errands, typing scripts, printing revisions, organizing files, putting revision pages into scripts, etc.) . . . but the experience is priceless. You learn how a TV show

> works from the inside. You see how stories are broken. You read lots of scripts . . . not just the ones that are written, and endlessly rewritten, for the show . . . but the specs that come in clamoring for the showrunner's attention. You see how freelancers succeed . . . and how they fail. You see how the producers deal with writers, studio executives, network executives, managers, actors, and everybody else associated with making a show. You make lots of contacts . . . not just with the writer/producers on the show and the freelancers who come in but, if you are any good at what you do, with the network and studio executives who call the office 178 times a day. [. . .] A job as a writer's assistant is a graduate school education in television . . . and, in your downtime (on the rare occasions when there is some), you can write. And I know it works. Not only have a lot of showrunners I know started out as writer's assistants, most of our assistants have gone on to become professional screenwriters themselves.[5]

How you get these jobs is sticky, because every wannabe writer wants them. You'll be competing against people who are extremely well- or just plain overqualified. Some of them will be prettier than you, with better typing skills. You'll be hoping that no relatives of the writers are applying. Make sure your people skills are polished. You're trying to convince the writers they'll enjoy your company for twelve hours a day. Make sure your screenplay formatting program skills are polished, too. Spend a few hours learning Movie Magic Screenwriter and Final Draft.

You could try to get a writer's assistant job by shotgunning an extremely charming, polite, and funny query letter, with a great résumé, to every member of the Writers Guild whose TV credits suggest they can afford an assistant, and to their agents. Agents know everything. But I have never in my life landed a job or anything else this way.

A better way to break in if you're not related to a writer is to intern (work for free) for a writer who's not currently on a show. Part-time is fine. If you do a great job as an intern, when your writer gets on a show, he or she will try to get you hired on.

Personal connections are crucial in show business. Get out there and meet people, and leverage those people you do know. TV and feature writer John August (*DC, Charlie and the Chocolate Factory*):

> Personally, all the assistants I've hired have been either referrals from friends, or people I worked with before. For instance, two of my assistants worked in the production office on *Go*. My current assistant came to me via my agent, who taught one of his classes at USC.[6]

Which suggests that taking classes at USC might help. Meeting screenwriters at symposiums might work, too.

Whomever you talk to, if they don't have a job for you, ask if they know anyone who does. That will vastly increase your possibilities. Don't be embarrassed. Embarrassment is a luxury no one in show business can afford, and life is short. Michael Benson (*The Bernie Mac Show*):

> I came to L.A. in 1990 and started as a production assistant on *Golden Girls*, while writing spec scripts at night. With each spec I got better. After getting to know some writers on the show, I showed them the specs and asked them for advice. Those writers and execs later hired us, so it proved very helpful to create relationships with them early on. For instance, the next year Richard Vaczy and Tracy Gamble created a *Cosby Show* spin-off in New York, called *Here and Now*, and they made me an assistant on it.[7]

Unfortunately, the very best way to get these jobs is to go to Beverly Hills High School. You know, the one in 90210. Then when your best friend's dad needs an assistant, your best friend can remind him that you're looking for a job. In New York, the high school to go to is probably Dalton. You know, the one in the movie *Manhattan*.

There are sometimes ads in *Variety* for assistant jobs, but these are generally for feature writers. As you've probably gathered by now, motion picture writers work in a different, lonelier, more easygoing world, with shorter hours. Working for a feature writer, you'll never sit in the room with the writing staff as they break a new story at 6 P.M. for the replacement script that has to be writen by noon tomorrow. You won't learn the ins and outs of production. If you want to be a TV writer, assisting a feature writer may not be that helpful.

If you do get to be a writer's assistant, be cool about your own writing. We know you want us to read it. We know you'd like a shot. The more you can suppress the impulse to ask, the more we're likely to offer.

If you're in the writing room, be cool about your own ideas, too. Try to get a sense of whether they're welcome. Some writing rooms are autocratic. Others will take an idea from the sandwich lady if it's good. It depends on the head writer.

If you're not sure what the room's protocol is, ask the writer you feel closest to. If your ideas are welcome, then offer them, but only when you're pretty sure they're on the money. If the room is prickly, then you can always mention your idea later on. (Or, if you absolutely must, pass a note to your writer friend.) After all, it's not your responsibility to write the show, it's the writers'. If you only offer the rare, brilliant comment, people will assume you're suppressing other, equally brilliant comments. Don't prove them wrong.

Writer's assistant jobs rarely exist as such in Canada. But even impoverished Canadian shows will have a script coordinator during production, who's responsible for tracking changes in the drafts and getting the drafts out to the production unit. Sometimes, to save money, the script coordinator will actually be a beginning writer who's also guaranteed a script. American shows shooting in Canada will also sometimes have a production assistant (P.A.) assigned to deal with script stuff, and that person will deal with the writers even if the writers mostly work in L.A. All these jobs get you close to the process.

Other Back Doors

If you can't get a job as a writer's assistant, get any job that gets you close to the right people. Jennifer Crittendon (*Seinfeld, Everybody Loves Raymond*) got a summer internship cutting pineapple on *Late Night with David Letterman.* "I started submitting monologue jokes to head writer Steve O'Donnell, who liked them. He passed them on to Dave, who started to use them."[8]

You do hear from time to time of impossible-luck, Lana-Turner-discovered-at-Schwab's stories. Kay Reindl once told me she and Erin Maher were discovered on the *Millennium* newsgroup. Kay wrote some biting comments about how the series had, in her opinion, screwed up an episode. Glen Morgan, who'd been lurking on the newsgroup to check in with his audience, wrote back to ask how she'd have done it better. She answered. Morgan asked if she had a sample. She said she did, she and her partner just had to polish it. They went back and wrote a spec *Millennium* in three days, and got hired on the show.

Or something like that.

The moral of this particular story is: great writing will out. And eventually your break will come; when it does, be ready to jump on it. Oh, and, lying your pants off is fine in showbiz, so long as you can deliver the goods.

8

GETTING HIRED

If a show's story editors like the spec scripts your agent has sent in, they will ask you to come in and pitch ideas for episodes. You don't need to convince them you can write; they've already decided you can. You need to convince them of three things:

1. You have great stories to tell.
2. You have passion for these stories.
3. You're going to be fun to work with.

If they don't like your pitches, but like you, they could possibly assign you a script, but don't count on it. You want to give them pitches they can say yes to.

Killer Story Pitches

You want to come in with a half-dozen killer springboards for the show. Eric Estrin (*McGyver*):

> The starting point of the perfect pitch is the pitcher knowing the show very well and exhibiting an understanding of the main characters and the types of stories that work for them. Ideally, the pitcher would have five or six stories pretty well worked out, all of them being in the ballpark for that show. The pitch would have the show's stars doing things they've never done before—if possible, things no one on TV has ever done before—in ways that are uniquely suited to them. The pitcher would not get bogged down on story beats but would highlight a few twists and turns that might serve as act breaks, while bringing new depth to the main characters.[1]

The better you know your story the stronger your pitch will be, but don't go into too much detail. The details are for you to know and the story editor or showrunner to ask for if they want them. You should know what your acts and act outs will be, not only because they may ask you for them in the meeting, but because they could okay your pitch only for you to discover that your concept doesn't actually work and you can't find good act outs. Then you're stuck trying to make an unworkable concept into a decent episode. If you can't break the story inside of an afternoon, there's probably something wrong with the story idea; don't bring it up in the meeting.

You don't need to know the beats. You certainly don't need to pitch individual scenes, unless you've got something truly exceptional—a killer teaser, an amazing confrontation, something memorable that the audience will talk about after the show.

Great springboards for a freelance script are like great springboards for a spec script, except they're more focused. These will get on television, you hope. Therefore stunt episodes—crossover characters, pushing the envelope—are less welcome. You're trying to make the writing staff's lives easier. Crossover characters require delicate negotiations at the network level, and pushing the envelope could run afoul of the network's Standards and Practices department.

On the other hand, your episode doesn't have to float free of the season's chronology the way a spec does. If you've been able to get a sense beforehand of where the core characters are headed in the season you're writing for, then you can try to fit the episode into the season arc.

Try to avoid episodes that require big new sets or big set-piece action sequences. Go slightly smaller with the story than the show goes. Try to stick to the core cast. It's easy to come up with an episode where an outside character shows up and turns everyone's life upside down, but that's not what they need a freelancer for. They need a freelancer to give them a new perspective, a fresh take, on the show they already have. Unlock an aspect of the show they haven't already thought of.

If you can, miraculously, come up with a *bottle show,* by all means pitch it. A bottle show is an episode that takes place inside a "bottle." It uses only the standing sets, and ideally only the core cast. This makes a bottle show cheap and fast to shoot. Bottle shows get a production back on budget and back on schedule.

A great bottle show doesn't feel like a cheap episode. Its story naturally restricts the characters to the sets. A good example would be the "Abraham and Isaac" episode of *The West Wing,* in which the White House is on lockdown due to a terrorism scare. The characters can't leave the White House set because the Secret Service won't let them.

It's hard to come up with a convincing bottle show. If you, as a freelancer, can pitch a plausible one, the odds are good you'll get a script, and you'll be a hero to boot.

It's not a bad idea, beyond your well-worked-out half-dozen pitches, to have a couple of wild story concepts you can pretend you just came up with off the cuff. Sometimes your listeners are in a grumpy mood and will shoot down every good idea you have. They may latch on to something truly offbeat and send you home to work that one up. Any port in a storm, mate.

Be Fun

You're coming in with stories to sell, but first of all, you're selling *you*.

A pitch session is simple. You come in and meet some of the story editors. The showrunner may or not be there. The head writer probably is there. You have cleverly confirmed beforehand (through your agent or by yourself) whom you're going to be meeting with and what they do on the show. You have checked out their credits on IMDB (the Internet Movie Database, www.imdb.com) so you know what shows they're alluding to.

A pitch meeting is a bit like any other job interview. The people in the room want to know you're qualified to do the job, but they already suspect that, or you wouldn't have been invited into the room. They want to know you're going to be a fun person to work with—someone who can handle the job *and* would be fun to go out with for a beer afterward.

This is a job interview, so all the usual job interview rules apply. Get to the office half an hour early, so you can hang out in the parking lot and walk in the door exactly on time. Dress appropriately. In L.A., a guy can't go wrong with the writer's uniform: a white Oxford button shirt, brand-new jeans, and blindingly white new sneakers. Weather permitting, add a leather jacket.

Women can dress up a bit if they feel like it, but be careful not to dress like a secretary—or a producer. The look is active, casual, and not too threatening—e.g., a feature writer or a showrunner can get away with biker or cowboy boots, but they might be a bit much for a TV freelancer. As a rule of thumb, a writer will never go wrong looking as if he or she is about to go to, or just came from, a barbecue.

Once you're in the room, take the time to get to know everybody you're meeting. If you've been able to dig up any personal stuff about them, engage them personally. If your interviewer rides horses, talk horses. If he believes in UFOs, talk about Area 51. Remember, they already know you can write—they read and liked your specs, or you wouldn't be here. Now they're trying to figure out if they want to work with you personally. The story editor who's supervising your draft will have to work closely with you. Be personable.

Let them ask you about yourself. It's not a bad idea to have a funny story ready to break the ice. It could be something you saw in the trades, or something about the vacation you just took, or something upbeat about the last job you did. If they don't ask you about yourself, give them a way to get to know you.

As with any interview, remember, they're just as worried as you are. They're wondering if they'll hire a difficult person, or someone who's good at writing a spec but bad at delivering under pressure, or a psychopath who'll show up at their door in the middle of the night wearing a hockey mask. They're *writers*, remember, which means they're probably not the most socially ept people you will ever meet. Just because they're sitting behind a desk doesn't mean they feel confident. Charisma is largely a matter of giving people a positive impression of themselves. Make them feel good about the whole process and they'll feel good about you.

Just Do It

After a bit of chitchat, there will be a lull, and they'll ask to hear your pitches. Now's your chance to tell them some stories that they'll want to commission you to write. *Be positive.* Your attitude should be, "I have some ideas I'm really excited about, and I hope you're going to be as enthusiastic about them as I am."

Start with your best pitch. Meetings sometimes get interrupted. If they like your first few pitches, they may just stop you there and buy them.

When you come to pitch, you want to stay on your toes, but don't get nervous. Hah! Of course you're going to be nervous. Only your whole career depends on this. But if you stay focused on the people in the room and the story you came to tell, and not on your own performance—focus out, not in—you'll forget your nerves and achieve what you came to achieve.

Don't rush. They've gone to the trouble of inviting you in to pitch, so figure you have at least a good twenty to thirty minutes. If you're getting in and out any faster than that, you're rushing. Chris Abbott (*Magnum, P.I.*):

> I think you should basically give the people you're pitching to a beginning, middle, and end. And you should give them anything really, really cool and unexpected—but not because of custom but because that's how you'll sell it.
>
> If you really know your pitches backward and forward, they should come out naturally. Remember, you're telling a story. If you have any doubt whether you can tell a story on your feet, practice! Pitch your story ideas to friends before you get to the pitch meeting.
>
> Practice, practice, practice. Ask others to listen to your pitch and give you feedback—not on the story, but on the pitch. Did they get lost? Were they pulled into the story? Are there any

> places that dragged or that went by too fast? I think it'd be good to offer to do the same for your fellow writers. It's good to hear how someone else pitches and discover what works for them and what doesn't. But, in the end, the pitch is your voice, your vision, your idea. So it has to sound like you.[2]

It's not a bad idea to have notes on note cards. You probably won't need them, but you won't have to worry about drawing a blank. (Winston Churchill used to memorize his speeches, but would bring a paper copy into the House of Parliament anyway, so he wouldn't have to worry. He even wrote in the audience's riotous applause.)

All writers are a bit squirrelly, but TV writers have to be less squirrelly than movie writers, just as movie writers can't be as squirrelly as novelists. When you're pitching, you have to listen at least as well as you talk. Be prepared for the people you're pitching to to ask questions or make suggestions. If they do, it's a terrific sign. It means they're really listening.

Be Flexible but Passionate

A pitch session is all about bringing in stories that you believe in, but which you're flexible about. Believing in your stories means you're passionate about them. They move you. You care about them. You relate to them personally. Even if they're not the stories of your life, they're the kind of stories you became a writer to tell.

TV is all about process. The people you're meeting are not buying your stories. They're buying *you writing* your stories. They want to know that you'll put your heart and soul into them.

It's a bit ironic, because TV is not a medium for personal expression in the same way movies are. You're working with their characters in their template. You can't tell any old story you like.

You have to tell a story that delivers the goods on their show. But that's all the more reason why they want to see passion. Anthony Zuiker (*CSI*):

> The main thing is passion. Passion begets more passion in the room, and when you are excited about something it becomes fun and improves the quality of writing. Passion is the main thing we look for in hiring writers, along with intelligence and understanding structure and story. One pitfall to avoid is writing for other people's expectations.[3]

And here's Shaun Cassidy (*Players, Cover Me, Invasion*), who became a TV showrunner after being a Hardy Boy:

> I want you to come in with a specific point of view. It's the old actor trick. When you go up for an audition, make a choice. It may not be the choice the producers wanted or expected, but it will be specific, it will catch somebody's attention, and it may inspire the producers to think, "Oh, there's a different way to go." That applies to a writer. When you go in to meet the executive producer or the showrunner or whomever, don't just try and do what you think they want you to do; come in with something that you can run with. Be bold. Try things.[4]

Remember, your value as a freelancer is that you bring a fresh eye to the show. You can have a writing room of six people, and after working together for a while, they all start thinking the same thoughts. If all you do in the pitch room is reflect those thoughts, they don't need you. They're giving you their time so you can bring in something they haven't thought of.

Never argue with the people in the room. Just as you would if you were negotiating with an armed hostage-taker, discuss, but don't disagree. If someone makes a suggestion where you could take the story, don't you dare shoot it down. If they're giving you suggestions, they see the possibilities of your story. Run with their suggestions as far as you can. If it's a dead end, let *them* tell you so.

Part of being flexible is the ability to take criticisms. The better you can take criticisms in the pitch room, the better they'll figure you are at taking criticisms when you're hired to write. Since it is the essence of freelancing that you will get the show at least slightly wrong, and story editors will have to let you know in what ways you missed the target, you want to show them how well you embrace criticism.

Get a sense of whether the story idea you're pitching is going down smoothly. If not, wrap it up and move to the next one. (Remember, you have four to six pitches.) If they're really hating it, you may want to just cut it short—"Not so much with that one, huh?"—but if you're not sure, just wrap it up efficiently. Get where you were going without further ado and be ready to go to your next pitch.

Keep the energy in the room up and focused. Although a few jokes and personal anecdotes when you get into the room are good to give people a sense of who you are, once you're pitching, stick with the pitching.

Chris Abbott has devoted an entire handbook to how to behave before, during, and after the pitch. The essence of her very useful *Ten Minutes to the Pitch* is to be mentally and emotionally prepared, and then be ready to go with the flow. Be energized, but relaxed. Know what you came to do but be ready to do it in ways you didn't expect.

Here's Chris's checklist; to get the details, read her book!

1. Arrive early.
2. Make sure you're at the right place.
3. Bring a pencil and notebook.
4. Go to the restroom first.

5. Be pleasant to the assistants.
6. Don't forget to breathe.
7. Know the people in the room.
8. Turn off your electronics.
9. Don't start pitching till you're in the room.
10. Tell the story you came to tell.
11. Expect the unexpected.
12. Be memorable.
13. Don't leave until you're finished.
14. Have someplace to go after the meeting.

(For the last one, I can recommend My Father's Office, a pub in Santa Monica.)

Writing Your Freelance Script

So, they bought one of your pitches and hired you to write the script. Congratulations! You're a TV writer.

Guess what? You're still auditioning. Only now, you're auditioning for a staff job. If they like the job you do, and the way you worked with them, they'll hire you on staff when a staff writer position opens up.

Your job is to deliver the goods on your pitch, and to turn in the best script you can, in the time available to you, without unduly taxing your story editor.

It's a good habit to *underpromise and overdeliver.* Promise the script no earlier than whenever they seem to need it. If you think it'll take a week, but they seem to need it in three weeks, ask for three weeks. If you underpromise, you won't be in a jam if it turns out you needed more time than you thought. If the script is harder than you thought or personal problems intervene, you'll have that extra time to finish the script. If it's as easy as you thought, then you'll have that extra time to put it away and come back to it with a fresh perspective. You may be able to turn in a much more polished draft than they expected. Nothing wrong with that.

If you turn in a script too early, no one will thank you. If it's rough, they'll wonder why you didn't take the time to finish it. And if it's perfect, they'll just resent you. Anyway, it's probably not perfect. It just looks that way because you haven't had enough time away from it to get perspective.

Under no circumstances ever, ever turn a script in late, even if you have to pull one all-nighter after another. The story editors are counting on you to save them trouble, and if your script is late, you've created trouble.

When you accept a deadline, make sure that you have no other serious obligations during the writing period. If you've got a vacation planned for right after you turn in your first draft, be ready to scrap it if it might somehow get in the way of your obligation to rewrite your script.

Don't be afraid to ask your story editor as many questions as you need to, and even a few more. A phone call is good, a sit-down meeting is better if your story editor has the time. You want to get as good a feel for the show as you can. If the show is new and hasn't aired yet, now's your chance to come in and watch rough cuts of the early episodes, to hear how the actors speak. Ask for a tour of the standing sets. Read all the scripts you can.

A good show has a voice. If you can tell a story, you're valuable, but if you can tell a story *in that voice*, you're much more valuable. Whatever you write will get rewritten into that voice sooner or later—if not by the story editor, eventually by the showrunner. The less rewriting your script needs, the more likely they'll have you in to write another, or hire you on staff.

Ask what the tone of the show is. Ask if there's anything about the characters they'd like you to bring out. Ask if there are any overall themes that make the showrunner happy.

Once they buy your pitch, they may want you to write up a breakdown of your pitch—teaser, acts, act outs, and tag. Or, they may provide you with their breakdown. Some shows will actually provide you with their own beat sheet if they feel their template is particularly hard to nail, or if they're not really sure how to communicate it to you.

Under a standard WGA contract, you can be cut off after the outline stage if the show isn't satisfied with your work, so really take the trouble to get your outline right.

After you turn in your outline, you'll get notes. After you turn in your first draft, you'll get notes. All the rules of taking criticism apply a fortiori now: they're paying you to write this, so if you have a choice to make between what they want and what you want, there's no question. Go with what they want. In most cases, though, if you struggle with a note long enough you can find a way to address it that will make both of you happy. That's usually the solution they were hoping you'd find.

If you're not sure how to address a note, figure out several ways you can resolve it, and then ask your story editor which she likes the best. If your story editor is bumping on something—a plothole, something implausible, something unoriginal—try to find the fix yourself. Don't expect her to fix it for you. That's what they hired you to do. Chris Abbott:

> If they're stuck, it's better to call and ask for help than turn in the wrong thing. But I don't want them to call me and ask for every beat, or I could write it myself. Most writers I've known have been good about that. I've had writers come in and completely miss it. But in that case all the phone calls in the world wouldn't have made a difference. I like them to ask a lot of questions and then write a beat sheet, and I give them notes on the beat sheet.

> Once they've got the end of the outline they should be in pretty good shape.

The same goes for problems you discover on your own. No beat sheet is perfect. As you're writing your pages, you'll probably run across problems you never suspected. Sometimes you can solve them neatly, but sometimes it will be unclear which way to go. If you aren't sure, come up with several solutions, and then ask your story editor which she thinks is the best.

That said, don't deviate too much from your beat sheet without checking in. They bought your idea because they *liked* it. Just because *you* no longer like it doesn't mean they don't. If you truly hate your idea now, come up with a new approach and check in. But no one likes a writer who's constantly second-guessing herself. It just creates more work for everyone. If it ain't broke, don't fix it. Chris Abbott again:

> Executives like to participate in creating the script. If you change it substantially, you're insulting them. Now why would you want to do that? If there are specific parts the executives loved and you take them out and you don't warn them in advance—start looking for a new day job. On the other hand, if the spirit of the notes is in the script and you've given them essentially what they remembered buying, they're not going to haggle over a couple of minor changes.
>
> [On the other hand,] sometimes you need to change the beat sheet. What the story seems like in outline, once you start writing characters, it doesn't work anymore. Don't be too slavish to the beat sheet—don't go off in a whole new direction, but no one's going to be unhappy if you bring in a better script.
>
> I was working with a writing partner and we had sold a story idea to an episodic TV mystery show. After we had gotten the approval to "go to story," which, for those of your readers who don't already know, means we could go home and write up the story we had just sold in more detail, my partner decided he hated

> the story and we should change it. I didn't know that was a really bad idea, so I agreed. We came in, not with the fleshed-out story outline the producers had bought, but with an entirely different story, which, incidentally, they hated. I could almost see the blood pressure rising on one of the producers as we pitched him our new "improved" idea. I never made that mistake again.[5]

Don't get too fancy with your episode. Freelancers sometimes like to show off, using lots of cinematic techniques. Unless it's a show that's chock-full of flashbacks, match cuts, hallucinations, dream sequences, and so on, try to tell the story clearly. Leila Basen (*Mental Block, Emily of the New Moon*):

> Don't junk up the format. A lot of freelancers overreach. Keep it simple. Grasp the situation and love the characters. Sometimes scripts I get are too showy, too flashy—too clever by half.

If you turn in a great script, and everyone dealing with you has a great experience, you'll probably get hired for another script. If that goes on long enough, then you're a pretty good bet for the next staff job.

Multiple Jobs

It may happen that you're offered two freelance writing jobs at the same time.

If you have to choose, don't worry about the money. It will probably be Guild scale anyway. Worry about which story you feel closer to, which you'll be able to do the better job in. Secondarily worry about how impressive the show you've been asked to write for is. But writing a great script for a mediocre show may lead to more work faster than writing a great script for a great show: the competition will be that much fiercer.

Anyway, most experienced writers will take both freelance gigs. The amount of time you're usually given to write a freelance script is enough to do a good job on two scripts. That's why you under-promise on delivery dates. (Remember Scotty on *Star Trek*?) You can usually get two weeks to write your freelance script, sometimes even a month; you should be able to polish off an hour script in a week once the outline is locked. Also, when you're working on one script, you often have to wait for feedback on it. While you're waiting, you can work on the other script. Larry McMurtry (*Lonesome Dove*):

> I've done at least one draft of something like seventy scripts. . . . The only project I've ever turned down was a remake of *Rin-Tin-Tin,* a lapse of judgment I've regretted ever since. There's absolutely nothing wrong with Rin-Tin-Tin![6]

Of course, you have to know how fast a writer you are, and how many personal drafts you need to write to get to an official First Draft that you can turn in. (A writer's first draft, as turned in to the story department, is sometimes called the First Writer's Draft, to distinguish it from the White Production Draft, which is the first draft the story department turns in to the production unit.) You may not want to take a second gig if it comes too hot on the heels of your very first gig. Don't take a second gig if you believe it will interfere with delivering a great script for the first gig. But don't feel it's morally wrong to take two freelance gigs at the same time. That's what "freelance" means. So long as you deliver the goods to everyone, it's nobody's business how you allocate your time. If they want you full-time, all they have to do is sign you up as a staff writer!

9

MOVING UP THE FOOD CHAIN: WRITING ON STAFF

A freelancer writes on her own: anywhere she likes, any time she likes, taking as little or as much time as she likes, so long as she turns her draft in on time. But the vast majority of television episodes are written by the writing staff: writers on salary who work a regular, sometimes insanely long workweek. The writing staff range from those actually designated "staff writers," all the way up to the showrunner.

The writing staff make more money than freelancers. They get paid for their scripts *and* they get a salary on top of it. A one-hour drama script fee under the WGA is roughly $30,000. The *minimum* weekly salary for a story editor is roughly $5,000 to $6,000 depending on the number of weeks guaranteed. Veteran staffers make much more than that.

Writing staff also know how many weeks they've been guaranteed and how many scripts they've been promised. Their show may be canceled, and their contract may not be extended or renewed, but until then, they can plan to buy major appliances without actually having the money in the bank.

More important, freelancers work alone. Members of a writing staff get to know one another. They go into the same office every day. They hang out in the writing room. They solve one another's problems. They go drinking together after work. They drink together *at* work, if they are so inclined. Just like any office situation, the writer's office can be anything from one small dysfunctional but happy family to a seething cauldron of frustration, fear, and resentment. But it's never lonely.

Who Are All These People?

A staff writer is essentially a freelancer who works in the writing office instead of at home. He gets a salary as an advance against his script fees. When his script is finished, he gets the difference between the script fees and any salary he's been paid so far. If he winds up getting more in salary than he's owed in script fees, he gets to keep the overage; but if he's not being hired to write enough scripts, he should be on the lookout for his next job.

The next step up from staff writer is a story editor. She works on her own scripts *and* rewrites other people's scripts. She works with the other story editors to break story. She outlines scripts, writes scripts, and rewrites freelancers. She may even rewrite the showrunner if the showrunner's too busy doing other things.

Story editors get credits according to their rank. Story editors move up to co-producers, then producers, then executive story editors, then supervising producers, co-executive producers, and finally executive producers. The person in charge of the writing staff may be called a head writer, an informal title that means what you'd expect. The person who runs the whole show is called a showrunner, but gets an Executive Producer credit. (There is no "head writer" or "showrunner" credit.)

Story Editors

There's no qualitative difference in job descriptions between a story editor and a co-executive producer. Both write scripts. Both rewrite scripts. Both break story. One just outranks the other. A story editor could wind up rewriting a co-executive producer's script, but it's far more likely that the co-executive producer will be doing the final pass on the story editor's script; and of course the showrunner rewrites everyone, time permitting.

As in any office, different writing offices have different protocols. Some are egalitarian. The credits mean little more than who gets paid the most. Others are hierarchical: junior story editors are expected to keep their mouths shut in the room unless the supervising producer asks for their opinions. Marc Abrams (*The Bernie Mac Show*):

> As you go from show to show you learn that each has its own temperature and its own etiquette. You recognize your role on that particular show. Certain showrunners encourage the lower-level writers to pitch ideas, others don't. Some want ideas well thought out before they are presented, others like to hear the kernel of an idea that could be expanded.[1]

A good story editor is a team player. Although you need to get your scripts done on time, you also need to do your part to make sure the writing staff as a whole keeps the scripts moving smoothly through the pipeline. That may mean helping another writer rebreak a story, or brainstorming a scene he's having trouble writing. Sometimes, to help a writer meet a deadline, you'll write an act, or a B story. When a script is seriously late, everybody may write an act—called "gang banging" a script.

Whenever you're not busy—all your own scripts are done or waiting for notes—you should be working up new story pitches for later episodes. A thirteen-episode season may get picked up for the "back nine," and suddenly there are eighteen new story lines needed. Melinda Hsu (*Medium*):

> And you must always, always get along and do more than your share. Give other people credit for ideas that they had; thank people for their help; stay in the office until people who outrank you leave for the day; be at your desk even if nothing in particular is going on; don't talk behind people's backs, don't be demanding, don't be crazy or arrogant or disorganized or slow or difficult to work with. Don't miss deadlines, no matter how understanding your peers and bosses seem to be.

Being a team player applies not only to whose project you work on, but how you treat your own ideas. A good basketball player gets the ball to the person who's got the best shot at the basket; she only shoots if she's got the best shot. A good story editor helps the story go in the direction that seems best for the story. If it's your idea, great. If someone else's idea works better, go with hers. Melinda Hsu:

> You want to keep the conversation moving and the ideas flowing, but you can't just blurt out everything that pops into your head because you need to respect the direction that the story is already moving in (unless you have an unbelievably genius idea). And even if you have a genius idea and it gets shot down, you have to let it go right away and not take it personally. Some of the worst things you can do in a room are: a) stay immovably fixed on a single idea; b) not come up with any ideas at all; and c) fail to keep up with the discussion—e.g., for-

get discarded ideas that have already been raised, not follow the twists of the story that the other writers are proposing, not think fast enough and have to have things repeated and reexplained for your benefit.

It's an important skill to know when to say nothing, even if you'd do it differently if *you* were in charge, and how to catch up by listening when you realize that you didn't quite follow that last proposed plot twist.

As in any office, even in an egalitarian situation, you need to remember who's working for whom. I asked Paul Guyot (*Judging Amy*) what the biggest mistake is that story editors tend to make:

> Thinking they know more than the executive producers. No, I take that back. It's opening their mouths and *saying* they know more than the executive producers. You may be a story editor or even a staff writer, and you may very well know a lot more than the executive producer. But keep your mouth shut. It's his or her show, not yours. Shut up and do your job.

Chris Abbott seconds that emotion, warning against "not paying enough obeisance to the exec producer." As does Kay Reindl (*Millennium, Dead Zone, Twilight Zone*):

> Although a showrunner may insist that everyone in the room have equal voice, a staff writer who consistently gives unsolicited notes to someone above them is considered trouble. You may be the most brilliant writer of all time, but on staff, you're still a baby writer and you're there to learn. Nobody likes a cheeky staff writer! I've worked with eager staff writers who do a great job and learn a lot, and staff writers who really needed to stop talking. So just remember that you're there to learn both how to do things right and how not to do things.

It's not a bad idea to check in with your boss now and then to see if there's anything you could be doing more of or less of. Just because some people outrank you doesn't mean they're comfortable criticizing you. They may not say anything until it becomes a problem. Don't let it get that far. Make it easier for them to criticize: ask them to.

Your Master's Voice

Your job is to write the show the way the showrunner would if he had had time to do it himself. One of the greatest talents a story editor can have is not only to write well but to write well with the showrunner's style, in the showrunner's voice. Chris Abbott (*Magnum, P.I.*):

> I'm sure that every writer on staff thought I rewrote them excessively, but I would rewrite my staff *more* if I could. There are shows like David E. Kelley's—he just writes them all. But that's good because I think you need a consistency of voice and style—you have to find someone who can really do your voice well or you have to rewrite. I was always good at mimicking the exec producer's voice.

On the other hand, one of the temptations of being a story editor is rewriting freelancers' scripts too much. These almost never come in right on the money. Freelancers aren't in the room; they don't know as well as you do what's in the show's template and what's not. They may get a character's speech rhythms without really catching her character, or vice versa; either way the character's voice will be wrong. They may put in too much action, or too much drama, or too much witty banter. To someone who's been trying hard for weeks or months to capture the essence of the show, freelance scripts often feel atrocious, even insulting, in the way they mimic the show from the outside without getting its heart. Often after you've given notes, and the Second Writer's Draft comes back, it feels like the problems you noted have been fixed but new, more awkward problems have arisen.

It's tempting to do a "page one rewrite" every time: to read the script once, react in horror, chuck out all the dialogue and replace it with your own, and rewrite all the action, too. An experienced or talented story editor can do a blitz rewrite on a half-hour script in a day, or on an hour script in two days. Just go back to the approved outline, and write at top speed, taking your inspiration from the script you just read, without leaving much of it on the new pages.

The problem is, what you have now is not a second draft, but another first draft. It's a better-educated first draft. You know the show. But it defeats the purpose of having a freelancer do the script. The freelancer may have been struggling with problems you may not even have noticed yet. The script may have semi-good solutions to these problems that you can improve on, but if you don't take the time to understand them, you'll toss out the baby with the bathwater.

Nor can you assume you'll do better. You'll like the result better, sure, because it's your script. But even the best First Writer's Draft is a first draft, with flaws and brainos and bad segues. When Aaron Sorkin brags, "We pretty much shoot my first drafts,"[2] you only have to go to the front page of the actual scripts to see how many production drafts there are; and those are only the revisions made *after* the script has been released to the production unit.

Sometimes a total rewrite *is* inevitable. Sometimes you're forced to hire writers who aren't up to snuff, because they're friends or family of the showrunner, or because you're in a Ukrainian co-production and you have to hire Ukrainians to write at least five out of the thirteen scripts. Sometimes, too, if the story editors haven't nailed the template in their own minds, and they're still feeling their way toward the essence of the show, it may be impossible to get a freelancer to deliver something useful. In those cases a page one rewrite may be called for. But if you know your template, and you're dealing with competent freelancers, you should resist the urge to jump in and rewrite everything. Try to take the freelancer's draft to a second draft.

Unfortunately, this feels like more work. You not only have to remember what the scenes were supposed to do in the outline. You also have to read and make sense of the scenes and try to figure out what the writer was trying to do with it in her draft. What was she aiming at? If you take the time, you may discover things in her draft that don't completely work, but which, once polished, will make the script richer and denser. Read the script two or three times. Ask the writer why she did it that way.

Using as much of the freelancer's work as possible will not save you time in writing your first pass because of all the effort in understanding what the freelancer did. But reworking her scenes instead of refabricating them entirely may save you from having to do a *second* pass. If you can make the script she wrote work, then you've got a *second draft*.

(It's worth clarifying the distinction between a "draft" and a "pass." When a writer works his way through a script, writing or rewriting it, that's a pass. Writers will usually do a few passes before showing their script to anyone else, although the later passes might be solely to clean up the script. A "draft" may represent several passes by one writer, or passes by several writers—for example, a pass by a story editor, another pass by the head writer, and a pass by the showrunner. What makes something a "draft" is that it's turned in to someone. A freelancer's first draft is turned in to the story editor. A production draft is shown to the production unit. Each revision shown to production is a new draft—usually printed on different colors of paper and so called the "White Draft," "Blue Draft," and so forth.)

After all, the point of hiring freelancers is to save a little time and get fresh ideas and perspectives. If you completely rewrite freelancers, you haven't saved a bit of time, and you've obliterated their perspective. "When a story editor says, 'No one can write the show but us,' I feel it's just ego and greed talking," says James Nadler. If a freelancer isn't getting the show, "that means I have failed as a story editor to communicate the show to the freelancer."

Credit Where Credit Isn't Due

By the way, if you do a page one rewrite as a story editor, don't expect you'll get a credit on it. Under the Writers Guild of Canada rules, a story editor cannot receive credit for a freelancer's script. The Writers Guild of America has no such rule, but poaching credit from a freelancer is considered greedy. Chris Abbott:

> Another story editor wanted to put his name on every episode because he rewrote part of it, and that's ridiculous. Story editors and showrunners should never put their names on freelancers' scripts. You can't get that show's voice unless you're there all the time—that's how you get it: when you're around the actors, watching dailies every day, you start knowing how everybody talks. If you're not around the show they just can't get it. So it's not their fault they got rewritten. They did their best job, so shut up—you're getting a weekly salary to make the script closer to the show.

And demigod Joss Whedon (*Buffy, Angel, Firefly*):

> There are entire episodes of "Buffy" that I have written every word of that my name is not on. Which is gratifying to me.[3]

Production Notes

Once you're a story editor you start getting notes from people who are not themselves writers. These notes are much harder to deal with than notes from people in the writing hierarchy. When you get notes from an executive story editor, you take them. What do you do when you get notes from someone outside the room?

There is something good in almost every note. I may ignore suggestions on *how* to fix things, but I try never to ignore the criticism behind the suggested fix. Unless your vision is completely at odds with the note-giver, the mere fact that someone felt something needed fixing is evidence that something wasn't working for them. Just because they're wrong about how to fix something doesn't mean they're wrong that it needs fixing.

Try as soon as possible to discover what everyone's vision of the show is, and keep asking questions till you understand it. You need to know where people are coming from.

If you are getting notes directly from the network, you have to take them very seriously indeed. *They're paying your salary*.

On the other hand, while you have to *address* all the notes, you don't always have to *take* all the notes. In other words, you have to solve the problems the network is complaining about, but you don't necessarily have to take their suggestions on how to fix the problem. If this seems defiant, bear in mind they've hired *you* to write the scripts and to fix the problems. You tell a carpenter what you want the cabinet to look like. You don't tell him how to nail the thing together. While you have to be tremendously respectful of anyone at the network, you also have to respect your own job. If you have a question on how to handle a network note, check with your boss.

What if you just plain disagree? If it's your show, then follow what you know to be true, and hope you're right. If the show's a hit, then you'll probably be forgiven the disagreements if you presented them in a polite and respectful way. A wise man once told me, "You can be as difficult as you are talented." The flip side of that is, if the show's a flop, no one will send you roses for diligently following the network's suggestions.

If it's not your show, and you disagree, then make your disagreement quietly plain, then do what you're told. Then go out with your friends, drink some strong cider, and tell everyone what idiots you're working for.

Either way, pick your battles. If the note will make something different, but not necessarily worse, go with it. If the note will cripple the scene or the script, you'll have to find a way to fight it without pissing people off.

Notes from actors and directors are more problematic. When actors give you notes about their character, they are often excellent notes. Actors are trained to understand characters. They won't let you have a character do something that's convenient for the story but unmotivated by the character's situation. They will also let you know when they think you're missing an opportunity to take their character into deeper or less charted territory.

On the other hand, actors are not looking at the episode as a whole. For an actor, each script is about *his* character. Actors are not looking at the season arc, or the overall theme; or, if they are, they've taken their eye off the ball.

Sometimes the actor has a misconception about her character and you can get into real problems. This is the famous "my character wouldn't do this" argument. At that point it's up to the showrunner to straighten the actor out. Some actors respond well to arguments. They really need to understand where you're coming from. Others are just testing you, to see if you really do know what you're talking about; with them, the showrunner will just have to lay down the law.

TV directors, on the other hand, are looking for what will

make the episode look cool. It's not their story to tell; they have no control over the arc of the season. They're looking for a few good shots that will look good on their reel. If they have questions about a character's motivation, listen to them. If they have an exciting way to stage a scene, well and good. But this isn't features, it's TV. You are in charge of the story. If the staging is cool but doesn't sell the story, it's bad staging. The showrunner should back you up on this.

Taking notes is always bound to be stressful, especially when you disagree. It's worth remembering, though, that TV is not a medium for personal expression. TV writing is a craft. You serve the audience through their paid representatives, the network executives. *It is just a job*. It can be the most fun job in the world. You can occasionally make great television, when all the pieces fit together. But it is television; it is not your life. And those are *their* chips you're playing with.

Playing Nice with the Other Kids

The higher up you go, the more you're involved in the physical production. A story editor might get sent to the set to observe the production unit—someone has to make sure that the director doesn't miss an important story point. However, usually it's only a showrunner who would actually contradict a director. It would be the showrunner or, if the showrunner's too busy, a supervising producer who would be meeting with the production designer or running a tone meeting or dealing with a union dispute.

Part of the fun of television writing is being involved in the physical process. One week you're writing a beat sheet and you realize you need a scene in an extraterrestrial bar. Two weeks later you walk onto the swing set and you realize you're standing in an extraterrestrial bar. You're standing in front of a big, brightly painted box with blinking lights, and you realize that the production designer has designed something, and the carpenter built it, and the scene painter painted it, and an electrician wired up all the lights, and all you had to do was write:

```
In the corner is some kind of interstellar
JUKEBOX.
```

It's a rush.

A good story editor learns the nuts and bolts of television production. You learn to ask the assistant directors what locations they're too heavy on, which standing sets are underused, which actors are exhausted, and which are chafing for more stuff to do. You learn to take two scenes at different locations and rewrite them for one. You learn how to cut unessential scenes when the script supervisor brings in the timing and you realize you have to lose eleven pages. You get a feel for timing yourself, so your scripts never come in eleven pages over.

Never forget that the reason your office is next to the studio is so you can go poke your head in. You can visit the production designer's office and see what he's designing, and if it doesn't match the story, you can chat about it. You can talk to the heads of departments and let them know where the writing staff is taking the characters. Often they don't get all the nuances from reading the scripts. A writing staff member can clue them in.

Have lunch with the crew, especially the department heads. You can pick up a lot from all the bitching and moaning.

With experience, you learn what changes the production people *need* to make the episode shootable on budget and on schedule, and which changes they just *want* because it would make their lives easier.

By watching the dailies and listening to the directors gripe, and talking with the actors, you get a sense of what the actors are and aren't capable of. Sometimes you realize you could give an actor more to do. Sometimes you realize that an actor doesn't do an emotion well. Some actors are in touch with their anger, but won't let themselves be vulnerable on camera. Some actors want to play everything like Clint Eastwood. Some actors aren't articulate and sound awkward saying complicated sentences.

You can fix all these ills. Give one actor angry scenes, but no vulnerable scenes. Write all the scenes with your Clint wannabe so that it's the other characters who carry the emotion, while he merely reacts. Give your inarticulate actor nothing but short lines with short words in them. They'll look good, they won't balk at the scenes, and you won't be frustrated that they're mangling your lines. (You'd be *amazed* how much an actor can improve when he's no longer stumbling over long sentences and big words.)

The more you learn about production, the further along you are to becoming a credible showrunner.

How to Run a Writing Room

As you move up the ladder, you continue to write, but now you are also managing writers. Writers are hyperarticulate. But they are not by nature friendly, sociable people. Writers are by nature people who observe other people being friendly and sociable and then go home and mock them. Sometimes immediately, sometimes years later. In other words, they're fundamentally antisocial.

TV writers have to be much more friendly and sociable than novelists; TV writers have to have the most social skills of any writers alive, really, except for gossip columnists. If they're successful, they've generally conquered their shyness to the point where they might even appear extroverted; but they're still fundamentally shy.

They are also egomaniacs. But they express their egomania by bossing their characters around and creating worlds; in real life, they're used to not being listened to.

They are artists, full of pride, full of pain, a little touchy.

So you might expect that managing a roomful of antisocial people who are spending ten to fourteen hours a day together might be a nightmare. It's not, because writers also tend to be hysterically funny. After all, they're used to coming up with sharp dialogue. They've honed their wits. Some of the best dialogue I've ever heard was at lunch with writers trying to outshine one another verbally.

Running a staff is a lot about keeping egos from being bruised and, on the other hand, preventing egos from running wild. Especially when people bruise your writers' egos. When writers are angry or upset, they generally can't concentrate on their work. In fact, when TV writers are angry or upset, being friendly and sociable means they vent like crazy for hours. Often hilariously. But no writing gets done. A graphic artist can do their thing angry, but when the writing staff gets in an interpersonal jam, no work gets done.

Management is probably the same everywhere on some level. But it's always more dramatic with show people, because show people are all drama queens at heart.

Always Start with Praise. If you can't praise the execution, praise the effort. If you can't say "good work," say "good start," or "thanks for putting in the effort." If you start off with criticisms, your writer will only hear half of what you say. The other half of his brain will be thinking of how sorry you'll be when you hear he committed suicide or whether you'd notice him poisoning your tea.

I once forgot whether I'd told a writer "good work" on an episode, so I called him up to ask him if I had. He said, "You always say 'good work.' That's the way you start every e-mail."

"That's because it's always good work," I told him. "If it sucked, I would have said 'Good start'!"

I used to be in a writing group. We were all professional writers—novelists, a TV writer, a feature screenwriter, a comic book writer—but one of the rules was, praise first. We went around the circle and everyone said something positive. Then we got into the criticisms. But thanks to the praise, we did not have a single suicide while I was there.

Keep Responsibilities Clear. Make sure it's always clear who's working on which script. When you have freelancers, assign each one a story editor who can develop a relationship with them. If possible, keep the same story editor with them; he knows their weaknesses.

Keep Your Staff Working. Make sure everybody has something to work on. If one of your writers has turned in his script, give him a beat sheet to revise. If all the beat sheets are waiting on network approval, tell him to come up with story pitches for the future. Don't assume your writers are working productively just because they're at their keyboards. Writers have an unlimited ability to write e-mail, surf, and blog. Left to their own devices, they will even work on their next spec screenplay on your time.

That said, *don't expect your writers to work all the time*. Writers need to shoot the breeze. They need to hang out on the phone and send e-mails and sometimes even read books in the middle of the day. Judge a writer by his output, not by his *sitzfleisch*. *Try to sense when your writers are usefully letting off steam, and when they are just goofing off.*

The best deadlines are often the ones writers give themselves. Ask, "When do you think you can have this by?" Then encourage them to turn things in on time. You don't always have this luxury, but if you decide the deadline, sometimes you'll be too generous. You may think a script will take all weekend; only the writer knows he can do it by Friday afternoon. If you say "next

Monday," he'll turn it in next Monday and have a great weekend. If you say "Friday" he may feel pushed. But if you let him say "Friday," he'll feel good about handing it in on Friday. The writer who's actually writing is the one who knows best whether the notes are a week's worth of work or a couple of hours'.

Try To Let Your Writers Do Their Work. Only take a script away from someone if he's really not going to be able to do the job in time. You'd rather get a script that's 80 percent there from a freelancer than a script that's 90 percent there from a story editor or 95 percent there from yourself. First, it's less wear and tear on the staff and on you. Second, it makes writers devoutly unhappy to be rewritten, especially if they feel they could have done the job themselves. Third, you'll get more diversity in the scripts. Fourth, if you do all the fine-tuning, your writers will never learn to fine-tune things themselves.

Work Toward the Long Term. Remember that show business is small, and how you treat people less powerful than you is how you'll be treated when you need a break later on. There's nothing more heartwarming than being able to help someone who helped you when you needed it. Unless, possibly, it's watching some jerk drown in quicksand because he's stepped on everybody who could throw him a rope.

The flip side of this is to be aware when you, yourself, are written out and when you should suggest someone else take the episode over. When you have to, fire yourself as a writer. Don't worry, you still get to be story editor, and the episode credit stays yours. Assuming you've done all you can, it's no shame to let the people you work with know you've taken a script as far as you can. Everyone loses perspective eventually; everyone writes themselves out on a given script after a certain number of rewrites. Only absence from the script and time will restore you, and there's never enough time in TV.

Pace Yourself. Keep perspective. Don't burn yourself out on one episode or you'll have nothing left for other episodes. If you're so stressed that you're not having a life outside of work, you're probably working too many hours. Try to leave work earlier, but focus better during the hours you're there. If you're not a little stressed, though, you don't care enough.

Keep Up Discipline, but Don't Embarrass Anyone. If you disagree with someone you outrank on a creative point, you can discuss the pros and cons in the writing room, if you're really open to changing your mind. But if you feel one of your writers is screwing up, discuss it quietly, alone with that person.

Never tell off a writer (or anyone else for that matter) in front of other people. Take them aside and talk to them. They're less likely to feel humiliated if there are no witnesses; and if they do freak out and storm off, you can both pretend later that it didn't happen. The less often people see that you're getting your way, the more you're likely to actually get your way.

On the other hand, praise people in public, if at all possible. This makes everyone feel good.

Don't Hog the Vision. Make sure everyone knows the vision you're trying to put on the screen. It sounds obvious, but sometimes head writers and showrunners guard the essence of the show as if it's a secret. Maybe they're afraid that if other people know the vision they'll laugh at it. Maybe they're afraid they can be replaced if the secret gets out. Maybe it gives the showrunner a winning argument: "Look, I know my vision and you don't." Who knows?

It's silly, because the showrunner doesn't need another winning argument. He's the showrunner. But if he communicates his vision better, he'll need to argue less.

The more people know the vision, the more likely they are to deliver the goods on it. It's that simple. The job of a showrunner is to communicate the show to everybody working on it, so that everything the crew does forwards that vision. You're the keeper of the concept, yes, but the only way to keep everyone in sync with you is to give everyone a stake in it.

The Pronoun "We" and Why You Should Use It Exclusively

Some writers are hyperaware of what they've contributed to the show and want to make sure everyone knows it. These writers have a superb memory for their own contributions and a poor memory for anyone else's. This sort of writer is less than a joy to work with. You wonder how much these writers can be concentrating on the story if they're devoting half their brainpower to remembering what they thought of and what other people thought of. It is no fun working with this kind of writer.

It's hard to tell what people's contributions actually are. It's easy to see who wrote a line or who turned in a draft, and sometimes there's one person who crystallized an idea in a couple of clear sentences. But how much of the goodness of that line came from the bad version of the line that came before it? How much of the value of a good draft came from an offhand comment someone made two weeks before, which triggered a good idea that someone jumped on and promoted and someone else turned into a plot point and the writer of record turned into a draft? Is the person who first crystallized an idea entitled to credit, when he had the idea after a two-hour conversation and then everybody honed the idea for another two hours?

I once rewrote a feature script and found everyone applauding me for having "saved" it. Only I could tell that the previous rewriter had entirely fixed the script's structure, but had made it so dark and unhappy that no one could stand it. All I had to do was lighten the story and brighten the characters, and write lots of snappy banter. Fortunately for me, when I told people how little I'd done, no one really got what I was saying, and they continued to give me credit for the work both of us had done.

I think it's crucial to instill in everyone in the writing room the feeling that the writing room gets credit for everything that comes out of it. "What happens in the room stays in the room." Sure, on a first or second draft, where the writer had a lot of independence turning the outline or breakdown into the pages, he deserves a pat on the back. But when I send in a revision as a story editor, even if it's a page one rewrite that I wrote every word of, I send it in as "our revision"; and when producers ask whose idea something was, I say, "It came up in the meeting."

This prevents a lot of hurt feelings and encourages team spirit. It has the added advantage that when the producer despises the draft, no one person takes the heat.

Nor should any one person take the heat. A draft should ideally never go out without the whole writing staff having a chance to read it. If everybody read it, and none of them pointed out the problem before the draft went out, it's everyone's fault the problem wasn't fixed.

Ultimately, it doesn't matter who had which idea. The people on the show remember how much fun you were to work with, and how well the scripts turned out. People outside of the show know how the show turned out. The more you go around claiming this or that as your own work, the less likely other people are to believe you. The more you praise the whole team, the more people will want you on their next team.

How to Get to Sleep When Everything Depends on You

The more responsibility you have on a show, the harder it is to get to sleep. Part of the key to keeping yourself sane is delegating as much as you can. People may not do things as much to your taste as you would, but they can't learn unless you let them make mistakes; and much more will slip through the cracks if you try to do everything yourself.

Try to get enough sleep. Don't fret after hours. Fretting makes people irritable. People don't work as hard for irritable bosses. They may not quit, but they'll spend hours ranting behind your back. Make sure both you *and* your team get enough sleep.

Never call anyone after ten at night or before six in the morning unless there is a real-world crisis—an actor has been in a horrible car accident, or the set is burning down. "I hate this script" is *no one's* crisis but your own until working hours. Go back to sleep and deal with it in the morning.

Do not drink coffee past five o'clock. Do not order the espresso truffle cake.

Keep exercising.

Remember, it's just TV. No one is going to die if you get it wrong.

Surviving Getting Fired

> Get that son of a bitch writer out of here! I don't ever want to see him again until we need him.
>
> —ATTRIBUTED TO SAMUEL GOLDWYN

You will probably get fired sooner or later.

Getting fired is part of being in show business. Sometimes jobs are cut and someone has to go. The rest of the time, people are fired for "creative differences." It generally means people didn't get along. But it isn't just a euphemism. When passionate people get together on a show, sooner or later they're bound to see important things in different ways. And with enough friction, you get fired. When two people are in conflict, whoever has less clout with the showrunner and the network may get fired.

Not all marriages work, and working on a show is a lot like a marriage. In a creative job, you put more of yourself out there than when you're working construction. There's nowhere for your neuroses to retreat to. You can be a perfectly good writer and just rub someone the wrong way. You can be too cocky, and irritate or even intimidate someone above you. You can have a different approach to solving story problems. At a certain point, it's over, and if you're the low man on the totem pole, you're out. Agent Jeff Alpern:

> The biggest reason is not the writing but the writer's personality. Bad chemistry. The writers' room needs to be a well-oiled machine and if one of the parts doesn't fit properly, that part may have to go. Even with screenplays, I've seen writers fired because they antagonize the producer or the studio/network. If the writing is absolutely brilliant, that writer will be given a lot of rope before he/she hangs him/herself. But for most writers, they need to figure out a way to be firm in their beliefs without pissing off too much the people who are paying their salary.

No one enjoys getting fired. But there is an etiquette to it that makes it easier on everyone, and makes it more likely you'll get hired elsewhere, or possibly even by the same people later on.

When you're fired, you need to take stock and figure out what you did to get fired. Often the reasons given are not the real reasons. No head writer or showrunner wants to admit he fired you because he didn't like you, or because his girlfriend wants your job. He'll phrase it as "he wasn't contributing," or "he just didn't get the show."

Of course, maybe you weren't contributing. But maybe you just need to keep your head down more next time. Maybe you need to charm your boss more. Maybe you need to have a better sense of politics, and get on the good side of the people making the firing decisions.

Or, maybe, if you have a choice, next time you need to get hired by people who like you, rather than people who dislike you but recognize your talent. Not everyone is going to like you. They may hire you anyway. In show business you often have to work with people you don't get along with. Try to avoid working for people who hire you for your talent (or worse, your brilliant idea) even though they don't really like you.

Regardless of why you were fired, when you're talking to people not associated with the show, downplay the firing. If you read the trades, you'll notice all sorts of people who are "moving on." They've been fired. "Developing new projects"? Fired. You're in good company. If you keep quiet about it, people may not realize you were canned. Shows cut staff for all sorts of reasons. Your boss may get fired at some point. Then you're out because your boss is out. Or if you get hired on something new, you can say it was a better opportunity and your previous show graciously allowed you to jump on it. Your show will eventually get canceled. Then you haven't been fired, your show was canceled.

Never diss the people who canned you—not in public, anyway. Let your friends do that. It won't make you look good; it makes it clear that you were canned, when you should be glossing over that awkward fact. If you're not going to work with a company again, it costs nothing to be gracious. If you're classy enough, they may, out of guilt, or because they really do recognize your talent, recommend you to someone else.

Meanwhile, don't waste time bemoaning. Get on the phone to your agent for new work. Write a new spec. Ideally, write a new spec that's nothing like your old specs. Chris Abbott:

> I've often reinvented who I was. Though I never got fired, what I was writing got out of style. I was known for writing family shows, then chick shows, then action adventure shows, then back to family. Rethink who you are and what you write. Every time I've been out of work I've written a new spec pilot. I've never sold any of those scripts but they've always reinvigorated my career. It gives you something new for your agent [to show].

> People say, "Nah, I know her work," and your agent can say, "You *don't* know her work, this is completely different stuff than what you've read," and then they're willing to read you again. Nobody's willing to look at old scripts again, and nobody wants to see what you've been writing for hire.

Call everyone in your phone book and have drinks with them. (Separately.) Remind the world you're alive. Reenter the thick of things. Go to industry events. Do all the things you would do after successfully completing a show. One of the hardest things in the world is being positive when you've just been rejected. But people like positive, and they want to be around it.

Have a life outside the business. Not only is it good for your sanity, it gives you something to write about. Have something that feeds and nourishes your soul that isn't your writing. Even if you never get fired, and always get work, at some point your career will start to wane, and one day you'll be without work. If all you have is your writing, that's the day you're alone.

Don't put off having a family until you're sure of your career. No one's ever totally sure of his or her career. Many people's careers don't take off *until* they have a family. Who knows if it's the family-man vibe, or the focus, or having someone small who adores you? And, how can you write for the whole audience if you don't know any kids?

You should always keep a few irons in the fire, even when you're working. That way you have something to jump on when you suddenly find yourself with more time on your hands. Often producers have scripts that need rewriting if they can just find the right rewriter. Let them know you'd be interested once some time opens up. Then, when some time opens up, you can let them know you're available. Chris Abbott:

> Keep contacts, make contacts, keep friendly relationships with lots of people. Throw your friends freelance scripts. Throw

people who *aren't* your friends scripts—they *really* feel obligated to you!

Keep writing. One of the advantages to being a writer is that you can always write; you just can't always get paid for it. You should always have a spec feature or spec pilot idea on your back burner. The moment you're not employed, get busy with it.

One last thing to consider upon getting fired is: take a vacation. It is very hard to take a vacation in showbiz, because either you're working too hard, or you're working too hard to get your next job. While you still have money in the bank, take a week or two off and go somewhere fun. It will do you, your relationship, and your family good. Amazingly, it will also do your career good. It will give you a better story to tell in meetings when you get back; and meetings are all about the stories you have to tell. It will help your attitude. And I can't tell you how many people's vacations get ruined by serious, urgent job offers.

10

THE HOLY GRAIL: CREATING YOUR OWN SHOW

Few things are more exciting than creating your own TV show and getting it on the air. Love, sex, parenthood, and getting shot at, possibly.

It is extremely hard to get a show on the air. A network exec might hear three thousand pitches over the course of pitching season (June–October). A U.S. network might buy on the order of a hundred drama series pitches. Of those, they commission perhaps a quarter to go to script. They might shoot five pilots. They actually buy three shows, meaning they fund production and air at least a few episodes. There's no guarantee how long any of those three shows will stay on the air.

You don't need to get a show on the air to benefit from developing a series, though. A spec pilot can serve as a good screenwriting sample, showcasing your creativity. If your pilot gets bought, you are in business with a network. That may put you on the short list to staff other shows on that network, and it may get you hired to develop pilots and series projects for the network. Most of the times I've been hired on shows it's been at least partly because I'd optioned a series pitch to the production company; while trying to set up the series I'd sold them, they hired me for one of their "go" series.

Also, creating your own series may be a creative antidote to the frustrations of working on other people's ideas, in other people's idioms and voice. It can also remind you just how difficult the job of the showrunner you're working for actually is. The lessons you learn from creating a spec pilot or a bible will help you write other people's shows by teaching you to take a show apart to see how it works.

But the name of the game is still getting your series on the air. You will often hear that U.S. networks buy series pitches only from experienced TV writers. This is partly true. The network would rather have a great veteran writer with an idea attached than a great idea with an inexperienced writer attached. Bill Persky (*Cosby*):

> You take a mediocre show with a great show runner, as opposed to a great show with a bad show runner, and you have a better bet with the mediocre show.[1]

And Bruce Sallan (also *Cosby*), in *Creating Television:*

> Imagine me going in to pitch an idea for a series about a black family: "Dad is a pediatrician, Mom is a lawyer, and there's three kids. . . . We might do a whole story about the tooth fairy. Or we'll do a whole story about what happens if the cat got lost. Isn't that brilliant?" . . . *Cosby* happened because of Bill Cosby and they got a good writer and producer. . . . Bill Cosby in the right vehicle at the right time. Was the idea brilliant? No. It was the execution.[2]

To pitch a network yourself, therefore, you are typically supposed to have at least an Executive Story Editor credit. A Supervising

Producer credit is better. What they're really looking for is someone with an Executive Producer credit, who's already run a show.

But the number one rule of Hollywood is that there are no rules. There are other ways to get a show on the air. Tom Chehak (*Regenesis*):

> U.S. TV will take writers' ideas wherever they can find them. I know right now of a bunch of top showrunners who are nursing through the process several less experienced writers. Here's the deal—a network doesn't want to buy a show from somebody with no experience in the TV business. But they don't want to throw out the baby with the bathwater. So what they do is attach a "hot" showrunner—like a John Wirth who ran *Nash Bridges* for nine years and didn't sell a pilot of his own this year. So they put John with a bunch of writers (I think three writers with three different ideas) so he can shepherd them through the process. If a show goes, he'll be the showrunner and the network won't have to worry about their investment.

As with spec features, a truly great idea whose time has come will find its way onto the screen somehow.

How do you get through to the network in the first place? Any way you can. A writer can pitch to a lower-ranked executive at a studio. The exec can then take it to the weekly meeting. If her boss likes it, the studio might invite the writer in for a pitch. If the pitch goes well, they'll start calling around to see what showrunners might be available to mentor the writer and take over the project. Shaun Cassidy is now an accomplished showrunner; he was called in to take over *The Agency,* while its creator was kept on the writing staff as an executive producer:

> CBS bought the pilot written by Michael Frost Beckner, and produced by Wolfgang Peterson and Gail Katz, and then they called and asked if I'd be interested in running the show. The script was very much like one of Wolfgang's movies [*Das Boot,*

> *Air Force One, The Perfect Storm*] in that it was a very strong action picture. The network wanted more character development, so Michael and I worked on characters, and the show sold and got on. . . . Michael Beckner and Melissa Rosenberg [*Dr. Quinn, The Magnificent Seven, Boston Public*] did a lot of good writing together for the show.[3]

You can get your project to a production company that does business with the networks. Independent producers are producing lots of television these days. If Jerry Bruckheimer's TV development guy likes your project, he can get it packaged. Same deal at the major agencies (CAA, ICM, William Morris, UTA, Endeavor). If they feel your project would be interesting to one of their producers, directors, or unemployed television stars, they can put a package together that will open doors at a network.

Spec Pilots for Real

The best way to get the network to pick up your series idea is to marry the head of the network. The likeliest way is to write a spec pilot. A bible tells the reader what you want the show to be like. But it doesn't prove that you can deliver a show like that. A pilot script is proof of the pudding.

It's vastly easier to get network executives to read a spec pilot script than to read a show bible. Executives are often willing to read a spec pilot as a sample. So, many experienced writers spec a pilot from time to time as an alternative to speccing a current show. If the pilot doesn't get picked up, it's still a good sample and showcases the writer's originality. If the pilot by some miracle gets picked up, mazel tov. Chris Abbott (*Magnum, P.I.*):

> I never wrote specs of existing shows. I always write a spec pilot or a spec [feature] screenplay. And when I'm hiring writers, that's

> what I want to read. Can you write characters, can you write plot, can you write twists and turns, interesting dialogue . . . all of that will be in a spec [pilot] more than in a spec existing show. Agents would call me, "Do you wanna see their *CSI*"? And I'd say "no!"

A pilot allows you to show off your own style more than writing someone else's show. The risk is that it's far harder to write an impressive pilot than an impressive "center cut" episode of a running show, whose actors have already brought the characters to life. But the gain is that if your pilot truly is outstanding, it is possible that someone at the network may buy it. Not likely, but possible. Bob Lowry (*Huff*):

> My agent needed more material to start pounding the streets to get me a job. He said he either wanted a *West Wing* or new material. Going back to . . . wanting to . . . write in my own voice as opposed to Aaron Sorkin's, I chose to write *Huff*.[4]

There is a subtle difference between a spec pilot you write as a sample and a pilot you seriously hope will get picked up. In a writing sample, you only have to show that there's a show there. We need to get a sense of who you intend to be core cast, and what the template of the show is, but since they're just reading the one script, you don't have to have every creative decision nailed down. If you do intend to create a show, then you need to know where the show goes after the pilot. What's the second show? The fifth? The overall dramatic arc of the first season? What's the 100th episode? What's the season finale for the fifth season? Kay Reindl (*Millennium, Dead Zone, Twilight Zone*):

> If you're writing a spec pilot to be used as a writing sample, don't worry about a bible. Just worry about setting up the series

> in the pilot. I.e., you want the reader to see that there's a series here. It's a little different if you're pitching a pilot. It's always better, I've found, to go in overprepared. Have three years of your show figured out. Chances are you won't talk about it, but knowing where your show is going informs the pitch. The most important thing in a pilot pitch is making the executive feel comfortable that there's a show there.

If you want to sell your pilot as a potential series, you need to know your show forward and backward—not every single thing that's going to happen, but every aspect of the template. You need to know what is and is not your show, and what's going to happen every week.

The danger of writing a pilot without knowing the show is that you can write yourself into a corner. Shows sometimes get picked up with superb pilots only for the writers to discover that it's very hard to generate episodes. Either the pilot has torched the central question of the show already, or it hasn't created one. A show can get a big audience for its pilot only to plummet in the ratings when later episodes don't live up to it.

Such problems—you should be so lucky to have such problems.

Should your pilot get bought, it's unlikely you'll get to be the showrunner on your own show unless you have a lot of high-level staff experience. Sad, but true. There are famous exceptions. Josh Schwartz wangled himself an executive producer slot on his first show, *Wall to Wall Records*, which never got past the pilot, and then he did it again on *The O.C.* Moira Kirland (*Medium*):

> It's almost always the more experienced guy who gets put in charge of the show. I was surprised Josh Schwartz got to run *The O.C.* And he has had executive producer–type people backing him up. That's a new thing. If it hadn't been him and hadn't been Fox—on another network they would have hired a giant ape. Josh would have got a supervising producer title and would be allowed to, well, *comment*. . . .

> I think it's an absurd way of doing things. Because the creator had the vision, they're marginalized. The person who's running it didn't have that vision. Doesn't have that passion. You should allow the guy with the vision to be a journeyman showrunner. Back them up. I can't think of any shows [where they put the creator under someone else] that were wildly successful, either.
>
> The best show possible is when you have the creator involved and passionate about the show and do the show. They didn't want to let Joss Whedon run *Buffy*. He told them no, you can't have the show. To have brought in another executive producer over him—the show would have failed. You've got to have faith in the people who bring you these ideas. Marc Cherry hadn't run a drama before. Now he's running *Desperate Housewives*. He had had no showrunner experience at all in dramatic TV.

In other countries, it's often easier to set up your own show. In Canada, for example, shows by Canadians get substantial government support. That enables producers to give inexperienced creators a shot. I co-created *Naked Josh* when I had only one season's staff experience under my belt. The trade-off is that in Canada, show creators usually have less control of their own shows than they do in the States.

Pitching Festivals: Any Use?

Various organizations have "pitching festivals" where anyone can come pitch their idea to a panel of industry professionals, usually for a substantial fee. This sounds like a good idea, right? If you don't have an "in," you can buy access to professional ears.

The problem is that the people who take pitches for a living—the people who can really buy pitches—hear enough pitches, polished ones, from experienced professionals. They don't need to go to a pitching festival to hear pitches. They're sick of hearing pitches. On their time off, the only things they want to see pitched are baseballs.

That means that there may be professionals on the panel, but they're usually not the people who can really buy your pitch. They're junior execs who have no clout. They're other writers, who can give you their own opinion, but don't buy pitches themselves. They're junior agents.

If they are legit buyers, they may be getting paid to be on the panel. Or, they have a book to promote. Or they're trying to find a date for Saturday night. Either way they have some other agenda than finding a great pitch to buy.

I don't know of anyone who's sold a television show through a pitching festival.

The worst part of pitching festivals, though, is that you pitch in front of an audience. It's great to hear other people's pitches, because you learn what sounds convincing and what sounds lame. But if you have a good idea, pitching it in front of a crowd of would-be TV writers seems like a terrible idea. Someone may steal it. Or someone may forget they got it from you. (Writers often remember thinking up things on their own that they actually heard somewhere else.)

Practicing your pitching is good. But practice pitching to people you know. Pitch your friends. Pitch your writing group. They won't charge admission. And if they steal your concept, you know where they live, so you can hunt them down and beat them to death with their Emmy.

The Pilot Episode

Often, the pilot episode not only introduces the core cast, but shows them getting together: a *premise pilot*. In the *Mary Tyler*

Moore Show pilot, Mary gets the job at the station. In the *Miami Vice* pilot, Crockett and Tubbs team up.

Some say premise pilots are going out of fashion, but it's not clear that this is true. The *Lost* pilot shows the castaways in the aftermath of their plane crash. The *Alias* pilot shows Sydney being recruited as a spy. The *Grey's Anatomy* pilot shows the interns on their first day on the job. However, many pilots are simply good center-cut episodes that take a few extra steps to introduce the main characters. The *Sex and the City* pilot introduces the girls with a few lines of voice-over—no explanation of how they know one another—and then continues on its merry way.

You don't even necessarily have to write the first episode that will air. You may want an origin story to start off the season, but your origin story won't play like a typical episode of the show. It may not be easy to tell what the show's template is from an origin story. Taking the time to show how your core characters got together may leave you with little time for a good episodic story, known as the "Curse of the Pilot." You may want to write episode two or three as the pilot. There's no problem with that. It will still *shoot* first, but once the show is picked up, it can always be *aired* later.

Because of the Curse of the Pilot, some shows don't actually air their origin stories until later in the first season. To draw in an audience, it's more important to know where the characters are going than how they got this far.

A series pilot script should convey what the series is going to be. The pilot shouldn't *tell us* about the show. It should *embody* the show. It doesn't have to set up the series universe; it has to *be* the universe. By the end of the episode, we don't need to know everything there is to know about the characters—hopefully we will never know *everything*, since that would be the death of the series. But we need to *know* the characters. We need to have a sense of what's going to happen every week: what kinds of problems are going to drive the hero in the stories.

The spec pilot should embody the template—hook, characters, and franchise. If your pilot looks much different from your series, it will draw a different audience than your series. It may draw people who will walk away from the later episodes. It may chase away audience members who'd like the actual series.

The same goes for producers and network executives who will be reading your pilot. If they like the show your pilot embodies, they may buy the pilot *and then insist the show look just like that*. That's why you have to do everything in your pilot that you're going to want to do in the show. If you want your show to have sex, put sex in the pilot. If you want your show to have supernatural creatures, there better be supernatural creatures in the script.

Whatever drives your show every week has to be in your pilot script. If your heroes solve murders, whether they're spending the episode getting to know one another or not, there has to be a murder and they have to solve it. If your characters regularly debate sexual mores at lunch, there better be a lunch and they better debate sexual mores.

Coming Up with a TV Show

So how do you come up with a great TV show pitch? Every chapter of this book should have given you some sense of the answer. A great TV show pitch has *fresh and compelling characters* in a situation that allows you to tell entertaining stories in a consistent way. It may also have a fresh *hook* or possibly a fresh *format*—an original way of telling stories on TV.

Characters

There is no formula for an ideal core cast; it depends on what kinds of stories you want to tell. There isn't even a formula for how big your core cast is. A show with multiple story lines needs more characters than a show with only one story per week. A procedural show is driven by external events and episodic characters; the core cast can be small. A character-driven show needs a big enough core cast to generate new stories every week. But there are character-driven shows that keep bringing in new recurring characters to drive the stories, and there are procedural shows with large core casts.

The X-Files, a procedural show with one story line per episode, had a core cast of two FBI agents who solved paranormal mysteries. *Buffy the Vampire Slayer,* a procedural show with one story line per episode, started with a core cast of four and wound up with a core of seven to eight. *Friends,* a character-driven comedy, had a core cast of six; *Sex and the City* had four. The *O.C.,* a multiple–story line character-driven drama, has a core cast of eight but *still* keeps dragging in new recurring characters.

It's really a matter of taste. If you have a large core cast, you can tap in to many perspectives in a scene; but you are also stuck with coming up with something for everyone to do. If you have a small core cast, you can focus better, but when you need to cut away to another story line, you may not have the characters to go to.

As you might expect, in character-based shows, the characters have to carry more of the weight. If the conflicts on your show are external, your characters need to be compelling, interestingly flawed people. Your episodes will challenge those flaws. But the stories are about how each character deals with the new crime/victim/patient/case that comes in the door in each episode. You need to think primarily about what skills, backgrounds, and fresh perspectives each character brings to the party.

If the conflicts are internal, you'll be generating your stories out of the conflicts between the members of the core cast. Now you need to think of your characters as a web of relationships. They still need to be compelling, flawed people. But they need to have deep dynamic tensions *between* them.

In a cast of six, say, there are only so many ways you can pair up the characters. You want to build the relationships between the characters so there's inherent conflict in pairing any two characters. That creates a well out of which you can draw countless stories. Every character should have a fundamentally different perspective than the other characters, giving him something to do every time there's a different external threat. Every character should have issues with the other characters personally, so the characters have something to fight about *while* they're dealing with the external threat. Remember, a TV show should be able to sustain 100 episodes. If you don't have enough tension between every pair of core cast members, you may run out of stories to tell.

What does each cast member give to each other cast member that keeps them together or makes them get along? What does each cast member want, but is never going to get, from each other cast member?

It's always handy to create a *triangle* in your core cast, or several triangles. A triangle need not be a love triangle, though those are good. Two protégés competing for a mentor's attention is another good triangle. Any unstable family arrangement works. It's a rule of geometry that any four people can make four triangles.

Remember, you're trying to create conflict, not contentment. You have to love your characters, but not so much that you let them have happy lives. Happy lives are boring to watch onscreen.

By the way, if you are creating the show, be careful what you name your lead. If the network rejects your working title, you'll probably find yourself going to your lead's name for a secondary title. Think of *Angel, Tru Calling, Gilmore Girls, Will & Grace,*

Frasier, Felicity, Rhoda, The Dukes of Hazzard, and *Malcolm in the Middle* to name just a few. So make sure it's a name that you can make a title out of. When the network marketing people nixed our first title, *Sexual Anthropology,* we had to make a title out of our hero's name, Josh Gould. Josh Gould is not an easy name to make a title out of. We went with *Naked Josh,* but it's a stretch.

The flip side of this is, if you do name your show after your lead character, it's going to be that much harder to dump your lead if you have to, which means your lead actor is going to feel irreplaceable. What's *Buffy the Vampire Slayer* without Buffy? But on *Stargate SG-1,* the only irreplaceable element is the Star Gate.

A Word on Science-Fiction Characters

It's a common mistake in science-fiction and fantasy shows to skimp on the characters. Just because your characters have bat wings doesn't mean you don't have to make them recognizable people.

Two caveats apply to characters in genre TV:

1. If there are fantastical creatures, they should be interesting *as characters,* not just as fantastical creatures. One of the reasons *Winnie the Pooh* holds up is that all the Pooh characters are recognizable people. I always get a distinct sense that Eeyore is a particular friend of A. A. Milne who must have had a habit of oh-poor-me'ing. That's the sense you want: that there's a real person in there, even if the person is a gargoyle. Ambassador Koss in *Babylon 5* isn't a good character because he's hidden inside a space suit. He's a good character because he's a mystic who speaks in parables. The Beast in *Beauty and the Beast* isn't compelling because of his makeup. He's compelling because he's a deadly warrior who's a gentle, wounded romantic at heart.

2. The human characters should be *more* interesting than the fantastical creatures. We're supposed to care about and root for them, right? We'll probably identify with them more than with the characters wearing a lot of latex. So if we're more drawn to the fantastical creatures because they're more compelling, you've got work to do on the humans.

The same is generally true for regular dramatic shows. If your day players or villains are more interesting than your heroes, then you've got work to do on your heroes.

Hooks

A TV show does not *require* a hook. Shows like *NYPD Blue* or *Deadwood* are genre pieces. There's no snappy 25-word description of *Homicide* that would explain why people tune in to *this* cop show instead of other cop shows. It's all about the characters. Which means that if you're a known television writer, you can create a show based on some great characters and no hook.

If you are not known, though, and you're looking to sell a spec pilot, a hook will help. It will get your spec pilot read. It will get the pilot episode seen.

Moreover, it gives you more to sell. If your show has a hook, and the network is unconvinced that you're up to running your own show, they may at least buy your pitch and set someone else to run the show. If you have no hook, they're unlikely to buy your characters.

How do you come up with a great hook for a TV show? What makes a fresh hook is usually either a new story element—a new territory or a new character—or a new juxtaposition of elements.

By "new" I mean "new to television." Actually, it means "hasn't been done successfully on television yet." A flop show may spoil its territory for a little while, but eventually the taint will wear off. A successful show occupies its territory. If you want to write a show in that territory, you'll need a fresh twist on it.

A new element can be a character or situation we haven't seen before. *Quincy* was the first successful show starring a coroner. *CSI* was a hit simply by being the first series to focus on forensic pathologists. *Numb3rs* was the first investigative show starring a mathematician. *Sex and the City* was the first hit show about a sex columnist. *The Mary Tyler Moore Show* was the first hit show about a single woman on her own.

In science fiction and fantasy (SF&F), you can simply create a character we've never seen before. *Joan of Arcadia* stars a selfish high school girl to whom God has started appearing. *Tru Calling* stars Tru, a girl whom the dead keep begging to prevent their deaths—and who somehow keeps getting sent back twenty-four hours in time so she can do it. *Point Pleasant* stars a girl who's the spawn of the Devil but who doesn't want to become evil. Naturally, these series put their heroines in situations where their extraordinary differences will come into play.

Outside of SF&F, it's fairly hard to come up with a hook based on a completely new territory, since most of the good territories have been mined. What's left are mostly territories that are either hard to make drama out of or hard to shoot. Not too many shows are set in a coal mine, for example. Who wants to look at a coal mine for an hour? Not too many shows are set on an airplane—it's too hard to move the actors around, and you need all those extras. Until society or technology changes, creating new territories, situations, and careers for you to poach, you will have to make do with a fresh juxtaposition of elements.

Familiar Character in an Unlikely Situation. *Dr. Quinn, Medicine Woman* was hardly the first show set in the West, or the first show about a country doctor, but it was probably the first successful western starring a woman, and certainly the first one starring a woman doctor. Tony Soprano was hardly the first mob boss on TV, but he's the first mob boss on TV who's seeing a shrink and worrying about his family.

Familiar Territory in a New Genre. *Lost* was hardly the first successful series about people stranded on a desert island, but it took the concept in a new direction by weaving in aspects of *The X-Files*. They're not just on any desert island, they're on an island full of unexplained phenomena—and everyone has a past. In other words, *Lost* is the first mystery show set on a desert island.

Mixed Genres. At the heart of many new shows these days. *Desperate Housewives* is an odd combination. Partly the show is a comedy of manners about housewives leading lives of quiet desperation. But the rest of it shows a surreal suburb where mystery is piled on mystery. It's a sort of suburb where all the rumors are true: Do you suppose that nice plumber is really a spy? And do you think the hole in that family's swimming pool means they've buried a body there?

A hybrid genre TV show can give the audience something they haven't seen before. That's a double-edged sword. They may be intrigued and thrilled. Or they may just be confused. Joss Whedon's *Firefly* was a kind of space opera western. It never grabbed a big enough audience, and Fox aired just eleven episodes before pulling the plug.

On the other hand, the *Firefly* DVD boxed set of all 14 episodes shot has sold brilliantly and the show spawned a feature film. So go figure.

If all else fails, all you really need is a *compelling character and a situation that automatically places that character in conflict*. Say "CIA superspy" and you've obviously got adventure. But say "student by day, CIA superspy by night," and you know the heroine of *Alias* is going to go through a lot of dramatic conflict. Say "fugitive tries to find his wife's murderer," and you know that avoiding arrest is going to complicate Dr. Richard Kimble's investigations in *The Fugitive*. Say "spoiled, idiotic heiresses live among working class folk" and you can guess what sort of conflicts are going to arise in *The Simple Life*.

After any hook, there's an unwritten sentence that's taken for granted:

> Complications ensue.

(Which, curiously, is the name of my blog, complicationsensue.blogspot.com.)

The key to a good hook is that we should be able to imagine those complications. A screen story should have (a) a compelling character who has (b) a clear goal (or problem or opportunity), who must (c) surmount obstacles and/or fight an antagonist to deal with that goal. He'll gain something if he succeeds (stakes) but he'll lose even more if he tries but fails (jeopardy). With a great hook, the elements of the story are either part of the hook already or flow naturally from it.

How do you know if you've got a great hook? Easy. Ask people if they'd watch a TV show based on your hook. Don't do this with fellow writers; they may forget it was your idea. Do this with friends, waitresses, cabdrivers, relatives, customers—anyone without an ulterior motive. Pay attention to their response. If they say "sure," and change the subject, either you're not phrasing the hook right, or it's not much of a hook. If they are all immediately excited or (just as good) intrigued and want to hear more, you have a hook.

New Formats

Creating a new format is the hardest thing you can do. You're asking your readers to absorb an entirely new paradigm. Network executives are not very good at absorbing new paradigms. Betting on one is a good way to get fired.

A new paradigm, though, can lead to an immensely successful show. The creators of the original Dutch *Big Brother* introduced the entire subgenre of "voted off the island"–style shows; arguably, they spawned the reality show as we know it. They're probably sitting on a ton of money right now. It probably doesn't bother them that the entire Writers Guild of America hates them and the horse they rode in on.

Naturally there's no formula for creating a new format. You simply have to understand the formats people are using, and see where there's a hole—something that hasn't been tried before. Then you have to convince people it's a good idea.

Good luck!

Things You Don't Need to Worry About

There are some things you don't need to worry about when you're trying to create a show. Don't worry too much about what kinds of shows the market is looking for. Various genres go in and out of fashion at the networks. If *Deadwood* rocks they'll want westerns again. *Battlestar Galactica* succeeded? Everyone wants spaceship shows. Ignore these trends if they don't suit your muse. If your agent is asking you for a science-fiction pilot, so is everyone else's agent. If your best idea is SF, lucky you. Write it up. But if you've got a brilliant comedy idea, write that. By the time you perfect your pitch, another genre may be what they're looking for.

On the other hand, if a certain genre is currently dead, you may want to wait on it. If no one wants westerns, don't write a western, unless you can twist the genre so it feels new. Period drama has been a hard sell as long as I can remember, at least in North America.

Don't worry about bringing elements. If you can attach a bankable TV star to your show, that's major. But it's unusual, and not at all necessary. The network will attach stars once they've developed your show. Bear in mind, who *you* think is bankable and who a network thinks is bankable are usually entirely different. Network execs spend a lot of time pondering who draws an audience, and they have access to yards of expensive private research that you don't have.

It does not help to attach most actors. Any TV actor who isn't currently on a show is, by definition, looking for work. Attaching a character actor that people have heard of doesn't mean anything. People might tune in to watch Rob Lowe's next show, or they might not. They might tune in to a heavily promoted sweeps episode of a running show in which Bob Newhart guest-stars. They might not. Telling the network that you've "attached" a face we've seen before but who's never starred in her own series just makes you look unprofessional and desperate. Desperate is never good. If you're able to get to a TV star yourself, the odds are there's a reason she's not busy.

It's best to leave casting alone, unless you're actually hired by a star's own production company to develop a vehicle for the star.

It should go without saying that attaching a *director* is pointless, unless that director is also a producer (such as Ridley and Tony Scott) and/or a show creator (such as Thomas Schlamme). No one tunes in to a TV show because of the director, and no one buys a TV show because a director is attached.

Enjoying the Process

So . . . it's a lot to know.

There's more. But it can't all be crystallized into words, even if I knew enough to crystallize it.

London cabbies must know all the streets of London before they get their hack license; they're tested on what's called "The Knowledge." Fortunately, TV is not about having The Knowledge. They're not building new streets in downtown London, but TV is changing constantly.

TV is all about process. It's always moving forward. If you have a show, you're riding a tiger. You have to give it something to eat or it will eat you. But it will take you places you've never been.

There are few things more exciting than creating television . . . and *everyone working in television is creating television.* Everyone is adding something that the audience will see or hear or feel in some way. It is the popular medium of our times.

Archimedes said that if he had a lever long enough, and a fulcrum, he could move the world. While a novel may change a few people's lives deeply, television changes millions of lives incrementally. The stories it tells define how we see ourselves. While politicians may be able to make decisions that acutely affect people, few people have more power, ultimately, than the people creating television. TV changes what people *want.* It changes the minds of future voters *and* future politicians *before* they know what they stand for. It is the lever and the fulcrum by which you can help move the world.

If you tell kids it's cool to smoke, some of them will take up smoking. On your head be it. If you convince people that murderers always get caught, some would-be murderers will think twice. If you show us people dealing with real problems, then some of us will realize we're not the only people with those problems. If you show us humanity banding together against a murderous cyborg . . . then maybe we'll occasionally remember that all of us are in the same leaky life raft.

You should think about why you're writing television. Know yourself. Know what you stand for. The stories you tell will convince people they should stand for the same things; or if you tell them badly, they may rebel against what you're saying.

That's part of the challenge and part of the fun. It's also a huge responsibility.

But most writers are arrogant enough to take it on.

Aren't we?

A Parting Word

You've got your show on the air? Congratulations.

Write us something great to watch . . .

And let me know how you did it, okay?

· APPENDIX 1 ·

Resources

Where to Read Scripts

The absolute best resource for legitimate scripts on paper is:

Writers Guild (WGA) of America Library
7000 West 3rd Street
Los Angeles, CA 90048
(323) 951-4000
www.wga.org

Other sources include:

American Film Institute Louis B. Mayer Library (AFI)
2021 N. Western Avenue
Los Angeles, CA 90027
(323) 856-7654
www.afi.com/about/library.aspx

Margaret Herrick Library,
Academy of Motion Picture Arts & Sciences (AMPAS)
333 South La Cienega Boulevard
Beverly Hills, CA 90211
(310) 247-3000
www.oscars.org/mhl/generalinfo.html

University of California Los Angeles (UCLA)
Arts Library Special Collection
Young Research Library
405 Hilgard Avenue
Los Angeles, CA 90024
By appointment only: (310) 825-7253
www.library.ucla.edu/libraries/arts/speccoll/speccoll.htm

University of Southern California (USC)
Cinema-Television Library
Doheny Library
University Park
Los Angeles, CA 90089-0182
(213) 740-3994
www.usc.edu/isd/libraries/locations/cinema_tv/

Likewise, the library of any university with a television program ought to have at least some scripts. You can also buy TV scripts in book format from your local bookstore or Amazon.com. If you live in L.A., you can often find scripts at yard sales on the West Side, particularly Santa Monica, usually on Saturday morning.

Scripts on the Internet

Drew's Script-o-Rama (www.script-o-rama.com/) has a large number of scripts—sometimes even the actual scanned-in pages from a production script.

Simply Scripts (www.simplyscripts.com/) and **Twiz TV** (www.twiztv.com/) have many scripts, too, but make sure they're actual production scripts and not transcripts in script format, which they also carry.

Script City (www.scriptcity.com/) sells scripts for ten bucks a pop. You can get them as PDF downloads. I'm not clear where they get their scripts from, but they do have a large selection, for example around twenty *Third Rock from the Sun* scripts.

You can also buy scripts at **Planet Megamall** (www.planetmegamall.com/) and **DV Shop** (www.dvshop.ca/dvcafe/writing/tvscripts.html), as well as, occasionally, eBay (www.ebay.com).

Episodes on the Internet

If you've missed recording the run of a show you want to spec, current and recent episodes of popular shows (both domestic and international) are available on the Internet for free download via a Bittorrent client (available at www.bittorrent.com). I certainly can't recommend you download them; why, that would be piracy. And pirates are wicked. Wicked and bad. So definitely do not go to sites such as www.mininova.com and www.torrentspy.com to see what's available.

▪ APPENDIX 2 ▪

Writing Contests and Fellowships

Not all writing contests are helpful. Many are run to promote a magazine or website, or I suspect simply to garner entry fees. The following are associated with legitimate producers, production companies, studios, organizations, or networks.

Warner Bros. Drama Writers Workshop
Warner Bros. Comedy Writers Workshop
4000 Warner Boulevard, Building 136, Suite 236
Burbank CA 91522
(818) 954-7906
www.warnerbros.com/writersworkshop

The Don and Gee Nicholl Fellowships in Screenwriting
Academy of Motion Picture Arts & Sciences
1313 N. Vine Street
Hollywood, CA 90028-8107
www.oscars.org/nicholl/index.html
(The gold standard in feature screenplay awards.)

American Zoetrope
www.zoetrope.com/contests

Chesterfield Film Company
Writer's Film Project
1158 26th Street, PMB 544
Santa Monica, CA 90403
(310) 683-3977
www.chesterfield-co.com/html/application_process.html

Fox Searchlab
Fox Searchlight Pictures
Attn: Susan O' Leary
10201 W. Pico Boulevard, Building 667, Suite 5
Los Angeles, CA 90035
(310) 369-5423
www.foxsearchlight.com/lab/about/index.html

Slamdance Screenplay Competition
www.slamdance.com/screencomp/faq.asp#scq
(The "anti-Sundance" festival.)

Sundance Institute
Feature Film Program/Sloan Fellowship
8857 W. Olympic Boulevard
Beverly Hills, CA 90211
(310) 394-4662
www.sundance.org

Diversity Initiatives

Typically you have to be a woman, minority, gay, or over forty to qualify for these.

ABC/Disney New Talent Writing Fellowship
www.abcnewtalent.disney.com/html/writing_fellowship_mainpage.htm
On the lookout for minorities and women.

NBC's Diversity Initiative for Writers
www.nbc.com/NBC_Career_Opportunities/Diversity_Initiative_for_Writers.html

CBS Diversity
www.cbsdiversity.com

Fox Diversity
www.fox.com/diversity/programs.htm

WGA Writer's Training Program
www.wgaeast.org/wtp/

▪ APPENDIX 3 ▪

Final Draft vs. Screenwriter

Final Draft and Screenwriter are the main screenplay-formatting programs writers use. The following are my impressions of the Mac versions, with additional input from a dozen or so blog readers on both platforms. Your mileage may vary.

Final Draft is extremely intuitive and easy to learn. You almost never have to look at the manual to figure something out. It usually guesses right about what the next character name or the next location will be. It's smarter about which part of your slug line is time of day and which is location. The Mac version has the Mac look-and-feel and uses all the standard Mac menus and dialogue boxes. If you click "Command-G," it is the "go-to" command, just like on every other Mac program.

Screenwriter is harder to learn. Many of the commands are not the standard commands. Many of the specific screenwriting-program commands are impossible to guess, and tricky to find even with the manual. It isn't obvious how to put a parenthesis into a line of dialogue because the left-paren key has been hijacked for the "parenthetical style" command. If you look carefully in the manual, you will discover that a "control-paren" generates a parenthesis in dialogue, but you have to look. You cannot OMIT a scene unless you have locked the script; in Final Draft, you can omit a scene any time you like, and un-omit it right back into the script.

In Final Draft you can display your script full-page, or with page breaks merely marked, or without page breaks at all. Screenwriter only allows you to see your script as formatted for printing.

In Final Draft, it's a snap to do dual-column dialogue (when two characters talk at once) and displays it correctly. Screenwriter will print dual dialogue correctly, but it doesn't display onscreen as dual dialogue, and it's a bit more involved to create it.

The Screenwriter people promise me that the next release of Screenwriter (I'm using 4.8.12) will have a revised user interface that is more Mac-friendly. But I don't completely believe this. Final Draft seems to be constructed as a glorified word processor. So you can, for example, define all sorts of extra style elements. You start with the basics: dialogue, action, parenthetical, scene header, etc. Sometimes that's not enough. I like to create a dialog2 element when I'm writing the subtitles in a bilingual script. Final Draft will do so happily. It will let you create Dialog3, Dialog4, and Dialog5 as well. Screenwriter's architecture seems to be much more based on the specifics of motion picture scripts. It does not think you should have something called Dialog2. The only way to include subtitles is to hijack the script notes element and reformat it as secondary dialogue. Then, of course, you can't have any script notes.

Likewise, Final Draft doesn't have a clue what a tag is, so all you have to do is type TAG and style it as act header and you're ready to go. To start a tag in Screenwriter requires a specific series of commands; it took me five e-mails to tech support to get a new page that started with the word *tag,* centered, all-caps. I couldn't find anything about how to make a tag in the manual. If it's in the manual, it's not indexed, and it can't be found through a regular search. The arcane commands are apparently needed because Screenwriter needs to know how many acts you have, so you have to define your tag properly for the sake of its internal bookkeeping.

Where screenwriter comes into its own is in production. Screenwriter meshes seamlessly with The Write Brothers' other programs, the utterly indispensable Movie Magic Scheduling and Movie Magic Budgeting programs that assistant directors and unit production managers depend on. From my point of view, however, ADs and UPMs are paid well to read scripts and make schedules and budgets; you, the writer, should not feel obliged to use a cranky screenwriting program to make their job a little easier.

Final Draft has had problems with sloppy programming. There were all sorts of minor bugs in Final Draft 6. An early release of Final Draft 7 wouldn't run at all on Mac OS 10.4. Once the bug was patched, I still had one script lose all its formatting; I had to reformat by hand. However, people who have stuck with Final Draft 7 now report that version 7.1.1 is robust and that the problems have been ironed out.

Screenwriter phone support is free; you will probably use it plenty in order to figure out how to use the program. Final Draft phone support costs money, but their e-mail support is free.

Personally, I tried Screenwriter for two scripts, and I'm ready to go back. I do know many writers who have gone from Final Draft to Screenwriter and stayed happily with Screenwriter. I also know many who consider Final Draft to be the best program for Mac and Screenwriter the best for Windows. If you're used to memorizing arcane commands, and want to help out the production team, you may want to choose Screenwriter. If you don't mind the occasional minor glitch, like your programs intuitive, and own a Mac, I'd go with Final Draft.

• APPENDIX 4 •

Scale Payments

The following are the minimum contractual payments allowed under the WGA (Writers Guild of America) 2004 Theatrical and Television Basic Agreement for episodes written for network prime time series (ABC, CBS, Fox, and NBC). The numbers change every year, and nonnetwork channels are allowed to pay slightly less. For the full details, check out the WGA website, www.wga.org.

HALF HOUR

STORY: $6,986
TELEPLAY: $15,031
STORY & TELEPLAY: $20,956

ONE HOUR

STORY: $12,299
TELEPLAY: $20,278
STORY & TELEPLAY: $30,823

The comparable numbers for the WGC (Writers Guild of Canada) are:

Half-hour Story & Teleplay: CDN $6,799
One-hour Story & Teleplay: CDN $13,597

However, the credited writer on any WGC episode is also given a production fee, which is around 2.75 percent of the episode budget, less script fees. On a $1 million episode, this takes the writer's total compensation to CDN $28,325, or slightly over double the Canadian one-hour fee, though about three-quarters of the comparable U.S. fee. Full details at www.wgc.ca.

▪ APPENDIX 5 ▪

Samples

Here are a sample springboard, breakdown, and beat sheet, and a sample act of a one-hour drama script. They're from my writer's draft of episode 1.16 of *Charlie Jade,* a science-fiction drama series. For clarity's sake, I've rewritten the breakdown and beat sheet to match that draft. The real breakdown and beat sheet took some evolution to reach the writer's draft, and if you've seen the episode, you know that there was quite a bit of further evolution from the writer's draft to what was shot, edited, and aired.

Springboard

> Episode 16 "The Shortening of the Way"
>
> Unable to fend off Shikari much longer, Charlie tracks down Jodi again, hoping to learn how to stop his visions. Instead she teaches him how to have them intentionally. He sees multiple versions of himself, each worse than the last, until he finally confronts a nightmare version of himself—but this time he's actually in Nightmare Charlie's universe. Can he survive his confrontation and get back home to Betaverse?

Breakdown

Episode 16 The Shortening of the Way—Breakdown—A Story only

Teaser: Charlie's about to lure Shikari into an ambush. But a vision gets in his way. She nearly kills him. He barely escapes.

Act 1:

Charlie seeks out a Xhosa mystic to help him with his visions. But the guy won't help him: Charlie wants to deny his visions, and that's not the point. Is there anyone else who sees visions like his? Charlie realizes that Jedi Jodi does, and heads off after her.

Out: Shikari, hot on Charlie's trail, meets the mystic.

Act 2:

Charlie convinces Jodi's mum to let him talk to her. But Jodi won't tell him how to stop the visions. "It's like a sneeze," she says. You don't stop them. You let them go.

And with Jodi's help, Charlie has a vision. Of Alphaverse. Where . . .

Out: Essa Rompkin is overseeing the rebuilt Link. "My god. They're rebuilding it!"

Act 3:

Charlie discovers there are more universes than Alpha and Beta. He sees Gamma. And he sees ones we've never seen before. One where someone who looks like Charlie is the sleazoid who runs the Glass Door. One where someone who looks like Charlie is in Karl Galt's chair, ordering Lubinsky to be killed.

And one where a Hitler-like Charlie Jade is looking over the smoking ruins of his universe's Cape Town.

Out: This Charlie Jade *can see him*.

Act 4:

Charlie discovers the depth of this universe's Charlie's madness. The anger Charlie carries around has, in this world, made him a monster. A monster who thinks Charlie is his evil conscience . . . and wants to kill him.

Charlie and the Hitleresque Charlie confront each other over what they have each done. The Hitleresque Charlie knows that our Charlie is not much better than he is. And he wants Charlie to kill him.

Out: Charlie refuses. And steps out of this universe . . .

Tag: Charlie reappears in Betaverse just as Shikari is closing in on Jodi and him. He only has time to say good-bye. He knows where to go now. And Jodi watches as he dematerializes and reappears . . . in another universe. Is it Alphaverse? Tune in next week.

Beat Sheet

EPISODE 16 THE SHORTENING OF THE WAY

Teaser

- WAREHOUSE: Charlie's lured Shikari into an ambush. But the ambush goes awry when he has a vision at the crucial moment. Shikari spots him. Charlie barely gets away alive.
- LUBINSKY'S OFFICE: Charlie tells Lubinsky he's probably a dead man. Urges Lubinsky to get the hell out of town.

Act 1

- LUBINSKY'S OFFICE: Karl suggests Charlie seek out help with his visions. There are people who *try* to achieve visions. Charlie's doubtful. But finally agrees.

- BERGIE ENCAMPMENT: Charlie talks his way past TAKKIES, a big guy who doesn't like strangers.

- LUBINSKY'S OFFICE: Karl packs. There's someone at the door. It's not Shikari, though. It's Reena. But Reena's bad enough. She wants Charlie. Lubinsky tells her Charlie's gone.

- CHARLIE'S OLD LOFT (ALPHAVERSE): Sew Sew brings Jasmine a present. A C-1 insurance policy, encoded in a diamond pendant. It's a huge present—Alphaverse medical care is superb for C-1's. But he's not happy. He's troubled. Those missing Vexcor execs are still nagging at him. Jasmine doesn't understand why he won't drop it and be happy.

- BERGIE ENCAMPMENT: Charlie does a psychedelic ritual with a Bergie mystic, POENTSIES. But Charlie's not interested in a psychedelic vision or spiritual truth. Poentsies asks if anyone else has visions like Charlie's. CUT TO:

- DUNES: And there's Jedi Jodi, watching people in another universe.

- BERGIE ENCAMPMENT: Shikari shows up. Is Charlie still there? No, he's gone. But she finds out from Poentsies where Charlie is headed.

Act 2

- ROAD: Charlie drives out to the desert to find Jedi Jodi.

- LUBINSKY'S OFFICE: Reena's desperate for help to eliminate the "programmed personality" that takes her over from time to time. Lubinsky, against his better judgment, tells her that O1 Boxer might be able to help her. To his surprise, Reena knows him—from Gammaverse.

- DE BEERS'S OFFICE—VEXCOR TOWER (ALPHAVERSE): De Beers is freaking out talking to Cargrath—all the other Alpha execs who ever went to Betaverse have disappeared. He thinks he's next. From her reaction, he realizes that Cargrath knows exactly what happened to them.

- DUNES—DARLENE & JODI'S TRAILER: Charlie talks Darlene into letting him talk to her daughter Jodi.

- ROAD NEAR DUNES: Shikari takes the same road he just took.

- DE BEERS'S OFFICE: De Beers gets summoned to Essa's office. He realizes this might be the end of him. Cargrath tells him to run for it.

- DUNES: Charlie tries to get Jodi to tell him about "the invisible people" (the people in other universes that she can see). She only agrees if he'll tell her about Alphaverse. He discovers she only has visions when she *wants* to.

- NEAR DUNES: Shikari is getting closer and closer.

- DUNES: Jodi shows Charlie how to have a vision. It's like sneezing, she says. You just let it happen. . . .

- DUNES (ALPHAVERSE): Charlie sees Essa! He follows her . . . and sees that the Link is being rebuilt.

Act 3

- DUNES—DARLENE & JODI'S TRAILER: Shikari sees Charlie's car. Knocks out Darlene.

- GLASS DOOR NIGHTCLUB: Reena comes in. She's delighted to see O1. He's surprisingly hostile. And knocks her out.

- SEW SEW'S OFFICE: Sew Sew interrogates De Beers, who's been caught trying to sneak out of the Vexcor Tower. De Beers tells Sew Sew what Essa's doing. Sew Sew's interested—but Essa's secretary terminates the interview by having De Beers escorted upstairs. Now Sew Sew's really troubled. And he has a secret recording of the interrogation.

- GLASS DOOR—DELTAVERSE: Charlie, having visions of the multiverse, is disturbed to see himself—only the Charlie Jade of this universe is a sleazoid O1-style nightclub owner.

- VEXCOR BOARDROOM—EPSILONVERSE: In this universe, Charlie is the Karl Galt of his universe, ordering this universe's Karl Lubinsky away to be tortured. . . .

- DUNES: Charlie wants to know why he keeps seeing himself in these other universes. Jodi doesn't know.

- LUBINSKY'S OFFICE: As Reena's taking a shower, Blues comes in. She spots Reena. Pulls her gun—Reena's a wanted terrorist. Lubinsky convinces her that Reena's one of the good guys.

- DUNES: Jodi's alone, playing with a half-empty bottle of water, when Shikari shows up. Shikari is surprisingly gentle with her.

Shikari follows her footsteps to find two dry footprints in a patch of wet sand—which we know is the hallmark of someone who's traveled between the universes. . . . Not understanding, Shikari runs off.

- VEXCOR BOARDROOM—OMEGAVERSE: Charlie looks down at a city that's been devastated by war. And there's the guy who burned it down: this universe's Charlie Jade. *And this guy can see him.*

Act 4

- VEXCOR BOARDROOM—OMEGAVERSE: This Charlie Jade is dying of his wounds. Charlie does battlefield first aid, probably saving his life. Charlie discovers that this guy led a rebellion against Vexcor that killed everybody. "We had to rebel. So we could be free. . . . I had to destroy the city in order to save it."

- GLASS DOOR: O1's got Reena tied up. He provokes the programmed personality to come out. "If the Link is opened," it tells him, "it will all fall away in the middle." How to stop that from happening? "Find the Three. Urding, Skuldeman, and Verdandi."

- CHARLIE'S OLD LOFT: Sew Sew tells Jasmine what he's learned. Jasmine tells him to leave it alone. Sew Sew throws it back in her face: Doesn't she want to know what happened to Charlie?

- VEXCOR BOARDROOM—OMEGAVERSE: The Charlie Jade of this universe is convinced Charlie's the Angel of Death. He draws his pistol on Charlie. . . .

- GLASS DOOR: O1 tells the programmed personality to "integrate" with Reena's normal personality—or he'll kill them both. She goes nuts. Breaks out of her bonds. And escapes.

- VEXCOR BOARDROOM—OMEGAVERSE: Charlie Jade Omegaverse wants Charlie to execute him for his crimes . . . and goads him to do it. But Charlie, realizing something about himself, and going all Hindu on us for a moment, tells Charlie Jade Omegaverse that suicide won't redeem all the crimes he's done. What if after-death is just another universe where he's the same person. "What if that's all there is, one hell after another, and the same choices to make? Think another bullet's going to help you get it right next time?"And he leaves Charlie Jade Omegaverse to *not* kill himself . . . and steps out of this cursed universe.

Tag

- STREETS: Reena, the two personalities warring in her, staggers through town . . . slowly getting a grip on herself as they integrate.

- DUNES: Charlie returns to Jodi, having learned a lesson. He understands that Jodi sent him to another universe . . . which means he can travel at will (using water, of course). And, just as Shikari returns to find him and finish him off, he has her pour water on him again, and steps out of our universe. . . .

- DUNES—VERSE UNKNOWN: Charlie is . . . where? (Alphaverse, really, but we're not telling till next ep.)

▪ APPENDIX 6 ▪

Script Pages

Title page and Act 4 of the Yellow Production Draft of Charlie Jade, ep. 1.16, "The Shortening of the Way," airdate July 24, 2005, written by Alex Epstein.

```
Executive Producer: Robert Wertheimer
Executive Producer: Chris Roland
Executive Producer: Izidore Codron
Executive Producer: Robin Spry
Executive Producer: Jacques Pettigrew
          Producer: Adam J Shully
          Director: Neal Sundstrom
```

CHARLIE JADE

Episode 16

"The Shortening of the Way"

Written by

Alex Epstein

<u>Green Revisions</u> July 26, 2004
Previous Drafts:
Second Draft 7/05/04
Production Draft 7/19/04
Pink Revisions 7/22/04
Blue Revisions 7/23/04

ACT FOUR

44 INT. VEXCOR BOARDROOM - NIGHT (OMEGA) 44

Charlie stares at Charlie Jade Omega. He looks down: there is no sand on the floor. He really is here. He realizes:

CHARLIE
You're wounded.

CHARLIE JADE OMEGA
Am I?

Charlie Jade Omega is sweating badly, and pasty-faced. He's showing all the symptoms of shock.

Charlie looks around. There's a DEAD GUY slumped in an impressive chair by a desk. [This could be Galt's desk.] Neat bullet hole in his head. The guy is wearing a really nice suit. He could be this universe's Brion Boxer.

Charlie is taken aback by the dead guy. What's going on here?

But at the moment, he's got a combat wound to handle, and it's the only thing that isn't confusing him. He unknots and takes the guy's tie. Grabs a metal letter opener off the desk.

CHARLIE
We gotta get you to a medic.

CHARLIE JADE OMEGA
All the medics are dead. Everyone's dead.

Charlie comes over and starts binding a tourniquet above Charlie Jade Omega's leg wound using the tie and the letter opener. Charlie Jade Omega looks away, out the window, with a thousand yard stare.

CHARLIE JADE OMEGA
It's beautiful, isn't it?

Charlie glances out the window. And what he sees horrifies him.

THE CITY IS A HELL OF FIRE AND SMOKE. Everything's burning. An occasional EXPLOSION lights up a block of buildings, then subsides to smoke and embers.

Charlie stares in horror. He's never seen anything this bad.

CHARLIE JADE OMEGA
We had to rebel against them. So we could be free.

CHARLIE
Against who?

Charlie Jade Omega gestures around at the boardroom. At the dead guy in the chair.

CHARLIE JADE OMEGA
Him. His company. He wanted to control everything. So we had to fight him. I had to.

Charlie looks at him with a new sense of horror.

CHARLIE
You did this?

CHARLIE JADE OMEGA
I had no choice.

Charlie Jade Omega looks wistfully down at the city.

CHARLIE JADE OMEGA
I had to destroy the city in order to save it.

An explosion from the city below illuminates the two men in orange firelight. Charlie stares at Charlie Jade Omega with growing horror, realizing what he's done.

CUT TO:

45 INT. THE GLASS DOOR - DAY (BETA) 45

Reena is bound to a chair. The body language -- restricted as it is -- tells us this isn't sweet, victimized, human-pinata Reena. This is BAD REENA. [BAD REENA DOES NOT TALK LIKE A ROBOT. BUT SHE IS A PERSONALITY STRIPPED OF ALL HUMANITY - A PERSONALITY WITHOUT PERSONALITY. Her intonation lacks flavor and lilt. Everything is expressed evenly. As before, her voice is lower, spookier.]

01
So... one more time. Who am I speaking to?

BAD REENA
I was not named. I only exist to perform the task.

01
Okay. Then who put you there?

BAD REENA
You do not know them. But they know you.

01
Okay. Bored now. Boxer. Oh-eight-seven-theta-four-nine execute.
(she doesn't react)
Boxer. Oh-eight-seven-theta---

BAD REENA
--You will not control me with words.

01
Okay. So you're not a Vexcor job. Fascinating, Captain.

BAD REENA
Release me. I will execute the design.

01
Which is?

BAD REENA
If the Link is opened, it will all fall away in the middle. I cannot allow this to happen.

01
Krogg said that. This universe is toast.

BAD REENA
If the Link is opened, it will all fall away.

01
So. I blow up the link. Vexcor rebuilds it. Lather. Rinse. Repeat.

CJ "The Shortening of the Way" 7/26/04 Yellow Draft p. 40.

BAD REENA
There are only three left who can rebuild it. Find the three.

01
What's their names?

BAD REENA
Urding, Skuldeman and Verdandi.

01 cocks his head at Reena thoughtfully.

CUT TO:

46 INT. CHARLIE'S LOFT - NIGHT (ALPHA) 46

Sew Sew comes in. Jasmine is wearing a long silk dressing gown. She's all ready to welcome him home. But after he throws the locks, he turns -- he looks exhausted.

She comes to him, worried. Helps him take off his coat.

SEW SEW
A man told me some things today ... about the missing people. Vexcor--

JASMINE
(she's upset now)
--Your company.

SEW SEW
People were taken to Essa, they didn't come back. People who've been... "over there," he said.

JASMINE
Let it go.

SEW SEW
The mystery gets deeper and deeper.

JASMINE
I can't lose you, too.

She's scared. And she's scared of losing him.

SEW SEW
I have to know.

Sew Sew looks deep into her eyes. He loves her ... but how can he leave the truth alone?

SEW SEW
Don't you want to know where they went? Don't you want to know what happened to Charlie?

She turns away, confused, troubled. In turmoil.

Sew Sew looks at her -- Charlie's girl. At Charlie's apartment. Wondering what he's risking.

47 EXT. VEXCOR BOARDROOM - NIGHT (OMEGA) 47

Charlie's reeling. He looks out at the dark city. Another o.s. fire-orange explosion lights the ceiling.

CHARLIE
You grew up down there, didn't you?

CHARLIE JADE OMEGA
You have to be willing to sacrifice to accomplish great things.

And Charlie Jade Omega is, for a moment, stricken with grief. Charlie stares at him, torn between horror and sympathy.

CHARLIE JADE OMEGA
They were winning. I had to. There was no other way!

Charlie just looks at him. What can he say to that. And Charlie Jade Omega sees the accusation in his eyes.

Charlie Jade Omega reaches out. Touches Charlie's face, as if testing to see if he's solid.

CHARLIE JADE OMEGA
I was afraid you'd come.

CHARLIE
Why? Who do you think I am?

CHARLIE JADE OMEGA
You're the Angel of Death. Aren't you?

And he draws his pistol. Off Charlie's alarm, we--

CUT TO:

48 INT. GLASS DOOR - DAY (BETA) 48

At the bar, 01 swigs down a shot of whisky.

01 (CONT'D)
Okay. Maybe I was wrong. I liked the old Reena better. Better conversationalist. Why don't you get out of her and leave her alone.

BAD REENA
The program must survive.

01
Good. Because if you don't get out of there...

-- 01 pulls a BIG ASS KNIFE and comes over.

01
Lotta people have died in this club. I call the service one more time, cleanup's free. I got a card and everything.

BAD REENA
No. Our goal is the same. You need what I know.

01
But what I don't need is <u>you,</u> hanging around in Reena's head. See, she and I are family. If she's got something, I want it. So if you want the program to survive, you're just gonna have to give her the keys to the program.

And he holds the knife to her carotid artery.

01
Integrate. Or die.

Bad Reena strains at her bonds. He hits her in the forehead with his palm.

01
Integrate.

CJ "The Shortening of the Way" 7/26/04 Yellow Draft p. 43.

BAD REENA
Inadvisable.

01
Not asking your advice.

Bad Reena nods. Closes her eyes. And... begins to writhe in the chair. She starts to choke and wheeze. 01's shocked.

Her eyes snap open. She is shocked as ACROSS THE SURFACE OF HER EYES seem to play a million images.

It only takes a second. Then Reena sags, spent. 01 staggers to the bar and pours a drink.

01 (CONT'D)
And that, kids, is how we do that.

A beat as he downs the shot. Then from behind:

A CRASH. He turns, to find...

Reena, smashing the chair to bits and flinging the ropes off her. She stares at him, a wild, cornered beast--

He tries to go to her. She flings a chair leg at him. He ducks. She runs out. 01 doesn't try to follow.

CUT TO:

49 INT. VEXCOR BOARDROOM - NIGHT (OMEGA) 49

Charlie backs away from the gun. He eyes the WATERFALL in a corner of the room.

CHARLIE
I'm not any kind of angel. I'm just a guy from another universe. I just look like you.

FLASHFRAME: Poentsies laughs.

And Charlie Jade Omega flips the gun around in his hand so the grip is pointed at Charlie:

CHARLIE JADE OMEGA
You're here for a reason.

Charlie takes the gun. Aims it at Charlie Jade Omega.

CHARLIE
(almost persuading himself)
You have definitely got this coming.

But he can't bring himself to pull the trigger.

CHARLIE JADE OMEGA
What are you waiting for?

Charlie shakes his head.

CHARLIE JADE OMEGA
I've tortured people. I've killed women and children. ... I've let the ones I love die.

And Charlie, to his horror, knows he's guilty of the same things. He lowers the gun.

CHARLIE JADE OMEGA
Why don't you pull the trigger? ... Are you a coward? Go on! Who are you? I'm a monster! Destroy me!

But Charlie just tosses the gun onto the floor. There's been enough killing.

Charlie Jade Omega scoops it up. Stands up. Aims it at his own head.

CHARLIE
Stop! Wait! ... What's going to happen when you pull that trigger? You think the pain's gonna go away?

CHARLIE JADE OMEGA
It'll all be over.

CHARLIE
Will it? Not for the people out there. Some of them are probably alive. They're still suffering.

CHARLIE JADE OMEGA
Because of what I did.

CHARLIE
Exactly. What gives you the right to check out now? You owe. You owe big.

CJ "The Shortening of the Way" 7/26/04 Yellow Draft p. 45.

CHARLIE JADE OMEGA
(re: out the window)
There's no paying back for <u>that</u>.

CHARLIE
Oh yeah? Too bad.

Charlie Jade Omega cocks the hammer on the gun.

CHARLIE
What's going to happen if you end it here, huh? You think it's all over? What if it's just another universe where you're you again?

Charlie Jade Omega's shaken.

CHARLIE
And you kill more people, and you still see them every night, every time you close your eyes?

Charlie Jade Omega's shaking.

CHARLIE
What if that's all there is, one hell after another, and the same choices to make? Think another bullet's going to help you get it right next time?

Charlie Jade Omega wavers. And slumps.

CHARLIE JADE OMEGA
Help me then.

CHARLIE
I can't.

CHARLIE JADE OMEGA
Please.

CHARLIE
You've got to pay for your sins. I've got to pay for mine.

He strides over to the waterfall. Plunges his hands into the water.

Charlie Jade begins to shudder. And maybe he's in tears by now. Or maybe he's just so, so very tired.

He looks up to say something but...

CJ "The Shortening of the Way" 7/26/04 Yellow Draft p. 45A.

... Charlie's gone. All that's left is a puddle on the floor next to the waterfall.

50 MONTAGE 50

An infinity of backgrounds ... all the different universes we can represent... till we:

<u>END ACT FOUR</u>

CJ "The Shortening of the Way" 7/26/04 Yellow Draft p. 46.

TAG

50A EXT. STREET - DAY (BETA) 50A

Reena staggers in the sunlight, her mind whirling, disoriented, lost ... and yet not entirely overwhelmed. She's getting a grip on herself.

51 EXT. DESERT - DAY (BETA) 51

Charlie slams down onto the sand. Jody runs over to him. He's in shock: he just traveled between universes!

JODY
You're back!

Charlie eyes the half empty water bottle. Realizes:

CHARLIE
Did you ... pour water on me?

FLASHBACK: Jody pours water on Charlie. He SHIMMERS OUT.

JODY
If I'd told you I was going to, you would've thought about it too hard. You can't think about it too hard if you want to go for a visit.

CHARLIE
Is that what you call it? A visit?

JODY
I used to go for visits when I was young. But my mum doesn't like it. So now I just watch. If you don't use water, all you can do is watch.

CHARLIE
I saw some ... pretty strange places.

JODY
I know. I don't like them.

CHARLIE
I was ... different ... in them.

CJ "The Shortening of the Way" 7/26/04 Yellow Draft p. 47.

JODY
There's a woman looking for you.

CHARLIE
A police woman?

JODY
No. A black woman.

Charlie's alarmed. Stands up, looks around. Is there any place to hide? Doesn't look like it. He looks at Jody. Is she in danger?

JODY
She was perfectly nice to me.

Charlie looks at her half-empty bottle of water. He takes the bottle. Steps away from Jody so she's not in the line of fire. Raises the bottle over his head.

As Shikari comes over the rise of the next dune:

JODY
Are you going on a visit?

CHARLIE
No...

Shikari pulls a gun, bursts into a run, as--

Charlie lets the water drip down over his head.

CHARLIE
I'm going home.

Shikari FIRES as she runs towards him--

But Charlie's already gone. Leaving only WET SAND.

Shikari arrives at Jody's side. Looks around. She can see no sign of Charlie.

She looks down at Jody. Jody's shaken. Confused. Shocked.

Absently, reassuringly, Shikari brushes some hair out of Jody's eyes. She's trying to process what she just saw. Confused. Frustrated.

She walks off. Jody watches her go.

OMITTED (MOVED TO 50A) 52

CJ "The Shortening of the Way" 7/26/04 Yellow Draft p. 48.

53 EXT. DUNE - DAY (BETA) 53

Darlene gets up from near the truck. Her head hurts. She looks up to see Jody coming down from the dunes.

Relieved beyond belief, Darlene runs like hell towards her daughter.

Jody just watches her come on, upset by the confrontation she just saw.

CUT TO:

53A INT. VEXCOR BOARDROOM - NIGHT (OMEGA) 53A

Charlie Jade Omega stands looking sadly out at the burning city. He tosses the gun to the floor, in almost the exact way Charlie did earlier.

CUT TO:

54 EXT. DUNES - DAY (VERSE UNKNOWN) 54

TIGHT ON CHARLIE. Looking around. Amazed. We do not see where he is.

END OF EPISODE

Glossary

A story: The most important story in an episode, which takes up the most screen time.

act: Everything between two commercials.

act out: A cliffhanger or emotional whammy that happens just before the show cuts to a commercial, so the audience will stay tuned in to the show. "We make our money on teasers, tags, and outs."

action: Everything that happens that isn't people talking.

attractive fantasy: A life situation in which the main character of a series finds him- or herself that we'd like to be in. Part of the template.

B story: The second most important story in an episode, which takes up a medium amount of screen time.

baby writer: A writer without a lot of professional experience, regardless how old.

backstory: A character's personal history before the episode or series begins its onscreen chronology.

beat: A unit of storytelling, in which one significant thing happens.

beat sheet: The whole story of an episode told beat by beat, in order.

bible: A document that theoretically tells you everything you need to know about the show in order to write it, and practically almost never does.

bit: A series of related jokes.

blacks: The action description. So called because it makes big nasty chunks of black text on the page, while dialogue is nice and sparse.

bottle show: An episode that takes place in a physically restricted set using a limited cast, or takes place only on the standing sets using only the series regulars, to save time and money.

breakdown: A brief sketch of the episode's stories, showing acts and act outs, teaser and tag.

breaking story: Finding the acts and act outs in a story, often done in the writing room by the writing staff.

breaking the frame: Drawing attention to the fact that the events are taking place on a TV show, not in real life.

bumping: Being annoyed by a plothole. "I'm bumping on how they got to the transporter device." "*That's* what you're bumping on???"

button: A particularly neat bit of dialogue (a single line or a couplet) that ends a scene sharply. Also used as a verb: "That buttons the scene rather nicely, doesn't it?"

C story: The third most important story in an episode, which takes little screen time.

callback: Dialogue that refers to earlier dialogue, often twisting its meaning into something new.

character-based: A drama in which the stories arise primarily from conflicts between the characters. All comedies are character based.

civilian: someone who does not work in show business.

clip show: An episode that relies on lots of footage from previous episodes. Used to save money or, more often, time. Naughty, naughty, naughty.

co-executive producer: Courtesy title given to indicate a writer-producer who ranks just below an executive producer.

co-producer: Courtesy title given to a veteran story editor who ranks below a producer but above an executive story editor.

comedy: Anything that is supposed to be consistently funny.

comic drama: A subgenre in which the story structure and stakes are dramatic but the situations and dialogue may be played for laughs. Usually single camera.

core cast: The characters who are supposed to be in every episode.

couplet: Two lines of dialogue in a row, in which one character's line answers the previous line. "How do you sleep at night?" "I don't." A couplet that neatly ends a scene is called a *button*.

demographics: What sort of folks watch the show.

dialogue: Characters talking.

dopplering: Describes the sound of a car passing by offscreen.

draft: A version of a script. Defined in the standard Guild contract, but more flexible in real life.

drama (1): A TV series that isn't comedy or reality. Usually one hour.

drama (2): What happens when two people come into physical, emotional, or moral conflict.

drama (3): A TV show genre about characters going through emotional issues.

dramedy: A comic drama. No one uses this term seriously anymore, so just forget it. Not to be confused with *dromedary*, which is a perfectly fine word for a camel with two humps.

echo: Repeating a line we've heard before in the episode.

ep: An episode. No one can be bothered to write the word *episode* over and over again.

episodic: Describes a show in which nothing that happens on one episode significantly impacts later episodes; compare to *serial.*

executive producer: The top title on a show. Traditionally given to the showrunner, but not exclusively so.

executive story editor: Title that indicates a veteran story editor who outranks story editors but ranks below writer-producers.

expo: Exposition, that is, when a character explains stuff the audience needs to know. "So how does this machine work, exactly?"

freelancer: A writer who is hired on a per-script basis.

gilding the matzoh: Belaboring a joke to where it's not funny anymore.

go out on: To end an act (or scene) with a certain moment. "Let's go out on Jasmine deciding whether to kill him or not."

going to pages: Writing the script.

Guild: The Writers Guild of America or the Writers Guild of Canada. Your first line of defense against producers messing with your credit or money. (Nothing prevents producers from messing with your words.)

hand waving: Story material that sounds great in a beat sheet or treatment due to the writer's clever prose, but leaves major story issues unresolved. Hand waving will cause pain to whatever poor bastard actually has to write the pages.

hang a lantern on: To draw attention to a story element so the audience doesn't miss it; also called *hanging a sign on.*

head writer: The highest-ranked writer below the showrunner. May have a title of anything from executive story editor to co-executive producer depending on the structure and size of the writing staff.

hook: A series premise that makes people want to tune in to watch at least one episode.

Joss: The dark god of writers. Black lambs are slaughtered to him at the new moon.

laying pipe: Giving technical information now so we'll know it later when a story point turns on it.

like-a-joke: A comic bit that has the rhythms of a joke, and is followed by laughter on the soundtrack, but is not actually funny.

the long term: Three weeks from now.

make a moment: Drawing attention to the moment in which a character is saying or deciding something important.

negative fantasy: A life situation in which the star of a series finds him- or herself that we're glad we're not in. Part of the template.

on the nose: Dialogue that says exactly what the character means. Characters should usually avoid speaking on the nose.

out: An act out.

pages: The script.

pass: A writer's pass through a script, writing or rewriting it. A draft may represent several passes by one or more writers. "Pass" suggests that the current version will likely be critiqued and/or story-edited before anyone outside the writing room sees it. "Draft" implies it's being shown to nonwriters. Freelancers are only supposed to do two drafts, but nothing limits how many passes they do before they show their work to anyone.

plothole: A logical flaw in the story.

point-of-view (POV) character: A character through whose perspective the story is told, whether the hero or not.

pop: When a scene ends with a bang that propels you into the next scene.

premise pilot: A pilot episode that shows how the core cast first got together or how the basic situation first arose.

procedural: A drama in which external events provide the stories. Medical, law, and police shows are typical procedurals.

producer (1): A courtesy title given to veteran story editors.

producer (2): A salesman who sells a package of some creative material and some talent to organizations with money, such as networks and studios.

pushing: Giving the audience story faster than they can absorb.

reality show: A show that pretends not to have a script, in order to avoid paying the writers *scale*. The WGA is addressing this issue.

recurring cast: Characters who reappear in the series without being core cast.

room: The writing room. The magic place where the writing staff break story. One of the best places in the world to be, if you're a writer. Nonwriters in the room usually kill the magic.

runner: A recurring bit of action, like a running gag, not necessarily containing all the elements of a story, and therefore not a C or D story.

scale: The minimum payment allowed for a piece of writing under a Guild contract.

schmuck bait: A promised story turn that only a schmuck would believe will ever actually happen, like the hero dying or, in a science-fiction show, the hero dying permanently.

script timing: The process of estimating how long an episode will play onscreen.

segue: How you move from one scene to another. Sometimes misspelled "segway," which is the brand name of a sort of scooter that balances itself on two big wheels.

serial: A show in which the plot develops from episode to episode; compare *episodic*.

series regulars: The actors who are contracted by season rather than by episode.

serving a character: Giving a character something to do in an episode or scene.

shoe leather: Dialogue or action that exists purely to fill in a plothole.

showrunner: The person responsible for all creative aspects of the show. Everyone on the crew is responsible to the showrunner; he is responsible only to the network (and the production company, if it's not his production company). Usually a writer. The writer's job is not to make a good TV show; that's his job. The writer's job is to make the showrunner's life easier.

single camera: Any show shot using a single camera, rather than three at once.

sitcom: A half-hour comedy, often three-camera, usually one, that tries to provide three laughs a minute and exists solely for the sake of the humor.

soap: A character-based drama with a serial plotline. Not necessarily an actual daytime soap opera.

soapy: Describes a show with serial plot elements.

spec pilot: A sample episode of a nonexistent series, written either to showcase your originality or actually to sell the show to a network.

spec script: An episode of an existing series written to showcase your writing skills and get you a job, not intended to actually be sold or produced, though that has happened often enough to give some people false hope.

springboard: An episode idea in a nutshell.

staff writer: A freelancer who works in the office writing his or her own scripts.

staffing season: The part of the year in which writing staffs are hired, roughly March–May.

standing sets: Studio sets that stay up all season. Cheap to shoot in. Scenes that take place on standing sets make production managers happy.

story editor: A writer who works on staff, writing his or her own scripts, breaking story, and rewriting other people's scripts.

subtitles for the nuance impaired: Prose inserted into a treatment or into the action description in a script to make sure the reader gets the point. Only considered bad writing if the audience won't get the point, either. The reasons the audience might understand something the reader doesn't include *directing, acting, cinematography, editing,* and *music.*

tag: The scene or scenes that appear after the last commercial to tie up any loose ends or, alternately, to untie one loose end so the story can continue next week.

taking the curse off: Making a story point not feel like a cliché without changing the story point itself.

teaser: The scene or scenes that appear before the titles and the first commercial, to "tease" the audience into watching the episode. Normally sets up the episode story but doesn't have to.

telegraphing: Giving the audience too heavy a hint where the story will go.

template: The deep structure of a TV show. The template encompasses all the things that every episode in the series must do.

templing: When a character puts his fingers together thoughtfully, forming a temple.

three-camera: Series shot on a soundstage with three cameras constantly recording the action. Three-camera series are often shot in two performances on a single day, as opposed to single-camera.

tracking: Following a character's personal story line to make sure it makes sense by itself. "Josh's story doesn't track."

treatment: A beat sheet expanded and polished for delivery to people who haven't heard the verbal pitch, such as network executives. Often contains subtitles for the nuance impaired.

two-hander: A dialogue scene between two characters. Production managers love these.

writer: A godlike man or woman, worthy of worship and offers of marriage, fantastic in bed, whose every fault is simply adorable.

Notes

Chapter 1: The Hidden Structure of a TV Series

1. Robert William Kubey, ed., *Creating Television* (Mahwah, N.J.: Lawrence Erlbaum Associates Publishers, 2003), p. 103.

2. Al Jean et al., *Writing for Episodic TV,* http://www.wga.org/subpage_writersresources.aspx?id=156.

3. Popgurls interview, www.popgurls.com/article_show.php3?id=538.

4. Conversation with Terry Rossio, blog.myspace.com/terryrossio, August 12, 2005.

5. *Friends* 7.24, "The One with Monica and Chandler's Wedding, Part 2."

6. *On Writing #18,* https://wgaeast.org/newsletter_and_publications/pdf/onwriting18.pdf.

7. leegoldberg.typepad.com/a_writers_life/2005/03/proving_that_tv.html.

8. *The Economist,* April 11, 2002, "All in the Family"; see www.economist.com/surveys/displayStory.cfm?Story_id=1066632.

9. "Our Ratings, Ourselves," *New York Times Magazine*, April 10, 2005.

10. leegoldberg.typepad.com/a_writers_life/2005/03/proving_that_tv.html.

Chapter 2: Great Episode Ideas

1. Interview by Alan Waldman, www.wga.org/craft/interviews/abrams-benson.html.

2. Popgurls interview, www.popgurls.com/article_show.php3?id=538.

3. Robert William Kubey, ed., *Creating Television* (Mahwah, N.J.: Lawrence Erlbaum Associates Publishers, 2003), p. 168.

4. Interview by Alan Waldman, www.wga.org/craft/interviews/zuiker.html.

Chapter 3: Writing the Script

1. Robert William Kubey, ed., *Creating Television* (Mahwah, N.J.: Lawrence Erlbaum Associates Publishers, 2003), p. 168.

2. Thanks to John Rogers, kfmonkey.blogspot.com/2005/04/writing-jargon-preservation-2.html.

3. See the ZAZ rules of comedy, artfulwriter.com/archives/2005/04/zaz_part_ ii_the.html.

4. *On Writing #4,* p. 8.

5. WGA website interview, www.wga.org/craft/intervies/zuiker.html.

Chapter 4: Bad Writing and How to Fix It

1. Comment on my blog, complicationsensue.blogspot.com/2005/04/spec-conundrum.html.

2. kfmonkey.blogspot.com/2005/04/writing-jargon-preservation-4.html.

Chapter 5: Bringing the Funny

1. Aristotle, *Poetics*, Book II, "On Comedy."

2. Interview by Alan Waldman, www.wga.org/craft/interviews/kevin-bleyer.html.

3. Comment on my blog, complicationsensue.blogspot.com.

Chapter 6: Preparing to Be a TV Writer

1. kfmonkey.blogspot.com/2005/04/writing-jargon-preservation.html.

2. E-mail to author.

3. leegoldberg.typepad.com/a_writers_life/2005/03/usc_or_nyu.html.

4. Interview by Laurie Kilmartin, *Tough Crowd with Colin Quinn.*

Chapter 7: Breaking In

1. insidetv.blogspot.com. I know who this writer is, but since she chooses to keep her identity a secret, so will I. In fact, she's since removed the blog!
2. Interview by Lee Goldberg, leegoldberg.typepad.com/a_writers_life/2005/04/ qa_with_chris_a.html.
3. Interview by author.
4. paulguyot.blogs.com/inkslinger/2005/06/anatomy_of_a_pi.html.
5. leegoldberg.typepad.com/a_writers_life/2005/03/what_does_a_wri.html.
6. johnaugust.com/archives/2003/finding-assistant-gigs.
7. Interview by Alan Waldman, www.wga.org/craft/interviews/abrams-benson.html.
8. Interview by Alan Waldman, www.wga.org/craft/interviews/crittenden.html.

Chapter 8: Getting Hired

1. WGA interview, www.wga.org/craft/pitch.html.
2. Interview by Lee Goldberg, leegoldberg.typepad.com/a_writers_life/2005/04/ qa_with_chris_a.html.
3. Anthony Zuiker, WGA interview, www.wga.org/craft/interviews/zuiker.html.
4. WGA interview, www.wga.org/craft/interviews/cassidy.html.
5. Chris Abbott, interview with Lee Goldberg, leegoldberg.typepad.com/a_writers_life/2005/04/qa_with_chris_a.html.
6. "The Grand Acquisitors," *New York Review of Books,* April 7, 2005.

Chapter 9: Moving Up the Food Chain

1. Interview by Alan Waldman, www.wga.org/craft/interviews/abrams-benson.html.
2. *On Writing #18*, p. 7.
3. www.infocusmag.com/05augustseptember/whedonuncut.htm.

Chapter 10: The Holy Grail: Creating Your Own Show

1. *On Writing #4*, p. 10.
2. Robert William Kubey, ed., *Creating Television* (Mahwah, N.J.: Lawrence Erlbaum Associates Publishers, 2003), p. 277.
3. WGA interview, www.wga.org/craft/interviews/cassidy.html.
4. "There's No Such Thing As Writer's Block in TV," interview by Dylan Callaghan, www.wga.org/craft/interviews/lowry.html.

Index

Abbott, Chris, 16, 53, 56, 89, 112, 125, 154, 202, 213, 216, 219, 220, 227, 228, 231, 245, 246, 251
ABC, 72, 192
Abrams, J. J., 169
Abrams, Marc, 53, 225
act break, 65
action, 98–99, 104–7
actors, 233, 235–36
act outs, 67–74
  finding, 73–74
Addams Family, The, 42, 44
Agency, The, 250
agent, 114, 177, 183, 185, 245
  contracts, 198–99
  getting an, 195–200
  working for, 176–79
Alias, 8, 22, 68, 77, 124, 126, 127, 169, 190, 256, 263
Allen, Tim, 10
Allen, Woody, 151–52
All in the Family, 13, 73
All My Children, 17
Alpern, Jeff, 183, 185, 188, 190, 244
Amazing Race, The, 23, 44, 50, 167
American Idol, 8, 66, 88, 167
America's Next Top Model, 5, 17, 88
American Zoetrope Screenplay Contest, 181
Anderson, Pamela, 10
Andy Griffith Show, The, 42
Angel, 7, 27, 180, 259
Aniston, Jennifer, 11, 149
antagonist, 43, 44
anthology show, 15
Apprentice, The, 4, 13, 46, 167
Arrested Development, 73, 187
assistant, writer's, 203–7
A story, 63, 74, 79, 83, 84
attractive fantasy, 11–14
August, John, 205
awards and competitions, 180–82, 273–74
Azaria, Hank, 127

Babylon 5, 30, 57, 260
back door, 203–7
backstory, 25, 26
bad story ideas, 56–62

bad writing, 111–41, 178
  communicating without dialogue and, 138–40
  flavors of, 119–20
  geography and, 123–25
  go-tos, 133–36
  offscreen story and, 130–33
  point of view, 136–38
  pulling vs. pushing, 120–23
  rewriting, 119–41
  suspension of disbelief and, 125–30
  taking criticism, 116–19
Barr, Roseanne, 9–10
Basen, Leila, 56, 97, 170, 171, 221
Battlebots, 5, 66
Battlestar Galactica, 265
Baywatch, 57
beat sheet, 77–81, 219–20
  sample, 283–87
Beckner, Michael, 250, 251
Benny, Jack, 152
Benson, Michael, 205
Bernie Mac Show, The, 53
Beverly Hills 90210, 13, 19
Bewitched, 46
bible, 38–40, 54, 249
Big Brother, 8, 265
Big Wolf on Campus, 52
Bleyer, Kevin, 147
Blind Justice, 168
block shooting, 32
Boston Legal, 144
bottle show, 210–11
breakdown, 70
  sample, 282–83
breaking in, 3, 195–207
  back-door strategies, 203–7
  getting an agent, 195–200
  move to Los Angeles, 200–203
  staffing season, 199–200
  as writer's assistant, 203–7
breaking story, 70, 74–76
Bruckheimer, Jerry, 251
B story, 63, 74, 79, 83, 84
Buffy the Vampire Slayer, 9, 13, 31, 43, 44, 47, 50, 58, 103, 180, 185, 231, 254, 258, 260
button, 94, 99, 146

CAA, 185, 196, 197, 251
cable television, xvii, 66, 71, 72. *See also specific shows*
callback, 99
Canada, 115, 175, 201, 206–7, 254
Canadian Film Centre, 175
Carey, Drew, 162
Carlin, George, 152
Carter, Chris, 62
cartoons, 124, 143, 144
Caruso, David, 19
Cassidy, Shaun, 215, 250
CBS, 36
characters, 14–28, 43, 233, 258–61
  betrayed, 61
  comedy, 14–15, 19, 25–27, 151–55
  core cast, 21–23
  creating your own show, 258–61
  don't change, 24–27
  lead, 18–20
  point-of-view, 20–21
  recurring, 27–28
  relationships, 23–24
  science-fiction, 260–61
  springboard, 43–64
  triangles, 259
  weaknesses and strengths, 46–50
Charlie Jade, 35, 49, 69
Charmed, 18, 54
Cheers, 11, 19, 29, 45, 46, 47, 73, 131
Chehak, Tom, 20, 167, 250

Cherry, Marc, 254
Chico and the Man, 19
China Beach, 6, 131–32
cliffhangers, 67–68
clothes, 76–77
comedy, xviii, 6, 9–10, 14, 67, 94, 142–63
  arcane jokes, 158–59
  bric-a-brac joke, 156–57
  characters, 14–15, 19, 25–27, 151–55
  commitment, 147
  confusion, 150–51
  don't break the frame, 155
  funny word last, 146
  great premises, 144–45
  hook, 9–10
  juxtaposition, 147–51
  learning to be funny, 162
  overwriting, 160–61
  pauses, 153–55
  plausible surprise, 145–46
  point of view, 136–37
  production costs, 28
  Squiggy, 149–50
  stand-up, 162–63
  structure, 72–73
  two jokes at once, 156
  types of, 143–44
  underwriting, 159–60
  up and back, 157–58
  writing, 142–63
  See also sitcoms; *specific shows*
commercials, 35, 71, 72, 169
communicating without dialogue, 138–40
competition, 167–69
competitions and awards, 180–82, 273–74
complications ensue, 264
confusion, 150–51
consistency, 4–7
contests and fellowships, 180–82, 273–74
contracts and drafts, 115–16
cop shows, 45, 57, 126–27, 169, 261. *See also specific shows*
core cast, 21–23
Corner Gas, 159
Cosby, Bill, 162, 249
Cosby Show, The, 15, 19, 93, 98, 249
Coupling, 64, 73, 143–44
Cox, Courtney, 149
Crane, David, 11
creating your own show, 248–68
  characters, 258–61
  coming up with a TV show, 257–68
  hooks, 261–64
  new formats, 264–65
  spec pilots, 251–54
crime shows, 54. *See also specific shows*
criticism, taking, 116–19, 188–90, 216
Crittendon, Jennifer, 207
crossover episodes, 187–88, 210
CSI, 4, 5, 6, 14, 21, 47, 57, 87, 103, 126, 145, 168, 169, 183, 185, 190, 262
C story, 63, 79, 83
Curb Your Enthusiasm, 19, 167
Curse of the Pilot, 256

Daily Show, The, 133
Dallas, 12, 16, 33, 168
Dangerfield, Rodney, 152
David, Larry, 19, 57, 68
Dawson's Creek, 33, 42, 44, 103
deadlines, 218, 225–26, 238, 239
Deadwood, 261, 265
De Grassi Jr. High, 30
demographics, 36–38
Dennis Miller Live, 159
Depp, Johnny, 24

Desperate Housewives, 21, 22, 53, 91, 139, 145, 168, 254, 263
detective stories, 120–21, 123
Diagnosis Murder, 20, 26
dialogue, 101–4
  communicating without, 138–41
Dick Van Dyke Show, The, 17
directors, 233–34, 235, 266
disgust comedy, 143
Disney, 36
Disney Fellowship, 181
Dr. Quinn, Medicine Woman, 262–63
Dr. Vegas, 10
draft, 115–16, 172, 222, 229–30, 241–42
  first, 111, 112, 115, 121, 222, 229
  rewriting, 111–19, 229–30
  staff writing, 229–30, 241–42
Dragnet, 79
drama, xix, 14, 67, 70, 81, 121, 145, 152, 192
  acts, 70–71
  characters, 27
  hook, 10
  See also specific shows
Dukes of Hazzard, The, 260
DVDs, 7, 35, 168, 180

echo, 99
ego, writer's, 236, 237
Eight Simple Rules for Dating My Teenage Daughter, 132
embarrassment comedy, 143
emotional connection, 60–61, 95
Entourage, 184
episodes, 33–35
  crossover, 187–88, 210
  great ideas for, 41–64
  pilot, 255–57
  springboard, 41–64
ER, 6, 12, 31, 76, 169
Eriksen, Shelley, 69, 96
Estrin, Eric, 209
Everwood, 33, 48, 90
Everybody Hates Chris, 13
Everybody Loves Raymond, 10, 73, 124, 144, 154
executive producer, 224, 225, 227, 228, 250
expectations, tracking, 86–92

family life, having a, 246, 247
fantasy, 11–14, 260–261, 262
Farrell, Mark, 145, 159
fear comedy, 144
feedback, 116–19, 188–89, 190, 216
Felicity, 17, 169, 260
Ferris Bueller's Day Off, 11
15/Love, 132
film schools and classes, 173–76
Final Draft, 192, 193, 194, 204, 275–77
Firefly, 7, 34, 48, 55, 56, 180, 183, 263
first blurt, 161
first draft, 111, 112, 115, 121, 222, 229
First Writer's Draft, 222, 229
flashbacks, 139
flip cut, 94
Ford, Harrison, 104
4400, The, 48
Frasier, 153, 260
freelance script, 217–22, 223, 224, 228, 229–30
  multiple freelance jobs, 221–22
  writing, 217–21
Fresh Prince of Bel Air, The, 13
Friends, 11, 19, 22, 24, 25–27, 29, 34, 46, 62, 73, 123, 133, 148–49, 150, 153, 154–55, 258
frustration comedy, 144
Fugitive, The, 8, 264
FX, xvii

"gang banging" a script, 226
Garner, Jennifer, 190
genres. *See specific genres and shows*
geography, 123–25
Gersh, 196
getting fired, 243–47
Gilmore Girls, 79, 99, 103, 158, 185, 259
Global Frequency, 93
goal, 43, 44
Goldberg, Lee, 26, 39, 57, 179, 203
Golden Girls, 205
go-tos, 133–36
Grey's Anatomy, 139, 169, 256
Grillo-Marxuach, Javier, 18, 54
Guyot, Paul, 53, 116, 130, 203, 227

Hall, Barbara, 16
hanging a lantern, 94, 106
Happy Days, 12, 45
Harper, Valerie, 19
HBO, xvii, 66
Here and Now, 205
Herman's Head, 127
Hill Street Blues, 4, 76
"hip pocket" client, 198
hiring, 208–22
  back-door strategies, 203–7
  freelance script and, 217–22
  getting hired, 208–22
  story pitch and, 208–17
Hollywood Reporter, The, 196
Hollywood Representation Directory, 198
Home Improvement, 10
Homicide, 4, 11, 12, 58, 126, 169, 261
Honeymooners, The, 30, 168
hook, 8–11, 261–64
  creating your own show and, 261–64
  new, 261–64
House, 72
Hsu, Melinda, 52, 55, 180, 181, 184, 189, 226
Huff, 252
Hunger, The, 15
Hunter, Lew, 173

ICM, 185, 196, 251
idiot stick, 127
I Love Lucy, 4, 5, 22, 23, 46, 62, 73, 143, 168, 187
industry, television, 165–268
  breaking in, 195–207
  creating your own show, 248–68
  getting hired, 208–22
  preparing to be a TV writer, 167–94
  staff writing, 223–47
Innovative, 196
Internet, 117, 211

Jack and Bobby, 42, 134, 135, 136
jeopardy, 43, 44, 45
Joan of Arcadia, 16, 262
jokes. *See* comedy; sitcoms
Judging Amy, 52, 53
juxtaposition, 147–51

Kauffman, Marta, 11
Kelley, David E., 81, 169, 228
kids' shows, 36, 37–38. *See also specific shows*
King of Queens, 144–45
Kirland, Moira, 91, 167, 184, 188, 253
Kung Fu, 9

L.A. Law, 30
Late Night with David Letterman, 207
Law & Order, 4, 6, 14, 21, 33, 35, 91, 168, 183
lawyer, entertainment, 198
lead character, 18–20

Letterman, David, 207
Lewis, Jerry, 152
Lifetime, 36
literary agent. *See* agent
"like-a-jokes," 160
logline, 43
London, 201
Long, Shelley, 19
Los Angeles, moving to, 200–203
Lost, 13, 18, 27, 53, 72, 91, 123, 168, 169, 256, 263
Lowe, Rob, 10, 266
Lowry, Bob, 252
Lucas, George, 104
Lucci, Susan, 17
Lyon's Den, The, 10

Magnum, P.I., 16, 53, 70, 138, 202
Maher, Erin, 207
Malcolm in the Middle, 140, 260
Marcus Welby, M.D., 169
Markus, John, 98
Martial Law, 9
Mary Tyler Moore Show, The, 14, 17–18, 187, 255–56, 262
McCarthey, D. J., 146
McMurtry, Larry, 222
medical shows, 45, 169, 262–63. *See also specific shows*
Medium, 36, 52, 55, 88, 91
Melrose Place, 30
Miami Vice, xvii, 13, 62, 68, 79, 168, 256
Mighty Morphin Power Rangers, 36
Milch, David, 179
Millennium, 207
Miller, Dennis, 159
Montreal, 201
Monty Python's Flying Circus, 144
Moonlighting, 6, 45, 50, 61
Moore, Mary Tyler, 17
movies, xvii, xviii, 24, 65–66, 94, 141
  music in, 141
  production costs, 28
  writing, xvii, xix, 14, 65, 104, 206, 214
Murder, She Wrote, 91
Murphy Brown, 14, 98
music, 141
My So-Called Life, 20, 139

Nadler, James, 20, 52, 69, 76, 99, 123, 139, 167, 168, 231
Naked Josh, 34, 47, 73, 254, 260
Nash Bridges, 250
NBC, 192
negative fantasy, 12–13
Netflix, 168
network, xvi, 7, 8, 14, 17, 34, 66, 183, 248
  approval of material, 92, 113, 238
  creating shows for, 248–57
  demographics, 36–38
  episode length, 100
  fashion for genres, 265
  five-act structure, 72
  greenlight a series, 14
  internships, 178
  notes, 232–34
  prefer episodic shows, 34
  Standards and Practices, 210
  stars, 266
network executives
  creating shows for, 248–57
  hero should be likable, 16
  pitching to, 93, 248
  Sopranos, The, and, 168
  staffing season, 199
  want to know character's backstory, 27
  will read a spec pilot, 200
networking, 205–6, 246

network television, xvii, 72, 199, 248, 250, 266
demographics and, 36–38
series pitches to, 249–51
See also specific shows
Newhart, Bob, 266
Nickelodeon, 36, 143
Nimoy, Leonard, 17
Nip/Tuck, 167
nondescript (ND) locations, 32–33
Northern Exposure, 59
notes, 219
production, 232–34
Numb3rs, 262
NYPD Blue, 4, 5, 11, 19, 43–44, 58, 88, 124, 169, 261
NYU, 174

O.C., The, 11–12, 13, 16, 19, 36, 47, 187, 253, 258
obstacles, 43, 44
O'Donnell, Steve, 207
offscreen story, 130–33
opportunity, 43, 44
Orenstein, Bernie, 171
Outer Limits, 15
outline, 219
overwriting, comedy, 160–61
Oz, 12

Page 2 Stage, 193
partners, writing, 170–73
pass, 230
pauses, in comedy, 153–55
PAX, xvii, 36
Pee Wee Herman, 37
Persky, Bill, 98, 249
Peterson, Wolfgang, 250
physical pain comedy, 143
pilot, 190, 248, 249
episode, 255–57
spec, 190–91, 248, 249, 251–54, 257
pitch, 208–17, 249
dress for, 211–12
flexibility and passion, 214–17
fun, 211–12
killer, 209–11
pitching festivals, 254–55
series, 249, 254–55
pitching festivals, 254–55
placeholder jokes, 160
plausible surprise, 145–46
plotholes, 125–30
point of view, 136–38
point-of-view (POV) character, 20–21
Point Pleasant, 262
Politically Incorrect, 147
premise pilot, 255–56
preparation for TV writing, 167–94
awards and competitions, 180–82
film schools and classes, 173–76
screenwriting software, 191–94
seminars and workshops, 179–80
spec pilots, 190–91
spec script, 182–91
watching TV, 167–70, 186
working for a literary agent, 176–79
writing partners, 170–73
Preston, David, 170
problem, 43, 44, 80–81
producer, executive, 224, 225, 227, 228, 250
production, 28–29
costs, 28
notes, 232–34
time, 28–29
Project Greenlight, 181
Psi Factor, 99
pulling vs. pushing, 120–23
punch-up pass, 160
Punk'd, 49

Queer Eye for the Straight Guy, 5
Quincy, 262

Rabkin, William, 57
reality shows, xix, 8, 167
characters, 16–17
hook, 8, 9
See also specific shows
Red Shoe Diaries, 15
Reindl, Kay, 207, 227, 252
reruns, 29
Rescue Me, 33
resources, 269–71
rewriting, 111–41, 178, 229–30
bad writing, 119–41
contracts and drafts, 115–16
knowing when your draft is done, 112–15
taking criticism, 116–19
Rhoda, 260
Rock, Chris, 13
Rockford Files, 168
Rogers, John, 15, 27, 93, 115, 136, 137, 144, 162, 171, 173
Romano, Ray, 10
Roseanne, 9–10, 45
Rosenberg, Melissa, 251
Rule of One, 84–86, 130
runner, 63
Russell, Keri, 17

Sabrina, the Teenage Witch, 55
St. Elsewhere, 30, 169
Sallan, Bruce, 249
samples, 281–87
Sanford and Son, 14
scale payments, 279–80
SceneWriter Pro, 193
school, film, 173–76
Schwartz, Josh, 174, 253
Schwimmer, David, 11
science-fiction shows, 57, 185, 262
characters, 260–61
See also specific shows
Scooby-Doo, Where Are You?, 42
screenwriter, 192, 193, 194, 275–77
screenwriting software, 191–94, 275–77
script, 39–40
freelance, 217–22, 229–30
sample, 39–40
sample pages, 289–302
spec, 39, 41, 60, 61, 75, 93, 100, 112, 113–15, 117, 140, 141, 159, 182–91, 200, 208, 245
springboard, 41–64
writing the, 65–107
See also specific shows; writing
Scrubs, 73, 169
Seinfeld, 10, 13, 19, 28, 57, 68, 153
Seinfeld, Jerry, 10
seminars and workshops, 179–80
serial stories, 33
series regulars, 22
Seriously Weird, 52
Sesame Street, 10
Sex and the City, 12, 20, 62, 64, 72, 77, 124, 187, 188, 256, 258, 262
Shield, The, 4
Show Me Yours, 69
showrunner, 119, 209, 224, 225, 227, 228, 231, 233, 234, 240, 250, 253–54
Showtime, xvii
Silliphant, Sterling, 173
Simple Life, The, 264
Simpsons, The, 33, 42, 61, 153, 168
single-camera format, 72, 73
sitcoms, xix, 6, 9–10, 14, 28, 67, 98, 121, 142, 153, 160, 192
characters, 14–15, 19, 25–27, 151–55

structure, 72–73
See also comedy; *specific shows*
Six Feet Under, xvii, 66, 167
sleep, getting enough, 242–43
Smallville, 47, 48
Smits, Jimmy, 19
soap operas, 33
software, screenwriting, 191–94, 275–77
Sophocles, 193
Sopranos, The, xvii, 12, 46, 71, 84, 168, 187, 188
Sorkin, Aaron, 6, 7, 26, 57, 103, 229
South Park, 143
Spader, James, 144
Spears, Britney, 158
spec pilot, 190–91, 248, 249, 251–54, 257
spec script, 39, 41, 60, 61, 75, 93, 100, 112, 113–15, 117, 140, 141, 159, 182–91, 200, 208, 245
pilot, 190–91
software, 191–94
writing, 182–90
SpongeBob SquarePants, 37
Sports Night, 103, 184
springboard, 20, 41–64, 209, 210
bad story ideas, 56–62
basic elements, 43–45
character's weaknesses and strengths, 46–50
coming up with great ideas for, 51–56
mixing and matching stories, 62–63
sample, 281
template-breaking, 50–51
themed shows, 63–64
Squiggy, 149–50
Stacked, 10
staffing season, 199–200
staff writing, 3, 112–13, 140, 141, 170, 199–200, 201, 217, 222, 223–47
comedy, 142
credit, 231, 241–42
getting fired, 243–47
how to run a writing room, 236–43
production notes, 232–34
production people and, 234–36
salary, 223, 224
story editors, 225–28
your master's voice, 228–31
stakes, 43, 44, 45
standing sets, 29, 30
stand-up comedy, 162–63
Star, Darren, 62
Starlet, The, 8, 167
Star Trek, 6, 17, 22, 31, 67
Star Trek: Deep Space Nine, 50
Star Trek: Enterprise, 53
Star Trek: The Next Generation, 49, 54
Stewart, Jon, 133
stolen plots, 58–60
story editor, 118–19, 209, 218, 224, 225–28, 231, 232, 235, 249
story file, 52
story pitch. *See* pitch
structure. *See* template
subtitles for the nuance-impaired, 106, 141
Sundance, 181
Survivor, 8, 17
suspension of disbelief, 125–30
syndication, 34, 72

tags, 66–67, 71
Taylor, Doug, 174
teasers, 66–67, 71
Telefilm Canada, 182
television, xvii–xx
bad writing, 111–41
breaking into the industry, 195–207

television (*cont.*)
cable, xvii, 66, 71, 72
comedy writing, 142–63
creating your own show, 248–68
getting hired, 208–22
hidden structure of, 3–40
network, xvii, 36–38, 72, 199, 248–51, 266
preparing to be a TV writer, 167–94
springboard, 41–64
staff writing, 223–47
watching, 167–70, 186
writing the script, 65–107
See also industry, television; *specific shows*
telling a story out loud, 82–83
template, xviii–xix, 3–40, 41, 46, 169, 228, 257
bible, 38–40
characters, 14–28
consistency of, 4–7
episodic vs. serial stories, 33–35
fantasy, 11–14
hook, 8–11
network and time slot, 36–38
software, 192–94
springboard and, 41–64
venue, 28–33
That Girl, 171
That '70s Show, 59
themed shows, 63–64
Third Rock from the Sun, 8, 40
Third Watch, 6
three-camera format, 72–73
Three Stooges, The, 143
time compression, 76–77
time slot, 36–38
timing, script, 99–100
title sequence, 169
TiVo, 168, 169
topper, 156–57
Toronto, 200
Touched by an Angel, 91
tracking expectations, 86–92
Trailer Park Boys, 140, 183
treatments, 92–93
Tru Calling, 259, 262
Turtletaub, Saul, 171
24, 6, 8, 29, 33, 35, 79, 85, 88, 122, 131
Twilight Zone, The, 15
two-handers, 97

UCLA, 173, 174
underwriting, comedy, 159–60
UPN, 36
USC, 174, 175, 205
UTA, 185, 196, 251

Valerie, 19
Van Dyke, Dick, 10, 17
Variety, 196, 206
Venter, Dennis, 152, 158
venue, 28–33
voice-overs, 139–40

Wall to Wall Records, 253
Warner Bros., 192
Warner Bros. TV Writing Workshop competition, 180, 181
WB, 36
Weinstein, Jacob Sager, 159
Wells, John, 6–7
Wertheimer, Bob, 69
West Wing, The, 6–7, 10, 21, 26, 31, 47, 49, 57, 66, 99, 103, 123, 132, 167
WGA (Writers Guild of America), 115, 116, 197, 198, 219, 223, 231
scale payments, 279–80
WGC (Writers Guild of Canada), 115, 231

Whedon, Joss, 58, 169, 175, 231, 254
White, E. B., 142
White Production Draft, 222
Will & Grace, 22, 30, 152, 259
William Morris Agency, 185, 196, 251
Wire, The, 4
Wirth, John, 250
Wise, Liz, 180, 183, 184, 201
WKRP in Cincinnati, 14
Wolf, 11
workshops and seminars, 179, 180
writer's assistant, starting out as, 203–7
writing, 65–107
  action, 104–7
  act outs, 67–74
  bad, 111–41
  beat sheet, 77–81
  breaking story, 74–76
  comedy, 72–73, 142–63
  dialogue, 101–4
  mix it up, 83–84
  rewriting, 111–41
  Rule of One, 84–86
  the script, 93–100
  teasers and tags, 66–67, 71
  telling a story out loud, 82–83
  time compression, 76–77
  tracking expectations, 86–92
  treatments, 92–93

Xena: Warrior Princess, 37
X-Files, The, 5, 42, 61–62, 184, 185, 258, 263

Zack Files, The, 52
Zucker Brothers, 162
Zuiker, Anthony, 60, 103, 215

About the Author

ALEX EPSTEIN is the author of *Crafty Screenwriting*. He has worked as a development executive, television story editor, and television writer for more than a decade. He cocreated the comic drama series *Naked Josh*, and was head writer for the science fiction series *Charlie Jade*. A graduate of Yale University and the UCLA School of Film and Television, he writes the popular blog Complications Ensue, http://complicationsensue.blogspot.com.